FINDING THE BALANCE

LEADERSHIP IN HIGHER EDUCATION

FINDING THE BALANCE

LEADERSHIP IN HIGHER EDUCATION

Dr. Tim Dunnagan

ISBN (Print Edition): 979-8-9940662-0-1
ISBN (ebook): 979-8-9940662-1-8

Published by Dr. Tim Dunnagan
with the support of Boise State University

Cover Design by Cara Vanvalkenberg

Table of Contents

Dedication

I want to dedicate this book to two very important and influential people in my life. My father, Bob Dunnagan, nurtured the development of leadership within me at a very early age. He showed me the value and importance of good leaders and the difference between a good and poor leader. In short, he fostered my interest in the noble aspiration of being a quality worker and leader throughout my working career. The second person is my wife, Shawn Dunnagan. Shawn supported me in my pursuits of understanding leadership and becoming a leader while taking on a significant role in the care and growth of our wonderful children. She also acted as a sage sounding board for my most challenging leadership decisions and unlike anyone else, always gave me honest and insightful perspectives. Her understanding of higher education and leadership helped me make better decisions and improve as a leader.

Chapter 1
Introduction

This book is about leadership. Specifically, I will explore traits, skills and tactics needed to be successful as a leader in higher education. In this chapter, I discuss pivotal experiences that led me into leadership and enabled me to successfully engage in a job that can be rewarding for some and onerous for others. Many of the experiences that make up the core of this book, not surprisingly, relate to my professional life in private industry and higher education. However, some of the most impactful experiences relate to my childhood and early work experiences. After sharing select developmental experiences, I provide an overview of higher education that includes a brief history of the growth and maturation of the institution in the United States, its significant contributions to society over time, and trends and themes that have emerged, requiring higher education professionals to recalibrate and change direction. While everyone in higher education needs to be a part of the recalibration effort, balanced, capable leaders are essential in facilitating this imperative.

Early Influences on My Development as a Leader

As a child, my father worked for the National Park Service. You may have heard the phrase "military brat," which refers to a child who grew up in the military and was a brat because they lived all over the world. I was a "park brat," because I lived in national parks across the United States and Canada. By the time I left home to go to college, we had moved 15 times and I had lived in places including Carlsbad Caverns, Big Bend, Yosemite, Canyonlands, Cave Springs, Fort Davis, Banff, Fire Island, and Mount Rainier. Some of the locations were extremely remote, such as Cave Springs in Utah, where my mother drove 2.5 hours in a four-wheel drive to a bus stop so I could attend kindergarten in Moab. I still remember trying to sleep while I got bounced around the back seat along the rough roads of southern Utah. Similarly, in one of my father's assignments in Yosemite National Park, I attended a school with six kids in six different grades taught by one teacher. I represented the entire fourth grade.

We moved from his assignment in Yosemite to Fire Island, which is a barrier island off of Long Island. This move had me going from a very small school in California to a middle school with 2,800 children located outside one of the largest cities in the world. Prior to this move I had largely seen two occupations through my secluded world in remote parks... essentially you were either a ranger or a tourist visiting a park. New York exposed me to a very culturally diverse community since my life on Long Island (winter home) and

Fire Island (summer home) exposed me to a diversity of lifestyles and cultures by interacting with kids and families from Jewish, Puerto Rican, Italian and Irish communities. The time in New York was a real eye opener for me. Subsequently, we moved from New York for a short assignment in Banff, Canada, and I was able to live in another country. Being a park brat was a unique way to grow up and a powerful environmental force in my development.

Change

You may be wondering what my childhood has to do with leadership in higher education. From my childhood experiences I developed a number of orientations and skills that would become important in my work as a leader. One of the fundamental things I took from my childhood was that the world changes, and when it does, you need to adapt. As a child, I needed to be able to change and adapt or I would be socially isolated and without friends. Through my father's many assignments, I could move and not miss a beat. All I really had to do was help pack, say goodbye to my friends, and we were off to a new adventure—typically within 30 days or less! Therefore, I developed an ability to change and adapt to new circumstances. Being able to effectively and quickly change may not sound like much. However, as we will discuss later in this chapter and throughout the book, higher education suffers from an inability to change and desperately needs to make modifications to select traditions, operations, and practices.

Leadership

The other insight that my childhood provided was an understanding of and profound interest in leadership. The park service is similar to the military and living within this environment developed a clear understanding for me of leadership rank in the park service. Even as a young child I knew the difference between a ranger, district ranger, chief ranger, and superintendent. I also listened to conversations my father had with friends, usually when I was supposed to be in bed, about quality leaders in the park service and people who were respected because of their effectiveness as a leader. As I grew up, I got to know many of these people and picked up on their personalities, traits and styles. Whenever there was a conversation about good leadership, inevitably there was a conversation about poor leadership. I also got to know these people and made the same observations and learned things not to do as a leader. This type of learning came from my lived experience, but firmly embedded ideas about what to do and not to do if I ever became a leader. I had no idea I would work in a university environment, but I hoped I could someday be a good leader and this desire was formed at a very young age. Later in the book we'll examine the traits, skills and qualities of an effective leader.

Adversity and Making Connections

While much of my upbringing looks like an adventure and in many ways it was, it also helped me develop the ability to navigate adversity. I can remember huge snow years in the Sierra Mountains of Yosemite where we would shovel snow daily so our roof would not collapse. During big storms I would miss school for weeks because all the roads were closed and the teacher could not make it to our small community. Later I learned that much of the remote education I received delayed my educational development and made it difficult for me to thrive academically. Part of the inability to flourish academically was my lack of interest and focus on academics, however part of it came from the fragmented, inadequate education that I received in some of the more remote parks.

For some, moving 15 times would be very difficult to navigate and making friends over and over again would be an exhausting, never-ending cycle. This was the case for some of the more difficult moves, like when we moved right before the start of my senior year of high school from the Denver regional office to Mount Rainier National Park in Washington. However, my childhood experiences allowed me to grow and deal with less than ideal situations. I am not saying it was all rosy, because that was not the case. The many moves made it difficult for me to form enduring connections with other people, and I spent years and years working to catch up academically. Nevertheless, from these experiences I learned that when things got difficult, you doubled-down and addressed adversity head-on. It made no sense to complain about the snowfall when you needed to get outside and shovel the roof before it landed in the living room.

Similarly, when I moved to a new park or community I would go out the first day we arrived to meet kids and make friends. For many, making new connections in a new community is a hellish task. However, I never saw making new connections as an arduous effort. I had no fear or hesitation about making new connections... it was just something I did when I moved to a new location. As I moved into leadership positions in higher education I was better able to deal with adverse situations and make connections and partnerships easily and quickly. As will be discussed later in the book, dealing with adversity, forming partnerships and connections within and outside the university setting, are critical skills to have as a balanced and successful leader. I applied these skills to become an effective leader.

What It Is To Be a Good Employee

Understanding what makes a good employee came from watching my father and other park employees. They came to work on time, they took work seriously, and there was honor in a job well done. I also learned from my father that you needed to be honest about the quality of work, and slap-dash efforts or outcomes were not acceptable. In addition to my experiences with the park service and my father's influences, my earliest jobs also formed my work ethic and deepened my notions of a quality employee.

One of the first jobs I had was with the forest service, where I ran a chainsaw doing pre-commercial thinning and wildland fire fighting on the Salmon National Forest in Idaho. An important trait that working for the forest service instilled was the ability to follow through on a request from my supervisor (assuming it was legal and reasonably safe). Even if it was a very demanding request, it was my job and I did not question the directive. My job was not to debate a request, it was to execute effectively. Later I became a commercial fisherman in Alaska and I saw how a high-functioning team could produce amazing outcomes under adverse conditions such as severe weather, short seasons, and competition for a shrinking resource. I learned that truly good employees needed to be part of a crew to maximize outcomes. I can remember one trip where we caught, cleaned, and iced 40,000 pounds of halibut that were caught long-lining on baited hooks over a 48-hour period. To this day, this is one of the best team working situations I have ever experienced, and I really learned what makes for a good and poor team member. The ability to follow through on what was requested of me and the strength formed through being part of a high-functioning team provided invaluable insights as I moved into leadership roles. Communicating to employees what they should do and developing high-functioning teams is also explored later in this book.

After commercial fishing for several years, I went back to college and started my graduate work and entered the richest and most dynamic learning phase of my life. Because of a couple of mentors, wonderful faculty, and rich programming, I largely committed myself to working in higher education for the remainder of my professional life (I did have one role in private industry). I've worked in higher education for approximately 35 years. During this time, I've had the privilege of working as a director of Wellness Programming at the University of Kentucky and its 14 state community colleges; as a faculty member; a graduate coordinator and department head at Montana State University; and most recently for 14 years, as a dean of Health Sciences at Boise State University. Prior to my time in higher education, I did worksite health promotion for Blue Cross Blue Shield in New Hampshire within large corporations. While my formal academic training is in health and wellbeing, I was consistently involved in leadership positions and have been a student of management and leadership my entire working life.

In the final chapter of this book, I will suggest that you review your life and identify experiences that influenced your leadership approaches. I'll encourage you to consider what innate skills you have developed through these experiences. If you can identify these experiences and what strengths they offer you, you will find great insight in how you can best contribute as a leader.

I'm eager to share my thoughts on leadership and management because over the past three decades, I've developed some successful approaches. Higher education is in need of quality leadership. Because of the support I received from Boise State University in writing this book, an electronic version is available at no cost (a free electronic version of the book is available by scanning the QR code located at the back of this book). As I will establish in this chapter, higher education in the U.S. has gone through tremendous changes and is at a critical junction requiring competent, balanced leadership if it is going to continue to be valued and make significant contributions to the country and the world. Balanced leadership is vital for many institutions to even be financially viable in the years to come. In this book, I detail how leaders in higher education must engage if they are to be successful in a modern university in the 21st century.

A Brief History of Higher Education in the United States

Higher education in the U.S. was originally developed as formal divinity training for an elite few to propagate the Christian faith. However, this started to shift and in the 17th century with approximately 70% of students studying divinity and by the 18th century it had decreased to 45%. By the 19th century divinity training only represented about 10% of the graduates and the growth of the sciences, professional schools and the arts was spurred by notable figures such as Thomas Jefferson and Abraham Lincoln. Jefferson saw a need to expand the lens of higher education to create an "educated citizenry" and support the growing democracy. Jefferson's position was supported by others and influenced the direction of higher education. Lincoln also supported the notion of expanding the scope of higher education through the Morrill Act, which provided incentives such as land for states to create institutions of higher education, particularly through land grant universities dedicated to support agriculture and mechanical arts.

Despite these efforts, higher education in the early 20th century was restricted primarily to wealthy, white males. However, to create economic recovery after World War II, the passage of the G.I. Bill allowed approximately 8 million individuals access to a college degree. Many of these students could have never afforded a college education. This support almost doubled the number of students in higher education and helped create the middle class, while linking higher education to the American Dream. Similarly, civil rights efforts and Affirmative Action initiatives opened higher education to individuals from different ethnic groups. In the early 1990s, online education started and grew into a delivery platform that allowed students to take courses and study anywhere at any time. In the early 1800s there were only a handful of universities and by the early 21st century there were over 5,000 colleges and universities providing education to over 25 million students.

In sum, higher education grew from a small enterprise targeted to white males studying divinity to a ubiquitous enterprise offered to millions through on-campus or virtual platforms across thousands of universities, educating millions of students in a wide variety of majors.

Higher Education's Contributions to Society

The growth of higher education has had a significant impact on the United States becoming a thriving economic engine and superpower of the world. It has also been essential in the creation and dissemination of knowledge and art worldwide. Furthermore, higher education has played a key role in the growth and stability of communities and society, as well as fostering individual intellectual, social, emotional, financial and spiritual growth. It has been critical in creating and maintaining a competitive workforce, dramatically increasing earning potential, making transformative discoveries and addressing many of the world's wicked problems such as sustainability, literacy and delivery of healthcare.

Legitimate Concerns About Higher Education

Despite higher education's contributions to the world, the growth and maturation of the institution isn't without significant problems and concerns. More recently, many groups—especially republican affiliated individuals—have questioned the value of higher education and if it is something that should be supported by government. The lack of funding has led to huge costs being transferred to students and made college inaccessible for many. For instance, inflation-adjusted tuition and fees increased between 1980 and 2015 by more than five-fold (Hanson, 2024) and many students have mountainous debt without adequate employment after graduating. Instead of being seen as a clear path to the American Dream, it's become a path for financial hardship.

Similarly, many conservatives, students, and employers question the need and legitimacy of what is taught and promoted in higher education and find college curricula blotted with useless, inaccurate teachings. Others have appropriately questioned colleges and universities investing in overpaid faculty and administrators, building lavish entertainment centers, and growing costly athletic programs. Countless observers of college campuses note excessive student amenities including recreation facilities that resemble high-end amusement parks and spas, complete with plush student living accommodations. Consequently, a legitimate question has been raised nationally: Is higher education worthy of the time and financial investment students currently contribute? Many states have answered that question by decreasing government funding. For instance, Alaska's governor Mike Dunleavey decreased funding by approximately 40% in 2018-2019 and some have become very involved in controlling the business of teaching, learning and research, like Florida Governor DeSantis, who initiated efforts to restructure higher education using funding as a stick to enforce his policies. Furthermore, at the time this book was written the Trump administration was critical of the practices associated with a number of institutions including Harvard, Columbia, and University of Virginia. While academics bristle at these changes, it is important that these messages are taken seriously by academic leaders.

The change in support for higher education has also occurred as fewer students are graduating from high school. This change created an obvious drop in the supply of students who are the lifeblood of universities. This demographic shift has put tremendous financial pressure on colleges and universities which has caused many institutions to merge, eliminate programming, or close. The financial strain has occurred during a time when the delivery of higher education has evolved from traditional degree-based face-to-face class delivery on college campuses to online programming, certificates or badges in state, private, and for-profit education institutions packaged in student-centric scheduling. This has given students many options when it comes to getting an education, and if they don't like what they are receiving they can explore many other options.

People who worked in higher education in the 20th century could expect a very predictable environment. Most could expect small, consistent raises and change took place at a very slow pace in a democratic, methodical fashion. In fact, this type of work environment coupled with significant worker autonomy were some of the attributes that attracted many people into this work setting. Today, colleges and universities need to move quickly in significant ways; if this does not happen students will vote with their feet and these institutions will fail. Therefore, the workforce must work in ways and at a pace that they are not accustomed or necessarily comfortable with. This environment will require the use of skilled, balanced leadership. *I envision a balanced leader in higher education as an individual who exhibits a combination of 21st century business skills, a deep understanding of higher education's successful practices and traditions that nurture faculty and staff, while addressing the world's wicked problems.*

Success in the Future

In order to survive today in higher education, colleges and universities need to be relevant, impactful, innovative, engaging, and accessible. Michael Crow and William Dabars in their book *Designing the New American University,* (Crow & Dabars, 2015) concluded that higher education needs to address pragmatic, big problems that are critical for the success of our nation. They argue that higher education needs to come together around big issues and problems. Unfortunately, higher education has not adequately addressed this imperative. They assert that universities are currently moving too slowly to address changes that have needed addressing for decades.

To meet the standards of a high-functioning contemporary university in the 21st century, higher education needs to make a number of fundamental changes in the way it goes about its work. Administrators, faculty, and staff need to break with problematic traditions and ways of operating to better demonstrate their value to students, parents, communities, government, and society. To meet the needs of an ever-changing world, it is higher education leadership's responsibility to ensure needed change takes place. *This will require a balanced leadership approach.* For higher education to be successful in the future, all who are involved will need to contribute to necessary changes. However, leaders in higher education must be prepared to guide this process. This pivotal group is the focus of this book.

Book Overview

We begin with an overview of the fact that higher education has had a difficult time changing over the years. This is important because change is needed and higher education struggles with this in such a tradition-controlled environment. Next, I discuss how and why leaders need to care for themselves... care that includes physical, social, emotional and spiritual aspects. I start with this because it is almost universally ignored, and a leader cannot be successful in the long run if they are not healthy. Subsequently, we'll examine why leaders need to understand how they can influence people and strike a balance between developing and nurturing employees while also holding them accountable. This is somewhat unique in higher education because a key part of the workforce is faculty who bring their collective knowledge, wisdom, and insights out for the betterment of the world. Part of this effort involves creating fruitful environments that allow employees to innovate and produce needed change within the challenging bureaucracy of higher education. Without the development of this group, higher education will lose its most important ability to contribute.

As part of attaining a balanced approach, leaders are encouraged to recognize their strengths and weaknesses and allow others to counterbalance their weaknesses. Often, successful highly-trained and skilled individuals who move into leadership don't possess the equilibrium that is needed to be an effective leader. Finally, we'll discuss management and business skills such as good communication, strategic planning, team building, and creating systems and processes. While academics often bristle at the idea of using business skills and strategies in higher education, it is something that all leaders need to understand and support. This is the focus of this book... to communicate the balance effective leaders need in higher education to be successful in the 21st century.

Chapter Summary

1. It is important to explore the key influences in your life that may have formed or influenced your leadership style and approaches so that you can convert these strengths into becoming a more impactful and influential leader. I share many of my childhood and early work experiences to demonstrate how they formed my ability to navigate change, under-

stand characteristics of effective leaders, deal with adversity, make connections, and identify traits of a quality employee.

2. Higher education in the United States grew from a small enterprise targeted to white males studying divinity to a ubiquitous enterprise that is offered to millions of students through multiple delivery platforms across thousands of universities, educating students in a wide variety of majors.

3. Higher education has played a key role in the growth and stability of communities and society as well as fostering individual growth. It has also been critical in creating and maintaining a competitive workforce, increasing earning potential, making transformative discoveries, and addressing many of the world's problems.

4. Despite the many contributions made through higher education, it has now become a path to financial hardship for many, and political figures and citizens have increasingly questioned the practices, curricula, and efficacy of higher education in the United States.

5. Given the questioned value of higher education, change is needed if it is to survive. Higher education will need to change and become more relevant, impactful, innovative, engaging, and accessible. These changes can only happen through effective and balanced leadership; qualities that are often lacking in higher education today.

Chapter 2
Why Higher Education Won't Change

Introduction

It's an exaggeration to suggest that all colleges and universities can't change. In fact, the willingness and ability to change varies dramatically across institutions. However, change is particularly challenging in a tradition-based enterprise like higher education. Stellar examples of change are often highlighted at conferences and described in articles and books. For instance, BYU Idaho (Christensen & Eyring, 2011) has created a highly effective delivery platform and a 12-month online educational strategy at a price point that is among the lowest in the nation. Similarly, institutions such as Arizona State, under the powerful and futuristic leadership of President Michael Crow, have become worldwide deliverers of education to well over 100,000 students, while dramatically growing their research footprint. President Crow has adopted a number of progressive positions such as basing the value of a university on how many students are accepted, rather on the number that are rejected. (Rejection rates are promoted by many selective colleges and universities such as Ivy League schools to show their significance.) He also asked his leadership to work at a pace that demanded timely execution of initiatives—something foreign to many institutions of higher education. One could find similar impressive examples from the top 50 innovative universities in the United States. These stories are newsworthy because examples of timely, effective change are still infrequent. Many are using antiquated processes and faulty governance structures that are ill-equipped to address the realities of a contemporary higher education system. With the exception of religious institutions, higher education struggles more than any entity to embrace and implement needed change (Crow & Dabars, 2015).

One caveat to this trend is that numerous stories appear each year where a cataclysmic event, such as the drastic budget reduction, forces quick and dramatic change to take place. An example of such change occurred in 2020 when the Alaska university system was faced with a $136M budget reduction. The reduction created forced mergers that impacted hundreds of students and employees. More recently, in 2022, Alaska Governor Mike Dunleavy scrapped the four-year degree requirement for many state jobs, citing a workforce shortage. Given that colleges and universities present a major potential employer for job candidates, the cuts and recent policies seem to be in conflict. Nevertheless, these changes exemplify the dramatic and drastic decrease in support for higher education.

The decrease in support in states such as Alaska do not create change in the most thoughtful and productive manner, essentially running the university faculty and staff to the edge of a cliff and telling them to jump. This approach is especially challenging because higher education is process dense and not accustomed to moving quickly. While some positive changes may occur, the process does not support innovative thinking, better processes, worker commitment, positive outcomes, or value. They do, however, reflect a robust desire by many citizens and political leaders to change higher education. Many cataclysmic events happen because people and political entities are tired of waiting for needed changes. Declines in enrollment and the COVID pandemic were part of the driving force for the cuts and policy changes in Alaska. Therefore, in this discussion I am advocating that we consider change of a proactive type that allows for thoughtful and impactful transformations that will create universities that better serve society, students and the states where they reside. Before change can happen, there must be an understanding of the impediments to change to remove barriers and create circumstances conducive to this evolution.

Prevailing Sentiment Towards Change

In 2018, I attended a national conference focused on higher education. One of the keynote speakers outlined his vision for the future of higher education, which included the deep integration of business practices into the traditional academic enterprise. His ideas attracted a group of speculators to invest $50M based on the potential of his ideas, so it was reasonable to assume that some of his ideas had merit. I have worked in higher education for more than three decades and I have yet to receive $50M for any of my ideas, so I was interested to see what he had to offer. While the viability of his ideas may have been debatable, what was most amazing was the visceral response from hundreds of attendees who were reduced to pounding their table, leaving the room and heckling the speaker. One person shouted "Outrageous!" and stormed out of the room, and another claimed that it was just another example of "corporatizing higher education." At several points they booed the speaker. The spectacle felt more like the House of Commons with a two-drink minimum than a conference on higher education.

It was striking to observe the strong resistance and even anger toward someone suggesting new ways of approaching higher education. This sentiment remained throughout the conference. The session demonstrated that most of higher education is not only resistant to change but unwilling to even consider it. The reasons for this opposition are embedded in a number of realities that exist in higher education. While many authors have written about change and the difficulties associated with a change process within any setting, higher education is especially challenging. The strength of the resistance is largely a result of problematic decision-making, inflexible work cultures/environments, and deficient leadership.

The Ongoing Use of Democratic
Decision-Making Structures

Higher education predominately utilizes decades-old processes for decision-making involving committees, voting, and faculty/professional/classified governance policies that focus on involvement rather than timely, high-quality decisions. In fact, there is often the false assumption that if a prescribed process is used, the purpose of the decision-making effort has been met. This assumption omits a critical concern... was a good and timely decision made? These decision-making processes are ubiquitous and are often outlined in policies that are created at the department, school, college and university levels, or are simply part of decades-old practices, adhered to through university traditions. Even though each university or college is somewhat different, the vast majority share this approach. Many institutions have constructed policies to ensure a democratic process through voting, giving everyone equal input into decisions through a process that says each vote counts. This can be tricky because people who may not have enough experience or knowledge to cast a meaningful vote are voting, while others with significant insights have a vote that carries the same weight as the uninformed voter. While the process may appear fair and embedded in our election processes, it is an inefficient and imprecise way to make many decisions.

There is also the assumption that everyone is casting a vote with the best interest of the enterprise in mind, and not their personal preferences. This is simply often not the case. The use of broad-based inclusion can be helpful in certain instances and we will discuss the examples of this exception in the strategic planning section in a subsequent chapter. However, routine use of these cumbersome, time-intensive processes creates a number of problems in an educational environment where timely, informed decision-making is so needed.

An example of this ineffective decision-making process happened at a university where I worked and the administration was considering offering students courses year-round via three semesters a year instead of two semesters (fall and spring) and an abbreviated summer session. I was in support of the idea as it had several strengths, such as better utilization of facilities. Buildings are largely a fixed cost, so using the existing space throughout the year made financial sense. The idea could also help students who wanted to complete their degree in three years instead of four years. This option would eliminate an entire year of student room and board costs and readied them for employment after three years of schooling. It was also a way for the university to increase revenue by generating more student credit hour production during the summer session. Furthermore, it could help some faculty increase personal revenue, assuming student growth took place through the new approach.

This change was a big lift and required many curriculum and scheduling changes, but it was very feasible. After more than a year of discussions, committee work and presentations, the idea was put to a faculty vote and was voted down. Even though faculty could still have a nine-month contract (they could take a spring or fall semester off if they worked the summer session) or elect to receive additional compensation for supplemental teaching, they did not want the disruption to their work and private lives. Was this the best decision? I guess it would depend upon who you asked. I saw this as an opportunity for the university to differentiate itself from other universities, provide an alternative option for some students and allow some faculty to increase their yearly income, while increasing the financial viability of the university. However, the vote killed the idea and that was the end of it.

The World Has Changed and So Should Decision-Making Processes

Historically, the number of 18-year-old students who showed up for classes at the start of a fall semester determined the delivery of courses and degrees. The courses were largely taught by tenure-track faculty and augmented by a relatively small number of graduate students, lecturers, and adjuncts. This process was fairly stable and predictable year after year. In fact, a person could teach a given class at a certain time and day and be teaching the same course with the same schedule 10 years later. Historically, the number of students graduating high school was growing, and the value of a degree was not questioned. This environment allowed for slow, participatory decision-making, even for basic day-to-day decisions.

Today, the successful university needs to work within an environment that is dramatically different. Successful institutions have a mixture of educational platforms including face-to-face, remote teaching at worksites, hybrid, and online class delivery. The typical degrees are augmented by stackable certificates, workforce development training, and partnerships that create customized educational products for public and non-profit entities. Programming is tailored to allow education to fit into the busy lifestyles of students who now view education as a lifelong relationship with an institution in addition to obtaining a baccalaureate degree. Furthermore, the programming must be financially viable because new programming is not commonly supported with university budgets or new governmental funding. These changes have dramatically increased the complexity, volume, and speed of necessary decisions. Chairs and coordinators in an online program may have 10 to 20 different cohorts a year that may include students from around the world. Instead of offering one or two sections of a course, programs may offer 15 or more sections taught over a seven-week period. There has been a dramatic increase in the use of part-time adjunct workers, clinical faculty, master course leaders, course designers, and adjunct faculty. Similarly, sophisticated relational databases, customized educational programming for public and private entities, all have changed the way decisions need to be made in higher education.

These factors make it too cumbersome to have everyone involved in decision-making. Utilizing broad-based input instead of core individuals familiar with the system often results in gridlock and a decision is either not made or delayed. Haste can also lead to a poor decision, but not making informed decisions in a timely manner will kill programs, frustrate students and faculty/staff. Later in this book we'll examine approaches to making effective decisions in a timely manner.

Decision Processes Vary Across Units and Committees

I once had an external community leaders advisory board for our college that was implemented to ensure our programming was relevant for current workforce needs and to identify future programming needs. A member of the board asked me a very simple question which was hard to answer. How do you make decisions at the university? Obviously, the board member had a defined process that was used across his entire organization and was interested in our process. The answer felt very disjointed when I said, "Well, we rely heavily on committees and some committees follow a defined process for making decisions such as promotion and tenure committees and the same is true with some hiring committees. However, most committees are ad hoc in nature and vary depending on the unit (college, student affairs, etc.) or the committee chair associated with the process." I went on to add that decision-making also varied depending on leadership. For instance, a new dean could come into a college and create a new set of decision-making processes. In three to four years, another dean could be hired and change many of these processes. In fact, often the committee chair or the loudest person on the committee can have inordinate influence over the procedures and the decisions made. With this lack of consistency, much time is lost and familiar procedures and techniques for making decisions are often omitted. The variability in methods results in considerable time discussing items that lack focus or purpose. After long discussions, people become fatigued and a less than adequate decision is made or it is delayed so more discussion can take place at the next meeting. The variability eats considerable time and can result in marginal decisions.

Partisan Nature of Units

When I first started my career in higher education as a faculty member, I remember a meeting where my department chair announced that most of the discretionary college resources for the year would go to our department and the other departments would receive very little additional funding. The group immediately broke out in cheers and applause. At one level I understood the excitement. However, I was also shocked because as a new faculty person I naively thought we were part of an enterprise with cohesive units working towards big, integrated outcomes. Therefore, receiving the support should have been received with some level of humility and sense of responsibility. The excitement of the group came because we got the support, and the other departments lost out. People made comments like, "It's about time we got some resources," and others talked about the inferior quality of the other departments and the people who worked in the unit. The experience felt more like a high school football game competing with cross-town rivals... not departments within the same college and university.

The substance of why we were funded wasn't offered. In fact, I never really heard why we got the resources. This partisan attitude did not build bridges within the college. In fact, a faculty member from another department that did not get funding commented that he wished our department had never been moved into the college 13 years ago. When a university needs to consider macro-level changes, this level of competition for resources does not allow people to galvanize around change, partner, and be focused on the benefit of the university and society.

Administrative Turnover and Loss
of a Long-Term View

A curious aspect of higher education is the rate of turnover in leadership. Many academic departments have a process whereby the chair is rotated every two to four years and the existing chair rotates back into the faculty. The chair is a key position in that faculty directly report into this person and much of the academic work within a university is executed at this level. Years ago, this practice worked because the flow of new students was steady and predictable, states funded current and new programs, there was no online programming with varying starts, and colleges largely closed during the summers. Work life on a campus was less complex and a different pace.

Today this practice is dysfunctional because it takes years to acquire the skills and experiences to be an effective department chair. Furthermore, many faculty see taking a two- to four-year rotation as a tour of duty and is something they would rather not do. Many say, "I would rather not do this but I will take the position because no one else wants the job." Often a new chair will say they will do this for a while and will then get back to the "real work of being a faculty member." I would argue that both jobs are real and important work. One department did the selection process by rank (professors) and alphabetical order! Not the best way to end up with a strong leader. I know when I was made department head, I was excited. However, faculty shared their condolences with me and hoped I would survive my tour of duty before going back to being faculty. The way I was treated by many was more like having a cancer diagnosis than a promotion. Having people who are not necessarily committed or enthusiastic, with a short appointment timeframe, creates a short-term view for leading and causes many problems, particularly if difficult decisions need to be made.

The average time for a dean or provost is three to five years, but some do not even last two years. Presidents tend to be somewhat more stable once they are established, but they often leave after two to five years. The turnover creates change fatigue for faculty and staff and makes change that requires a long-term view (more than three years) very difficult to implement. This problem is compounded because leaders at this level are usually requested to come in with their agenda and vision for a unit or the university. I have been asked more than once what my legacy as department chair or dean would be. Often to create a legacy or implement an agenda change is required. However, starting and stopping initiatives every three years is very disruptive and dissuades engagement because change happens each time a new leader is appointed—especially a leader external to the university. The recurring change is like the movie "Groundhog Day" with Bill Murray, but nobody learns from the repeated experiences... they just become numb to the quick and often disjointed requests for change. The changes often accompany new initiatives, strategies and directions for work units to embrace. For long-term faculty and staff, the constant adaptation creates fatigue and causes more senior employees to disengage from the planning and execution of new initiatives. In fact, they often try to protect the department members from a leader who will be off to the next bright and shiny thing in a couple of years. Faculty and staff do not want to clean up administrative messes that are partially implemented, so they resist change. This resistance was exemplified by a faculty member who told me two years into my deanship, "You know what they say about deans—they come and go." Basically, it was her way of saying she would not change and instead just wait until I left to avoid the disruption.

Risk-Adverse Environments

Many mid-to senior-level administrators want to create needed change within institutions, but few are willing to deal with the resistance associated with change. I can think of very few changes that will fundamentally improve an educational enterprise that will not create resistance. In fact, one way to lose your leadership position in higher education is to take the risk of making change and having people push back and question your suitability as a leader, even if change was needed. This can result in a vote of no confidence in faculty-based units, and in non-academic areas leaders can be quickly removed and another put in place. People lose their jobs and possibilities for future employment growth when they take risks and things do not go well. There is an obvious moral hazard associated with change if it can adversely affect your current and future employment status. Not many people want to hire someone with a vote of no confidence from the faculty, and they do not tend to be sympathetic with the explanation that it "needed to be done for the betterment of the college or university." So a culture is reinforced where administrators avoid change to avoid jeopardizing their current and future employment.

My Area Is Too Important To Fail

University faculty are highly trained and passionate about their areas of study. Their discipline typically does much to improve the world, so individual worth is frequently coupled with their areas of expertise. Just ask a faculty member why their area is important and you will get a convincing and often long explanation. Faculty are frequently nurtured and trained to contribute and create a deeper sense of importance for their discipline. In fact, it is not uncommon for a faculty member to find their discipline and area of expertise more important than their department, college or university. Also, considerable accomplishment, time and effort go into becoming a faculty member. Given these circumstances and the daily interaction they have with like-minded colleagues in their department who reinforce these beliefs, faculty think what they do is too important to fail. This belief can lead to employees dismissing the possibility that they need to change or unable to recognize that their area or application of their area to students is no longer relevant. This orientation creates blinders for change.

Higher Education Is Unquestionably Indispensable

Higher Education has held a high place within our country for centuries. This has led many in higher education to take the stance that higher education is good and important and those who question this enterprise are ignorant and simply lacking the faculties to understand the importance of it. In short, they feel that people or groups who question higher education have no idea what they are talking about. Consequently, concerns outside the university are not taken seriously and efforts to address the concerns are explained away or disregarded. Unfortunately, the individuals and groups that question higher education—students, parents, legislators and competitors—are also critical to the future success of higher education. This orientation does not go unnoticed by critics and they are understandably offended by people unwilling to consider their view. This positioning creates a tone deafness to rethink how and what is done in higher education, which deepens the critics' resentment, and a negative feedback loop is created across both groups.

Culture of Not Being Strategic

While all universities have a strategic plan in part because it is required for successful accreditation reviews, many do not use the plan as a true systematic guide for success. I remember a university that was making preparations for their site accreditation visit and had consultants attend to help with the process. A consultant asked if the university had a current strategic plan. The provost answered, "Yes," and was then asked some general questions about the plan. The provost responded by saying, "I said we had a plan... I did not say I knew what was in the plan." Everyone in the room thought that was funny and laughed. That was not funny, it was embarrassing. Many universities have operating budgets of over $500M a year, thousands of employees, diverse academic programming, profound community engagement efforts and robust research agendas. There is a lot going on. Creating impactful movement within an institution, e.g., growing a research and creativity agenda or dramatically growing student recruitment without a strategic plan is doomed for failure. For institutions to be successful a well-communicated strategic plan with employee buy-in and a process for holding people accountable for the successful execution of the plan is mandatory. In short, a strategic culture across the entire institution is needed to make large system-wide changes. Without this commitment, the best that can be hoped for are individual units doing as much good as possible within their area of interest. Local optimization of units is typically not enough for institutional-level change and success.

Tenure

Faculty come to a university excited to engage as members of the university and hungry to support their community and profession. However, they are placed into a promotion and tenure (P & T) process that forces the faculty to think individualistically (my publications, my teaching scores, etc.). The tenure process essentially determines if a faculty member has exhibited the skills, productivity, growth and expertise needed to retain them at the university as a tenured member of the faculty. Once tenured, they typically are promoted at the same time to associate professor. Some universities provide other pathways, but this is the most common. If they do not meet this criteria, they are given a final one-year contract and asked to leave the university at the end of that year. Understandably, this creates great anxiety for many faculty members who are constantly worried about their effort and productivity. It also creates anxiety for administrators who conduct reviews and determine the future of non-tenured faculty members. People often talk about the stress faculty are under during their first five years of employment, however, few discuss the stress that administrators (department chairs, deans, provost and president) and faculty review groups experience as the evaluators in this process. The decisions of leaders involved in the tenure review invariably become public and they personally deal with the impact of their decisions on a faculty member's career for years. It is important to note that faculty committees also review candidates, which can also create anxiety for these individuals. In total, the process is very stressful and the candidates work to try and please multiple reviewers and reviewer groups.

In many institutions, P&T requires faculty to be adequate in teaching and good in research/creative activities. Service is another component of tenure, but it is very rare to have someone not tenured because of their service contribution (service to department, college, intuition, discipline and community). I have reviewed more than a hundred P&T candidates and not a single faculty member has failed in the area of service. In rare cases, individuals are not tenured or promoted because of poor teaching. The primary reason for failing the review process is inadequate research and creative engagement, and failure in this area is infrequent.

Therefore, the P&T system causes a focus on research and creative activities and then teaching. Given this focus, it is not typically in a faculty member's best interest to contribute to creating a high-functioning enterprise or meaningfully engage in service unless it helps *their* research and teaching. In fact, if a decision is made in the interest of the university that is perceived as a threat to a faculty member, i.e., time away from research/creative activities, they will often avoid these contributions. This single process makes large-scale systematic change very difficult because 500 faculty are focused on *their* productivity and not necessarily the strategic priorities of the university. Furthermore, tenure makes it difficult for administrators and committees to prioritize areas for investment and growth because the feedback they receive is often from 500 faculty with an individualistic orientation created by P & T. This is not the fault of the faculty member, but a systems problem created by the P&T process.

It is important to remember that most faculty do not come to a university with this orientation. The system requires faculty to engage in this behavior through the fear of being denied tenure and terminated from their position. At the same time, it is hard for leaders to change the P&T process because it is the treasured policy of faculty. Many faculty view P&T as protecting them from evil and unscrupulous administrators who would deny tenure or promotion for petty or non-legitimate reasons. Many see tenure as job security and will fiercely protect this cherished feature of their job. Therefore, a stalemate is created between faculty and administration, and P&T continues to be a part of almost all institutions in higher education and an impediment to many macro-level strategic initiatives.

Insufficient Leadership Development

Some universities are starting to have leadership training academies, which is a step in the right direction. The in-house supervisory training for new leaders varies dramatically, from excellent to poor. However, the excellent programs are few and far between. New leaders (coordinators and department chairs) are given a job and told that if they have questions to visit with their dean or chair. In many instances, this could be the first time a chair has supervised a professional employee or faculty member, so their skills are probably lacking. Their experience prior to their new appointment was likely watching other people who were put in a similar position. This is akin to people learning how to teach from people who are teaching but never trained as instructors. The dean may or may not have relevant experiences or knowledge of leadership in academic settings and are busy with other responsibilities such as fundraising, personnel issues and resource constraints. This situation can result in oversight of faculty and staff that is less than optimal.

As the chair moves into their new position, the complexities of the day-to-day operations overwhelm many. The work related to managing costs, revenue production, personnel issues, conducting performance reviews, class scheduling, technology, facility constraints, student retention challenges and faculty pay all close in and can have a paralyzing effect on the new leader. Many chairs often maintain teaching loads and try to engage in research and creative activities while running an academic department. The administrative assistants typically provide the continuity from chair to chair, which turns over regularly to ensure that the enterprise keeps running. Given the struggle in this leadership position, most chairs have limited bandwidth or interest to engage in meaningful change efforts. They simply do not have the training, mentoring, time or energy to engage in effective change efforts. They do their best and typically go back to their faculty position after two to four years of service.

Leadership and Faculty Hires

Another common practice in higher education is for faculty, staff, and administration to vote or give feedback on who they want to hire as a new leader. The feedback is often helpful and needed, however, depending on how it is executed can create complications. For instance, the orientation of the respondents may not be aligned with what is best for the future of the unit or institution. In fact, many have a limited understanding of the position and what skills and experience leaders need to be successful in higher education. For instance, faculty may focus on the candidate's research agenda, which has almost no relationship to the candidate's supervisory and management skills. Many are concerned with how a new hire might change their role, program, and/or college. Certainly, these concerns are ubiquitous and human nature, but not necessarily the best perspective for making a hire. The problem with this feedback process is that self-interest is very strong and makes it hard for many to consider the greater good and what is really needed in a leadership hire, especially if sweeping change is needed. Balance is typically attempted by having administrators and faculty involved in the decision making, but the same problematic thinking can come from administrators... will they be a disruptive force in the college? Will they question my authority? Will they adhere to the leadership team's group thinking? Again, this orientation may result in feedback that can lead to hiring someone who is not the best candidate. New hires can be an outstanding way to facilitate needed change at a university. However, the process does not always result in this outcome.

Chapter Summary

1. Institutions within higher education typically have difficulty making timely, needed changes. In fact, many are not only resistant to change, some will not even consider the possibility of it. This is particularly problematic because the complexity, volume and speed at which decisions and change need to take place in higher education require that these changes are executed in a timely fashion.

2. A number of factors contribute to slow or ineffective change with individuals, groups and entire institutions. The factors include poor processes for making decisions and the partisan nature of individual/work units and frequent leadership turnover. Additionally, work culture and environmental factors hamper this process and include leadership's avoidance of faculty resistance and job security. Furthermore, many feel that higher education in general and their area of expertise specifically is too important to fail, so the incentive to change is often minimal.

3. Other factors that can act as a barrier to change include poor or non-existent strategic planning and policies such as promotion and tenure that promotes individual rather than organizational thinking. Finally, poor leadership execution and insufficient leadership training contribute to problems with change in higher education.

Chapter 3
Take Care of Yourself!

A Leader's Cautionary Trail

If you ignore this chapter, the rest of my advice on leadership may not matter... It is that important! I am referring to a critical area that is ubiquitously ignored by leaders: Health. The signs of neglecting this area may start with too much time devoted to work. You are dedicated to being successful, so you put your best foot forward and this requires time. Initially, the excessive time investment is explained by things that make sense. For instance, you and people you know say it's a new job and you will be busy at first, but once you get it down things will go back to normal. You tell yourself, friends, partner, kids and community groups this message and promise to spend time with them in the near future. Unfortunately, getting this job down ends up being harder than you anticipated and even when you are away from your leadership position your thoughts are consumed by this effort. You start apologizing to significant people in your life and say it is this damn job, but you *hope* things turn around in the near distant future. This statement concerns you because a mentor once told you that hope is never a good plan and how long is the near distant future? You decide to double down to figure the job out and work harder to be successful as a leader and start coming to work early and staying late. To take care of new budget and personnel issues, you start working part of the weekends. Each time you solve a problem others pop up, and you constantly have more work to do. You are getting some positive feedback about your work which is good, but you wonder if you can keep going at this pace.

After a year of working non-stop you make a commitment to start taking care of yourself and spend more time with important people in your life. You start your commitment to a healthy lifestyle with a bang and are eating better, taking a yoga class and not going into work on the weekends. It feels good! But a department chair unexpectedly leaves the university and you are asked to take on her role along with your current responsibilities until a new chair can be hired in approximately six months. You are uncertain about taking this on, but it obviously means that you are doing a good job, or you would not have been offered another department to administer. As you think about the request, it was really a compliment that you were asked to lead another department after only being in your position a little more than a year. Also, this could look very impressive on a resume if you want to be considered for more revered positions in higher education administration. Unfortunately, the department is a mess and this addition to your current job takes up even more time and energy. Your commitment to health and wellbeing vaporizes and you end up working even harder. Not only do you have more problems to address, but you are confronted with significant litigious human resource issues. This is new ground and unnerving and intimidating work. The search for a new chair fails (could not find anyone to take the job) and you end up taking on the extra department for the next year and a half.

As you move into your third year you consider applying for a new job at the university that is highly coveted, complete with a higher salary and more influence. Several prominent university administrators and faculty encourage you to apply because of the good work you have done since becoming a leader. You apply for and get the job! But a familiar cycle starts again. It is a new position with different responsibilities, so you need to double down and work harder so you can gain proficiency in your new position. You excel at all you do so your idea of proficiency is a very high bar. Two years into your new position you feel like you have an understanding of how the job works. However, over the past five years your health has really declined. You have a hard time sleeping and even sleeping pills and melatonin tablets don't allow you to get a full night's sleep. You find yourself anxious in a variety of circumstances and it is now an ongoing part of your life. The recent university-wide restructuring of administrative positions has only added to that anxiety and your workload. Your doctor's visit that you had put off for two years reveals that you have put on 25 pounds in the last five years, your cholesterol and blood pressure are both elevated and your blood sugar numbers classify you as pre-diabetic. Your absence from your partner, kids, and friends is starting to take its toll and these key relationships are suffering. You also find that it is hard to concentrate at work and you are losing interest in things that used to be exciting. Sadly, the best method you have found to help free your mind of the senseless chatter associated with your job is to have a few stiff drinks when you get home. These side effects of being a leader were something you had not anticipated.

A leadership story like this is too common. Almost everyone has the best of intentions and they really believe they will be fine as they step into a leadership position. Many leaders sacrifice overall health because they think it is necessary to be effective in their position. This is especially true if people have not had nor will they receive adequate training or support. While this unhealthy behavior may provide short-term dividends professionally, long-term it will negatively impact job performance and psychological, social, emotional, physical, and spiritual aspects of wellbeing. Addressing your health as you initiate your leadership position is by far the best option.

How Do I Take Care of Myself?

Do a search and see how many papers, books and talks are given on the topic of self-help. The volume of literature, supplements, techniques, equipment, facilities, retreats, mentoring, and training devices that are dedicated to this topic is staggering. I used to be a health researcher and devoted time trying to understand why people don't engage in health-enhancing behavior. In all fairness, adherence to health behaviors is a complicated area and despite tremendous efforts studying health behavior, modest progress has been made. When other competing responsibilities such as a demanding job influence health-enhancing behaviors, the quest for wellbeing becomes even more arduous. Despite this challenge, it is possible to be a leader in higher education and have health and wellbeing. The great scholar Peter Drucker wrote almost 100 management books and said, "Always be true to yourself and give only part of your life to the organization," (Edersheim, 2007). Similarly, leaders such as Colin Powell profess, "Take leave when you have earned it," and, "Have a life outside of work," (Harari, 2002). Meaning, there is strong encouragement from scholars and leaders to take care of yourself!

You Are Not a Superhero

Even though there is some correlation in performance across job responsibilities, many leaders are recruited into a leadership role because they were good at something else, like teaching or research. Therefore, the individuals recruited into these roles tend to be very hard working and successful. The work and success over time can reinforce feelings of superiority and lead one to think that they do not operate under the same rules as the average human being because they are above average. I have noticed that an above-average notion of self, born of success, can also transfer to the way leaders view their susceptibility to illness and disease. In short, they do not view their limitations the same as the average person.

Sleep

One common practice of superheroes is not getting enough sleep. Most everyone has heard that on average a person needs eight to nine hours of sleep each night. There is a wealth of research supporting this statement and many health issues are associated with sleep deprivation such as increased risk of cardiovascular disease, cancer, dementia, metabolic problems and a weakened immune system (Knutson et al., 2010). However, the words "on average" really throw a superhero off. If most people need eight hours of sleep, that means that they need less than eight hours, so surely they can excel on five or six hours of sleep a night. They may not say it so plainly, but this is often the outcome of their belief.

I remember a senior administrator saying that they slept four hours a day and did fine with that pattern. These statements are damaging to themselves and make other leaders think that is what they need to do to be a senior administrator in higher education. While a very small portion of the population (approximately 1%) can function well with limited sleep, the vast majority cannot. In fact, I hesitated mentioning that 1% finding because the superhero will just assume that they are in that group! Similarly, the strong sense of self associated with this orientation means that unlike most people, recovery is not needed after an especially demanding period of work. An example of this behavior relates to travel across international time zones. The superhero will arrive home after crossing multiple time zones at midnight and be in the office the next morning at 7 a.m. Often, they will let others know this to show that they truly are a superhero. People do not have superpowers and most of the population needs to get eight to nine hours of regular quality sleep. Also, after particularly challenging episodes at work, additional time is needed to recover. So, for your health and wellbeing, get the sleep and recovery you need to perform at the top of your game!

Check Your Health

Superheroes also forgo basic health examinations and the feedback given through these services. Once a person is in their 40s they should get examinations and meet with their physician once a year. They will advise you on what tests should be run, but yearly check-ins are wonderful to see how your health has progressed during the past year through blood panels, blood pressure, general examination of your body, a discussion about your behavioral health—especially anxiety and depression—and anything notable that has changed with your health during the past year. One problematic aspect of being a leader is that leaders typically spend most of their work life sitting on their butts. This can increase a number of health risk factors associated with a sedentary lifestyle that involves sitting, talking and typing.

The superhero can run into a couple of barriers in getting regular examinations. First, they are very busy and do not have time. Again, the idea that they are above average allows them to forgo examinations and tests because they are fine... just ask them and they will tell you. Even if they do get the test, the second barrier is that they dismiss the results because they know why their cholesterol or blood pressure is high and they will take care of it by exercising and changing their diet. If those changes happen, great, but that is not usually the case. They tend to keep putting off the needed behavior changes to address their health issues.

These yearly visits are a good way to get objective and qualitative feedback from people who are experts. If their feedback and advice is taken seriously, much more severe problems can be averted. Your primary physician can also be very helpful in getting you more focused help through specialists such as endocrinologists, physical therapists, counselors, acupuncturists, dietitians, and others to maximize your chances for success in a proactive manner. Similarly, many universities have extensive wellness programming that can give you access to screenings and programming to address your health through the convenience of the worksite. Moreover, every university I have familiarity with has good to excellent health insurance benefits. Collectively, these benefits afford employees excellent access to a high level of care. Through hard work you earn these benefits, so take advantage of them for your health.

The superhero syndrome can pop up in several ways, especially for successful leaders. Just because you excel at your work and other dimensions of life does not mean that you are not susceptible to the impact of poor work/life choices. Reflect upon the way you work and live and decide if you are living the superhero syndrome and need to rethink what is needed to allow your body, mind and spirit to run optimally.

You Need a Coach

People who have never been in a leadership position may not realize how isolating being an administrator can be —especially a senior administrator. I remember attending a management development program and our speaker who was a president of a prominent university was asked how they dealt with all the stress and strain of their job. The answer was their faith (he was also a Catholic Priest), a few close friends and his black label (Irish whiskey no doubt). The point being that he had very few people he could share his work concerns and challenges with. One of the hardest parts of being a leader is that information often cannot be shared that would help employees understand their actions. Therefore, having a thoughtful and knowledgeable person to process issues with on a regular basis can be invaluable.

During my first 25 years in higher education, I was not aware of many leaders using coaches. At least they did not share that they were using a coach. However, this is a very common practice in other industries. In fact, for many it is boiler plate support that they received when hired. Some leaders did see therapists which can be a good choice, but this information is typically very guarded and is not always associated with work issues unless the university has a very robust Employee Assistance Program (EAP). I have never worked at a university that had what I would describe as a robust EAP. Therefore, you will likely need to obtain this support through discretionary funds you can access through your unit budget or through your health insurance that allows for personal counseling to address maladaptive stress and strain.

I have used both work coaches and therapists and found them invaluable. A coach typically has more management and administrative skills but less training than a therapist on how to effectively deal with psycho-social issues. I had a wonderful coach who I could freely share my most sensitive and intractable work problems with. The coach had over 20 years of experience in the banking industry and had been a worksite coach for over 10 years. It was a bonus that he had some clients who were in higher education. I could share issues and he responded with neutrality, as someone with substantial experience with fixing problems across a host of worksite settings. I also knew that I could talk about my supervisor and other senior administrators and my conversations were safe. Confidentiality is not necessarily as secure when discussions are initiated with colleagues and co-workers. In total, the coaching relationship gave me an essential outlet and sounding board that offered sage advice. The modest investment for my monthly meetings was invaluable.

Depending on your situation and the availability of professionals, you can work with a coach and/or a therapist. The contribution this investment can make in your work and wellbeing can be significant. If it is not significant, then you probably need another coach or therapist. Unfortunately, about half of the coaches and therapists have moderate to poor skills, so do some searching before forming this relationship. Today you have many options afforded through technologies such as Zoom that allow recruitment of coaches and therapists across a broad geographic area (even another country) for meetings in the comfort of your office. This action can do wonders to help you address work issues such as the stress and strain associated with difficult decision making, budget reductions, poor institutional leadership, performance improvement, using support services such as legal and human resources to enhance work outcomes, and more.

Don't be Surprised

As a leader you are given access into your employees' life circumstances and their good and bad behaviors. I had worked in higher education for over 10 years as a faculty member and thought I had a good grasp of the behaviors associated with students and employees. However, this was not the case. I did get a decent lens into good behaviors because the universities I worked at did a wonderful job of celebrating success and achievement of the students, faculty, and staff. But the less desirable behaviors were not as evident.

As a leader I was struck by the volume of legitimate issues that take place in employees' lives that impact their ability to work effectively. This makes sense when you consider all of the significant events and changes that take place in a person's life. Just think of your life and events and circumstances that can impact your work quality and productivity. Health is an area that impacts everyone. Employees and/or the people close to them will have significant health issues to address throughout their career. I once had a high-performing employee who suddenly started having performance issues with meeting deadlines, missing meetings, slapdash work and they became difficult to communicate with. After several months they shared that they had been diagnosed with cancer and were going through treatments that zapped them of their energy. Maybe there was a larger issue to address within my department or the university in general, because she did not share this information for three months! However, I should not have been surprised because health is a very private issue and people are often reluctant to share health information, especially behavioral health issues. In addition to personal health issues, psychic energy is also diverted when friends and family members have health issues, elder care obligations, and processing the grief associated with the loss of a loved one. Generally, people assume "things will be dealt with" in a week or two. In fact, for the death of a close family member, five days of sick time can be used at many institutions for this life event. Don't be surprised if it takes much more than a week to recover from or deal with chronic health issues. In some cases, it involves a lifetime of management and work.

As a supervisor you will have the honor of presiding over celebrations where faculty, staff, and students have done extraordinary, impactful work. I fondly remember students talking about the work and contributions that they made during graduation ceremonies. Through my leadership positions, I attended over 100 graduation celebrations and the impact and growth of the students was reinforced after each ceremony. The faculty and staff who mentored these students made similar contributions. At these times, I am taken aback by the good work, kindness, empathy, and constructive drive of these amazing individuals. It is one of the things that makes working in higher education wonderful.

At the same time, you will see and work with people who will demonstrate inappropriate and shocking behavior. As soon as you think you have seen every kind of inappropriate behavior you will be shocked again. I know because it has happened to me many times. This poor behavior can be somewhat minor, where people in a public forum will degrade a co-worker in front of their colleagues. Other behaviors can be more grave. I remember an instance where candidates were visiting campus and a question was asked of the candidate after their presentation about how they would side on issues where administrators want to go one way and faculty want to go another. The candidate started answering and the faculty member who asked the question yelled out, "Wrong answer," because they did not fully side with the faculty. When you have a room full of people listening to a guest invited to the university for recruitment, this behavior is alarming. It seemed ludicrous that I was going to have to take action as the leader to ensure this did not happen again. Another ripple effect of the behavior was it made recruitment even more difficult! Would you want to work in this type of antagonistic environment?

There will be many instances like this that surprise you. For instance, I have seen employees reduce other employees and students to tears because of their uncaring and condescending feedback. When you hear what was done you will likely think how easily all of the drama could have been avoided if they just had some basic communication skills and treated people with dignity and respect. As a leader it may even be more shocking when you discuss the problematic communication with your employee and they have no idea why their communication was inappropriate and they see no need to change their behavior in the future. I remember one instance where a dean took someone's lab while the faculty was on vacation without telling them. They literally had all the equipment moved to storage, had it painted, carpeted and turned it into a dean's suite. Can you imagine being gone on vacation and when you return the dean is sitting in what used to be your lab? I have had employees steal from the university, take another job and give four days' notice before the semester started, use university resources to run a side business, abandon their job, falsify documents, prevent employees from accessing benefits, post pictures of themselves with students wearing inappropriate (very little) attire, and request sexual favors for grades. I had a colleague who had an employee who urinated in someone's office! The behaviors are appalling.

While these are the actions of a very few people and this type of behavior happens in all work settings, it can shock and surprise you. It can also be very stressful for a leader even though someone else engaged in the behaviors. What I would recommend is that you are prepared for anything and normalize what a small number of people do under your watch. By normalize, I do not mean to say that what they did was acceptable. These types of behaviors are not acceptable and need to be dealt with, generally by leadership. However, do not have a visceral response each time someone does something stupid or surprising. By normalizing the issues, you expect that surprising and stupid things will happen and take it in stride. This orientation minimizes the energy wasted over the fact that an employee, often someone who you thought would not engage in inappropriate behavior, does not rob you of your energy and composure. It is their behavior, not yours, so deal with it from that perspective. The lesson to be taken from all of this: Don't let people's poor behavior surprise and zap you of your ability to effectively address your work and maintain your health and well-being.

Set Boundaries

Steven Covey, the author of *The Seven Habits of Highly Effective People* (Covey, 1989), once said at a training I attended that "the important thing is to make the important thing the important thing." I heard that statement over 30 years ago and it has stuck with me. I would sit at my desk each morning and ask myself, "What is the most important thing for me to do today?" It has been a great way for me to prioritize how I spend my days. It is also helpful for long-range planning and focusing of time so that you are better able to address your health and wellbeing. Often, we are busy at work doing a lot of things... this orientation can change being busy to actually contributing in meaningful ways.

Priorities

Greg McKeown, in his book *Essentialism* (McKeown, 2014), does a good job of diving deeply into the question of what is essential in work and life. He points out that a leader's most precious resource is time. Therefore, deciding what you can and cannot spend time on is one of the most important decisions you can make. In higher education, if you do not prioritize your time, others will gladly do it for you, even if they have no supervisory responsibility associated with your position. Many management and leadership scholars have applied the Pareto Rule as a way of conceiving time allocation. Essentially the rule states that 20% of your efforts will produce 80% to 90% of the critical results. The rule is fascinating when you consider that essentially 80% of your efforts produce almost nothing! The obvious question is, why are you spending 80% of your time achieving almost nothing? For some it is a belief that if you are busy you are successfully executing your job, and can honestly say, "I am doing all I can do." Others feel they have no control over their work life and move from task to task like a leaf in the wind. There are many possible reasons, but it is ultimately an inefficient use of time.

The use of your time has powerful applications to your work performance. It also has critical applications to your health and wellbeing and life outside of work. One of the most common reasons people give for not caring for themselves and nurturing important relationships is lack of time. One of the dominant sources of time use is work. To begin to focus your time on important things you need to let go of the idea that you need to attend all meetings and events or you'll miss out. I remember a president from a large research-intensive institution who said that even if he and his wife attended an event every night, people still would not be satisfied. Given this assessment, maybe identifying what is most important makes sense because you cannot please everyone, even if you give all of your time.

Analyze Your Time

Obviously, you need to attend some meetings and events, but are they all worth your time? As a way of confirming this idea, look at one month's worth of meetings and see how much time was spent in these meetings. Just before I left the University of Kentucky, I reviewed my schedule and I was spending about 27 hours a week in meetings. That was a lot of time! What was fascinating was that almost half of the meetings involved ideas that I felt were not going to work and oftentimes I left feeling I brought no real value to the meeting... I just came because I was invited. After reviewing your meetings and totaling the hours, decide which are essential to what you do. It is important not to confuse the fear of missing out or concern over what your colleagues/supervisors think with what is essential. Surveying your past year's schedule may clearly show that you need to say No more frequently. In fact, it is not uncommon to have to say No five or six times before you can say Yes to a significant idea. Similarly, consider how many conferences or trainings you have attended out of habit or fraternal obligation. Do the conferences or trainings add value? Are the social events you engage in the most important way to spend your discretionary time? The findings of this exercise can be very illuminating. Another way I better allocated time was to be thoughtful about the people I spent time with at work. Despite it being uncomfortable, I could not say Yes to everyone. Certain individuals required a lot of attention, but there was not much output created from the interactions, so I minimized time with these people. The ways of prioritizing are many and varied. The hard part is learning how to say No, even if it is your boss.

Sunken Costs Bias

Another consideration associated with boundaries relates to the bias of sunken costs. Essentially, the cognitive bias states that we continue to invest time, energy, money and other resources despite the evidence indicating that the effort outweighs the benefits. We do this because we have put too much in to stop. I know I have experienced this phenomenon with academic programming that experienced little interest from students and lost money every year they existed because of low enrollments. I continued these programs too long because of the convincing pleas of leadership and faculty involved with the programs. Also, when I considered the time and money that went into feasibility studies, faculty recruitment, course development, advertising, space renovations and efforts given to convincing the powers that be that this was a good idea... I hesitated closing the programs. I simply did not have firm enough boundaries to call it quits, thinking too much was invested to let the program die. The problem was that each year the program continued it extracted money, time and energy because people were trying to fix a program that was not viable. There was a wonderful quote by Peter Drucker (Edersheim, 2007), who encapsulated this dilemma by asking, "How much more money are we going to spend trying to get this dead corpse to stop stinking?" The obvious clarity made by the statement was that no matter how much money was thrown at the problem it would continue to stink. Therefore, the answer was to stop funding and supporting the dead corpse. Maybe you can think of similar situations where considerable time and energy was put into your version of a dead corpse and how time and energy could have been enhanced just by letting it go.

Negotiation and Being Able To Say No

Fisher and Ury wrote a book entitled *Getting to Yes, Negotiating Agreements Without Giving In* (Fisher & Ury, 1981), and in 2008, Ury wrote *The Power of a Positive No* (Ury, 2008). I have found both publications helpful in allowing me to frame and negotiate how my worktime is spent. Essentially, they teach how to effectively communicate your perspective in a clear, respectful way that is firm and compelling. Often people walk into a discussion without doing the reflection that needs to occur before the conversation. The authors provide some good ideas on how to prepare and engage in conversations that can maximize your chances for the desired outcome while maintaining relationships.

One of the strategies I have used if I am surprised or unsure about a request is to thank the person for the offer and communicate the need to take a day or two to see if I can work it into my current workload. Similarly, Ury (Ury, 2008) suggests saying you have a *policy*. Maybe your policy is reserving the summer for your writing. Pre-planned responses can be helpful in preventing over-commitment. Other methods of gracefully giving a No response include "Maybe another time," saying you're "over-committed," or that you want to do quality work and that it is not possible with all of your obligations. Still another approach is to say No to a proposal, but with changes it could be a Yes (assuming that this change makes sense within your prioritization). Ultimately, the process is designed to be clear but respectful of the people and your relationships. It is important to use methods that fit your style and of course to be honest.

Often an example can help illuminate how some of the methods can be applied. I worked in the College of Health Sciences and our faculty and staff had a very positive and strong working relationship with the College of Business and Economics (COBE). In fact, the former dean of COBE worked with me to create a minor in business that went from 30 to 40 credits to approximately 18 credits and was adopted by many majors in the College of Health Science (COAS). Similarly, we co-created an institute (Blue Sky Institute) to address wicked problems such as health care delivery, behavioral health, poverty, and sustainability. Individuals in one of the business programs wanted to take their current management program and turn it into a health administration program. However, I had some concerns because we were already in the implementation or growth of eight online programs in the college. We had recently said Yes to several programs which required a lot of work for many people in the college. I also had some curricular concerns in that only two to four health-related classes would be included inside an MBA program. It seemed like a bolt on to a current degree. The business department—to their credit—was geared up and ready to move, while we felt more work needed to be done before we could move forward on the proposal. These differences are common when academic groups come together and work to hammer out a partnership.

My approach was genuine. I first said how much I appreciated our current partnerships and the difference it made for students and the university. This created an honest platform of respect and a visible way for me to demonstrate the value of our relationship. I really prepared for the meeting to understand what was being proposed and considered how to communicate my decision in a respectful but firm way. During the meeting, I outlined the number of online programs that we were engaged in and the need to have more dialogue and discussion about the curriculum offerings and integration across the two disciplines.

In this example, I used several approaches by first indicating we were overcommitted (eight online programs). I also offered that if the curriculum was changed and different dates were selected, we could partner on this new degree (No, but a Yes if...). I also shared the need for more discussion with my college's leadership and the faculty most likely involved with this effort, and that I could not move forward until they had time to work more closely with the management faculty. This is critical in higher education and the consequences of not having this conversation would likely doom the program to failure (faculty and leadership not on board with a proposal is typically a non-starter). Given their timeline and the extensive work they had already put into the programming, there was no way for them to delay for another year. They were understanding of our current commitments and understood that we did not have the bandwidth to implement a new program. We also understood their need to start the program as soon as possible. At the end of the conversation, I agreed to let COBE pursue other partners and not include COHS in the new program. This decision protected my bandwidth and that of many others in the COHS through a "positive No" and allowed our partners to use another avenue to address their needs. The process was authentic and respectful of the people in both colleges.

To maintain clarity and strong working relations I met with the COBE dean and the university provost (my boss) to explain my position, reasoning, and to ensure our relationships were still strong. It is important to note that the university was interested in growing programs, so communication on why we would not move forward on the project was important. There needed to be an understanding of why a college that had moved on developing and implementing many new programs was suddenly saying No. People often ask what a dean does, which is a legitimate question. In this instance, I spent significant time not doing something and ensuring that the parties involved were communicated with and working relationships were maintained. At the end of the day, my workload and the workloads of others in the college were addressed and the relationships remained strong. However, considerable time was spent on the best way to say No, which is not always an impressive outcome on the year-end report.

This is an example of deciding what is essential at work. It was done because taking on too much at work compromises quality and in this case did not allow the workforce to best direct their time and talents. Also, taking on another major effort would negatively impact the health and energy of my staff, as well as my health. There were simply too many arrows pointing to No on this big decision. Therefore, you can improve work performance and spend more time addressing your health and wellbeing and important relationships by doing something that is not always easy... Say No.

There are some difficult tradeoffs that need to be made in order to spend your time on what is of most value. I just gave an example where everything worked out and people were understanding of a No response. The only downside was that it took a while to communicate this. I have also said No and it ended up damaging work relationships. Even though relationships may have been compromised, the No response was still the right thing to do. So be sure you want or need to say No, because it can harm relationships, despite your best efforts.

In addition to saying No at work, No replies happen in other areas such as family, health practices, friends, and community requests. When all of these areas are considered collectively, saying No becomes more critical because *not* saying No in one area may prevent you from saying Yes in another area. For instance, not saying No at work may prevent time with family or other priorities. In a sense, your ability to say No in one area determines what the Yes decisions can be in the other areas of your life. Then you are left with daunting decisions to decide what is most important; family, friends, work, community, or health? Saying Yes to everything simply does not work. Ultimately, if you have thoroughly considered your time, saying No in this calculated fashion helps prioritize what is of most value to you. Deep reflection can help clarify what is most important across these areas.

Reflection

Shortly after I started working in a leadership position, I would take a few days away from work each year to reflect on the past year and think about how I was spending my time. When I first started doing this, my reflection process only consisted of one leg on a stool—work. While this helped my work performance, other aspects of my life writhed, including health and relationships. It was much later in life that I started considering all the parts of my life as an integrated whole. This ultimately helped me find a balance that supported my health and wellbeing. Given this experience, look at your life as an integrated whole as soon as possible.

Schedule a reflection period to evaluate how you are spending your time, to avoid getting lost. Author Greg McKeown (McKeown, 2014), offers three questions that can be helpful in your reflection process around work. They include: What am I passionate about? What taps my talent? And, what makes a difference? In other aspects of my life, I used questions like, what has happened with my health in the past year? Am I spending *quality* time with the people that are important to me? Am I finding ways to engage in activities that replenish mind, body and spirit? McKeown offers a wonderful quote from Socrates that is relevant to this topic: *"Beware the barrenness of a busy life."* We can learn a lot from this statement. The key is to spend time in the areas that create the most value for you and are intentionally chosen.

Be a Leader of Health Promotion

During my career, I worked at three universities and met many people who worked in higher education across the country. I was always struck by their reluctance to share how they spent their time away from work. Weekends were especially strange in that the socially correct response at many universities was to say, "I worked." While I know this is true, we all have to work on weekends or evenings occasionally, but the hesitance to share recreation or down time pursuits seemed really strange, especially when I knew people were engaging in these activities. It was like they were doing something that was wrong or violated a precious work ethic. This was especially true for people in the tenure process who didn't want colleagues seeing them not working, for fear that they might not get tenured. I remember at a conference where a group of people were visiting before a session started. One person mentioned they had been reading a novel and her research colleague overheard the conversation. The research colleague said, "I thought during the next five years all of our work is focused on generating publications and here you are reading a novel!" Fortunately, the session started and the awkward moment ended.

As a leader it is important to model healthy lifestyles. You do not have to be perfect, but it needs to be communicated as a priority through your actions. We all have times when we must put in extra work, but we all must find ways to step away and take care of our health. Some universities have better climates for this pursuit than others. I often asked others what they did during the weekend. When they asked me, I made it a point to share the non-work personally enriching things I did. I would talk about my hunting, fishing, kids ski races, hikes, wood working, floats, and whatever I was doing. Sometimes I would work and I shared that also... I was not making this stuff up. I also took time to work out on campus when my schedule allowed during lunch and walked to work or rode my bike. I took time off for trips and given my family's interests, this generally included being active in a pretty place.

I did this for a couple of reasons. First, I wanted to normalize taking care of myself and having fun. I could think of no better way than to share what I was doing. I was fortunate to largely work in institutions that supported this perspective. I also took a genuine interest in the people I worked with and was interested in what they did outside of work. Most people enjoyed and engaged in this exchange and some did not, which was fine. As dean at Boise State University, I spent the first 30 minutes of my initial college-wide meeting introducing myself to the faculty and staff. The session included pictures of me with family and friends floating the Salmon River, fly fishing in Montana, and a story about what it was like growing up in national parks across the United States and Canada. I had talked extensively during my interviews about my work, which is why I was hired. However, from the start I wanted people to know that I did many things to replenish my tank and, in some ways, how I got to be the person that I was.

So, to be a leader of health promotion you do not have to run races, cycle across the country, summit peaks, and eat a vegan diet. If you want to do that it is fine. Rather, you need to find the things outside of work that you can do that promote your health and wellbeing. Maybe that is reading a book or taking a walk at lunch. Whatever it is, share it and normalize giving time to your health. Allow faculty and staff to engage in these types of activities, especially through worksite wellness programs (nice if you can show up as a leader), and encourage them to take breaks and vacation time. At one university I called all the employees who reported to me who were losing vacation time. As you probably know, you can accumulate vacation time to a maximum number of hours and it no longer accrues... you lose it. I asked these employees why they were losing their vacation time. I had to be careful, but I essentially said I'm not trying to tell you what to do with your vacation time, however, I am concerned that you are not using it. I communicated that vacation is given to get away and rejuvenate and I want to encourage you not to lose any more time. Some took my advice and others did not think it was any of my business. Nevertheless, as a leader I thought it was important.

Being Present and Not Listening
to the Chatter in Your Head

Being a leader in higher education is a demanding job with many external forces to consider such as defunding of higher education, public opinions, and demographic shifts, which were discussed in chapter two. Additionally, there can be stress created trying to be successful at work, maintaining health and navigating the many struggles in life such as financial burdens, relationships and family. The collective demands often create an environment conducive for the creation of narratives in our mind. The narratives are the stories we tell ourselves about why things did or did not occur at work, formed to help make sense of what is happening. These narratives are often fueled by our egos. Our egos love drama and will die without the creation of dualities such as good and bad, being a victim in a cruel world, needing confrontation, and access to unending success. The narratives are varied, and they can promote fear of losing things of value (e.g., a leadership position), the need for more in the future (e.g., a promotion), anger, and the dilemma of being a victim. For a deep dive into this sobering and enlightening area, writings by authorities such as Eckhart Tolle (Tolle, 2005; Tolle, 2003; Tolle, 1999), and the Dalai Lama (Lama, 2002; Lama, 2000), are helpful. Becoming more present and reframing narratives has been transformative for me and has contributed to all aspects of my life, including my work.

The interesting thing about narratives is that they are stories we make up, roughly based on our experiences, but designed to feed our ego. The intrusion of our ego typically shapes narratives that are not true and after running them over and over in our mind, we believe the stories we tell ourselves. Unfortunately, the ego has a short attention span and as soon as it is fed it needs more and it is off to the next thing. As a leader there is significant content to create narratives and continue feeding the beast. Think of the narratives occurring in your mind. Are they accurate? Do they follow the pattern of an ego-infused story? Since people spend much of their waking hours at work, much of the feeding can be about work or the perceived problems in other aspects of our lives that are caused by work (at least that is what the narrative tells us). The narratives are typically distortions, which creates the possibility of misinterpretations and costly actions on the part of the leader. Just being present and experiencing life as it happens does not feed the ego. If the ego is not fed it begins to fade into the background, and you regain control of your life. Some examples may help clarify this perspective.

At work, I remember a time when my college had a very impactful year. In fact, we accounted for half of the student body growth of the university and had successfully started four new online programs. The faculty were showing impressive research growth and we had a record year with philanthropic donations. Each year at the start of the fall semester, the president gave a terrific presentation on what was done the previous year and what we could look forward to in the upcoming year. The president typically had over 1,000 people attend the onsite presentation and most of the other employees streamed the two-hour presentation. This was an event people did not want to miss. It was one of the best turnouts I have seen in my time in higher education for a yearly kick-off presentation.

The president was reviewing the past year and as the minutes ticked by, I realized that our college was not going to be mentioned. In fact, colleges that in my mind had done little or nothing were mentioned. I remember that I was so mad that I told a friend at the university that it was "the equivalent of a General Motors CEO giving an update and leaving out the SUV division." Lots of ego things going on in my reaction—anger, drama, being a victim, etc. Much of what I was doing and feeling was delusional. At the end of the day, getting lost in my narratives and wasting psychic energy on something that was not true was a poor way to focus my energy. Furthermore, railing about the president's omission was not a good career move if I wanted to advance as a leader. The sad truth was that I never even spoke to the president about my concern. Several months later when I settled down, I discovered that the problem was connected to not sharing our success effectively with senior administration. That omission landed squarely on my shoulders. I just assumed they were aware of our good work and this was not the case. As we'll discuss later, communication about what a unit does to contribute to the success of a university needs to be specific, succinct, accurate and delivered to the right people in a timely manner. I missed executing this important action. Therefore, the lack of acknowledgement could have been easily addressed; the omission of our college involved no ill intent on the part of the president and the narrative was caused by my ego.

One of the key teachings I have taken from this orientation is the need to be present and not spend too much time in the past or future. Yes, it is important to learn from the past and there are many practical reasons why the future must be considered. However, when most of the time is not spent in the present, problems occur. As Eckart Toole points out there really is only the present (Tolle, 2003). If you are anchored in the past, it is only an incomplete memory of what happened and if you are focused on the future, you are using the present to create something in the future. The future can only really unfold in the present, so the present needs to be the focus of your time. Time outside of the present often creates the narrative of what you would like to have happen in the future, which is typically driven by the ego... success, revenge, etc. Similarly, the past is the interpretation of what happened and how that will impact the future.

Therefore, the present is where life happens and it will be recognized by others because when you are present, you are giving yourself and others your full attention and focus. Have you ever seen leaders who are distracted and don't seem to really be hearing what you are saying? This behavior does not inspire others to follow. In fact, many just find this rude behavior. Also, by being present, you get a clear picture of where things are and what needs to be done to attain desired outcomes within your organization. Essentially, if your narratives and ego are engaged and strong, the interpretation of issues and subsequent answers are not accurate and consequently promote engagement in activities that miss the mark.

I have used this insight many times at work and wished I had discovered the importance of being present decades before I internalized it. Often, I will catch myself in a meeting and recognize that I am creating a narrative. Just by making this connection you can make great progress in disengaging the ego and being present. My thoughts start and I ask myself (it gets confusing to know who is talking and who is listening when it is with yourself) why the university would invest in this program when there are so many better options available. Before I go on with this story, I stop by simply noticing that I am creating a narrative in my head and reminding myself that it does not help. If I am on top of things, I probe why I had that response. Sometimes it is just the chatter of the ego, but sometimes it is something else that helps me understand the source of my narratives, like fear, or needing to be liked, etc. This can be very humbling and illuminating. I then pull myself out of this inner conversational stew to just observe what is happening... I am present in the moment and not thinking what this means in the future and how this same thing happened in the past. I also take a few deep breaths. This calms down my body and mind so I can engage in a very different way.

As a confession, I do not use this approach all the time and I have so much more to learn and practice about being present. I still create narratives, get lost in the future and dwell too much on the past. This will be lifelong work for me to be present in the moment and use it for my wellbeing, work and personal life. I have however, over the years, gotten better at just realizing that I am creating narratives through my ego in my day-to-day life. Today when I catch myself and can smile, I know I am making progress. When I smile at something my ego's power dissipates, and I can go back to being more present. I have also engaged in other practices to help with being present including breathwork, taking a sauna and Qigong. Breathing takes a matter of seconds and most of the Qigong practices I follow on YouTube take 10 to 25 minutes. There are many other quick and easy ways to develop being present such as meditation, yoga, being in nature, or visiting with others about your journey. However, just taking some deep breaths and clearing the mind can be a great start. If you are interested in this topic, I would recommend Eckart Tolle's book, *The Power of Now* or *The New Earth*. If you get his book(s) and like them that is great! If you think it is a bunch of junk, I would still keep the book. You might find it very enlightening later in life. So, for your health and wellbeing, find ways to minimize mind narratives spawned by the ego and aim to be more present.

First Things Last

Generally, when you read about health, it's advice about physical activity or nutrition. Both areas are very important. However, if you are going to engage regularly in fitness and nutrition behaviors, you need to get other areas of your life in order that have been discussed in this chapter. I did my master's degree thesis in exercise adherence (Dunnagan, 1987), and the findings were sobering. Although people have good intentions, the success rate for long-term behavior change in exercise was about 20% to 25%. When interviewed, participants gave many reasons for falling off the wagon and stopping an exercise program. I worked for years in the fitness and worksite wellness industry and if everyone who intended to exercise showed up, the floors would cave in. Despite well-crafted approaches to increasing long-term engagement in physical activity, not much progress has been made and nutrition has a similar track record. These behaviors are important but challenging to maintain. But by addressing some of the things discussed earlier in this chapter, you will have a better chance of establishing meaningful change when it comes to exercise and diet.

For instance, internalizing that you are not a superhero may help you pay more attention to exercise and nutrition. Also, setting boundaries in your life will help carve out the time and energy needed for exercise and proper nutrition. Furthermore, viewing part of your job responsibilities as being a leader of health promotion reinforces the duty to promote things like flexibility to exercise at work and selecting healthy food options at work functions. As you work on being present, activities like exercise and meal preparation offer wonderful opportunities to practice. There are a variety of publications, services, technologies and facilities that can help facilitate these behaviors. Like anything important, it needs to be treated as a priority in your life.

Integration

In this chapter, we discussed a variety of ideas to help you care for yourself. Maybe you are well on your way in this process and maybe you have a lot of work to do. My strong suggestion is *not* to try and do all of these changes at once. Years ago, working in worksite wellness programs in industry and at universities, I was often surprised by the list of changes people wanted to make immediately after the first of the year. If they really took on all they were planning to do, the chance of success was about zero. It was just too much change all at once. However, I found that if they started with one area and incorporated it into their life before trying something else, their rate of success increased dramatically. The practices discussed in this chapter are things I wish I had prioritized and incorporated into my life much earlier in my career. Like so many leaders, I dove deeply into my job and did not give the long-term care that was needed to maximize my potential as a leader and as a person. No matter where you are in your career, it is never too late to start caring for yourself!

Chapter Summary

1. Self-care is ubiquitously ignored by leaders. Addressing your health and wellbeing is critical for your long-term success as a leader.

2. Understanding that you are not a superhero and operate under the same susceptibilities and limitations as the average person better enables you to engage in self-care. Therefore, make sure you get eight hours of sleep each night, yearly medical examinations, and seek the expertise of health

professionals when you need them (therapist, dietitian, exercise specialist, etc.).

3. Consider contracting the services of a coach or therapist to help you navigate difficult work-related issues.

4. Don't allow others' problems to become your problems. As a leader, you will become privy to a host of employee and student tragedies and hardships and witness poor behavior that is void of professionalism. Prepare yourself for this reality so that you are not derailed by these surprising events and behaviors.

6. Set boundaries in your life and analyze how you spend your time in work and non-work activities to ensure that the allotments align with your priorities. Discipline yourself to say No to non-priority issues and have the resolve to sunset failing efforts.

7. Consider being a leader of health-promoting activities and support your entire workforce in these efforts.

8. Strive to be present in all that you do and avoid creating mental narratives that are stress producing and unwarranted.

Chapter 4
Being Human and Caring for Employees

What Is Leadership?

There is a lot of dialogue in higher education about leadership. This interest is in part because higher education needs quality leaders. However, the need for quality leaders is ubiquitous in all private and public enterprises. Many differentiate between leadership and management which is a valid dichotomy, even though both are important aspects of effective leaders. The most helpful definition I have found for leadership is, "The ability to influence," (Maxwell, 2007). I am not sure if John Maxwell was the first to craft this definition, but it is a succinct and helpful explanation that other leadership experts widely support. Even in a very hierarchical organization such as the military, leaders have encouraged the use of influence over authority (Harri, 2002). Management focuses on business skills and approaches to effectively execute the day-to-day functions and activities of a university. While some take a more disparaging tone towards management and describe managers as people who do things right and leaders do the right things (Bowman and Deal, 1991), management skills such as budgeting, accounting, program planning/implementation, etc. are critical in the successful oversight of a university or units within academic settings. Both roles are important and have their place, however leadership is a much more human-centered endeavor and is the focus of the next two chapters. In this chapter, I will explore authenticity and practices that demonstrate caring for employees.

Be Yourself

One of the best pieces of advice I can give someone considering a leadership role is to be your authentic self and identify how your attributes can make you an effective leader. Being yourself is essential to being human and allows your unique gifts to be harnessed as a leader. Leaders such as Jack Welch (Former General Electric CEO) and William George (Former CEO of Medtronic) also supported the notion of being yourself as a leader (Pandya & Schell, 2006). Working from a place of authenticity makes your interactions with people more comfortable, natural, predictable, and less work. It is tempting to emulate effective leaders you've observed, especially if you are new to leadership and uncertain of your abilities. However, it is exhausting not being yourself! Doing the work of a leader is hard enough without trying to figure out how someone else would respond in a situation. Invariably, you will slip back and forth between your natural self and the person you are trying to emulate, and this leaves co-workers wondering which person they are going to work with on any given day. Remember, nobody possesses all the talents and traits of a great leader. However, every person possesses some effective leadership traits. Great leaders tap into areas that they can naturally execute and most effectively bring to life to influence employees.

Although it may sound contradictory, I think that *studying* the talents and traits of other leaders is invaluable in a couple of ways. First, other leaders often show how qualities like humor can be used to reach and inspire employees. Observing other leaders is especially helpful for someone new to leadership who is still discovering their style. Humor was something I had seen other leaders use and applied to my leadership style. However, it takes practice and experience to effectively use a skill like humor as a leader. Also, humor needs to be something you are comfortable with and part of your natural style.

When I was a graduate student, I created a thesis proposal at the recommendation of my advisor. Essentially, I was studying whether a nutritional supplement could increase anaerobic capacity in rats. Part of the study involved swimming as an exercise protocol. I put together a line-item budget of the major costs of the study which totaled about $2,000. I had several small items that totaled $100 that I should have listed as miscellaneous. Instead, I thought I would use humor and listed rat bathing suits for the miscellaneous category of $100. After submitting the proposal my advisor called me into his office and started the conversation by saying, "Did you really put rat bathing suits as a line-item for your proposal to the vice president of research?" We then had a conversation about appropriate and inappropriate times to use humor. Needless to say, I did not get funded, but I learned something through the process. I have found leadership skills are something that need to be continually developed and refined. To do this a leader needs to be open to feedback and other ways of doing things. Watching other leaders (both good and bad), as well as learning from occasional mistakes and recalibrating, are ways to hone innate skills.

The second reason for studying effective leaders is that you may not be aware of your strengths, or that something you take for granted like humor, is even a talent that can be applied to leadership. Certainly friends, trusted colleagues and a host of personality inventories can help in this discovery process. However, I have found that studying good and bad leaders through observation and reading to be invaluable in this practice. For instance, I have seen a number of leaders move into new programs or institutions and implement quick and decisive adjustment. In some instances, this approach was efficient and created needed change. However, this was not the best strategy for me because I was interested in taking a job for an extended period of time (I spent 35 years at three higher education institutions). If I went into a job and adopted this approach, I could not stay for long because my actions would most likely impact the goal of having a trusting relationship with employees. So, I learned through observations and readings to avoid these situations because they are not congruent with my preferred and natural leadership style.

So be yourself and learn by observing, visiting with and reading about other leaders. However, avoid emulating the unique way another person leads.

Caring for Your Employees

Many leadership experts discuss the importance of developing others as leaders, but few have done a deep dive into fostering a caring attitude toward employees. Mark Crowley, in his book *Lead From the Heart,* addresses this important leadership feature (Crowley, 2022). A fundamental premise of his message is that people are human and have needs (challenging work, growth, success, etc.) that must be addressed. Without question, a key person who can support these needs is the employee's immediate supervisor. In fact, a crucial function of quality leaders in higher education is to match employee desires/strengths with organizational needs.

Marcus Buckingham and Curt Coffman in their book *First Break All the Rules,* compile information from two large studies conducted by the Gallup organization. The data were collected over decades by interviewing millions of productive employees and over 80,000 managers (Buckingham & Coffman, 1999). One of the findings established that most people leave a job not because of poor pay, benefits or location but because of their direct supervisor. Also, they found that retention and staying productive were all strongly influenced by the quality of the supervisor. The Gallup interviews showed that talented employees need great supervisors. These findings are relevant because recruiting and keeping quality employees is essential to the success of any organization. In subsequent publications, Buckingham and colleagues conducted work based on the Gallup findings showing that employees should work from their strengths rather than trying to improve their deficiencies (Buckingham and Clifton, 2001; Buckingham, 2015). Collectively, these and other findings from their research provide valuable applications for the care and development of employees.

Supporting Employees Requires Sacrifice

As a leader, supporting employees is a critical part of your job and requires time and passion. This level of commitment is key to effectively develop and support faculty and staff and to address the mission of the university. As a new leader, I actively made the decision to let go of the things that I was responsible for as a faculty member and redirect myself to the work of a leader. In fact, if a leader in a substantive leadership role in higher education is unwilling to leave teaching and research efforts, they may not be the best person for the job. I have never conceptualized leadership as a part-time activity... it is a full-time effort. I realize this orientation will not sit well with some considering leadership in higher education because they want to be a leader and continue with certain faculty responsibilities. I am also cognizant that the shift from faculty to administrator is considerable. Once I left my research and teaching responsibilities, I was leaving a career path that I had cultivated and nurtured for over 20 years. Making the decision to turn away from this body of work can create insecurity. It is also a decision that can be challenging to reverse. While I could have possibly returned to teaching with a lot of determination, my research agenda was gone. So I understand the desire to continue as a faculty member while leading. Nevertheless, it is a disservice to the leader, their employees and the university to try and succeed in both arenas. Leadership is a full-time job and focusing on employees is one of your chief responsibilities.

Supporting Employees Is Central to Your Job

After discovering Buckingham and Coffman's Gallup data, I applied this to my leadership role (Buckingham & Coffman, 1999). I focused on listening and understanding the strengths, weaknesses, desires and needs of the employees in my unit, especially my direct reports. I did this because one of the most important actions you can take in developing and understanding employees is to get to know them. With this orientation, one of the first things I did when I accepted the deanship at Boise State University was to visit individually with the faculty in the college. I used a small group approach to meet with all of the staff. Talking one-on-one or in small groups is my most comfortable communication style, so I did this a lot. The meetings were informal, but I wanted to better understand the employees' professional and personal interests and passions. This is what author Mark Crowley refers to as the human needs of people, and he notes that by addressing these needs, employees can achieve their greatest potential (Crowley, 2022). Author John Maxwell speaks to the importance of *connecting with people,* because people do not care how much you know until they find out how much you **care** (Maxwell, 2007). Listening is a basic and powerful way of showing you care.

Often leaders make assumptions about what is important to others, which is a big mistake. I have confirmed this many times: You can really never know someone's needs and passions unless you listen. As C.K. Gunsalus, author of *The College Administrator's Survival Guide* concluded that nothing will increase influence more than listening to people (Gunsalus, 2006). Listen and try to understand their motivation and interest. Years ago, I was interviewing someone for a leadership position in the college I lead. As I entered the meeting to offer the position, I worried about the salary and how I was going to address this difficult issue. However, having done this a number of times, I started our meeting by asking the candidate what would be important for him in taking this new job? It was a simple, open-ended question. I did this before leaping into my concern about salary. As it turned out, there was almost no concern about salary... he understood the salary limitations. What was important to this person was having time off every September for two weeks so he could bow hunt. That was his concern and it was a deal breaker if this could not be arranged. His need was easy for me to address. He was being offered a 12-month administrative appointment and would accrue about five weeks of vacation each year. Arranging a two-week vacation in September with advanced notice was an easy task and meant a lot to this person. Not making assumptions and listening are essential for a leader to work effectively with employees. It is something we'll discuss again in chapter five of this book.

Engaging People in Strength-Based, Meaningful Work

Since finding meaning and utilizing an individual's strengths is key for employee satisfaction, leaders need to discover how to make this important outcome possible within a multi-faceted work setting. What I did may not sound that creative, especially in a technology-focused world, but it was an approach that always worked for me: I made time to have coffee with employees and made time before and after events to visit with people in my units. Additionally, I checked-in regularly with supervisors to hear their insights about their employees. Direct supervisors were invaluable to understanding the employees in my unit. Earlier in my career, I tried to short-cut the process and used inventories to gain insights about the people in my units to better assign work and create teams. This seemed like a rigorous and time-efficient way to collect employee information. However, many of the faculty were suspicious of the information that I was gathering and in some cases were resistant to even filling out the inventory. The fears varied, but some questioned the validity of the inventories and others worried that the information would disadvantage them and be applied inappropriately. Based on the resistance, I gravitated back to visiting and observing people so I could identify employee strengths, aspirations, professional interests and skills in a way that better resonated with them. Engaging with people in this manner requires patience, dedication and time. Unfortunately, I have not found a speedier and more parsimonious way for doing this important work.

During annual reviews I asked employees about their future aspirations and supported their goals as much as I could. While meeting with leaders, I asked how they were developing and supporting their supervisees. The additional insights during these interactions allowed me to understand how to deploy people and groups in a unit to support their skills and interests, while addressing the needs of the unit/ university. Larger meetings provided opportunities to strategically gather feedback on group trends, concerns and interests. In a sense, I became a broker offering people project opportunities, partnerships and resources so they could engage in activities that energized them and contributed to the mission of the unit/university. These interactions offered many new ideas, ways to problem solve, and were one of the most valuable and important parts of my job.

Support, Don't Micro-Manage

As I worked to develop employees, I respected the chain of command. This was critical to avoid being seen as a leader who interfered with his leadership teams' employees. I was quick to work with relevant leaders to make them aware of my involvement with their supervisee. In fact, the employee's supervisor was often the first person I visited with. If my interaction or idea gained traction, I would let the faculty and staff do their work with minimal oversight through my office and they would typically also connect on their new assignments with their direct supervisor. This required three-way communication, but it typically worked. For employees, enrichment comes with the freedom and confidence to direct their own work. Micro-managing kills this benefit.

My job in supporting employees involved acting as a sounding board and creating guardrails related to timelines, costs, scope, etc. Their direct supervisor was often a part of these discussions. It was also my responsibility to find resources so people could have reallocations of their work assignments, effectively conduct feasibility studies, and receive training/support. If things progressed successfully, the resources to implement and run programming were often provided through my office or split with their home unit. This approach was utilized across areas including educational programming, research growth and community engagement. I did this employee development often with new leaders and it helped them gain confidence and pride in their work.

There are many ways to go about identifying strengths, areas for worker development, etc. My informal techniques of talking to people may or may not resonate with you. Nevertheless, it is key to find ways to accurately assess your workforce to better care for and develop your employees.

Share the Workload

Many departments in higher education allow everyone in a work unit to be involved in departmental efforts and decisions. Some even use voting as a way of making decisions. I think these are naive notions. One management approach that helped me match employees to rewarding efforts was only conversing with those who were going to be substantially involved with an effort. Certainly, regular updates need to be given to the entire unit on decisions, progress, delays, etc. However, including too many people or the wrong people in the process bogs things down and often paralyzes progress. I have had departments unable to make a decision because the entire group is involved with the examination of a new initiative. Each time we visited, they seemed stuck; contemplating the issue and unable to engage. In one instance, a department spent two years considering an idea and nothing happened other than to schedule another meeting to discuss the idea. When a more streamlined group took over, decisions were made. Chronic contemplation is common in higher education and can be frustrating because nothing progresses and time is wasted beating a dead horse. It may seem inclusive to allow everyone to have input but, it comes with complications and challenges. Limiting participation to key individuals who are intimately involved with a given effort helps create movement for fruitful programming.

Work units mature and gain capacity through trust. Everyone benefits when work is divided and allocated across individuals and groups because there is faith that co-workers have the knowledge, skills and drive to execute assigned responsibilities. Everyone cannot be directly involved. Other members of the unit are informed via regular updates, but they are not involved with decisions and day-to-day activities associated with a given effort. Developing this level of trust in a work unit is not easy. I have worked with some units for over a decade to generate this atmosphere and never fully succeeded. The effort felt like climbing a mountain composed of sand. Every step involved slipping back almost to where I started. However, if this can be achieved, the capacity of the unit fundamentally changes. Having too many people involved in too many projects and using a voting system for decision-making are typically signs of an immature work unit where individuals do not trust their co-workers. While this is difficult work, finding ways to develop trust throughout the workgroup(s) you supervise is an exceptional contribution and needed in higher education. It increases the quality and productivity of your unit and increases the satisfaction of the employees because they have a manageable, focused workload.

Work Latitude

Another helpful practice to demonstrate care and support for employees is giving latitude to faculty and staff. Latitude allows employees to design work schemas customized to their work. This is necessary in employee development because it allows them to have more ownership in producing outcomes. I did not engage in a lot of oversight unless there were serious issues with an effort. This approach allows employees to develop their skills and discover how they can successfully engage in their assigned work. I firmly believe in giving latitude because of the creative problem-solving skills and capacity of workers leveraged through this practice.

For instance, the College of Health Sciences at Boise State had nine separate online programs developed over a 15-year period. Through the Extended Studies unit, a quality-control process was developed and required of all university online programs in evaluating feasibility before launching a new program. I had a close and long relationship with this unit and was thankful for their guidance and expertise in developing and managing online programs. However, the way that the various units such as public health, nursing, respiratory care, and imaging science executed their efforts varied. They all executed the Extended Studies process, but they had different staffing models, work allocation policies, decision-making procedures, and recruitment and retention processes. Essentially, as the unit leader I was uncomfortable having a mandated approach across all areas in the college. In fact, I was fairly sure that a high level of central control would be problematic. Therefore, I was fine with the variability as long as they all eventually met certain requirements (they developed these in consultation with leadership) related to recruitment goals, cash flow, student satisfaction measures, etc. I knew that becoming overly involved as a leader would diminish their growth, program effectiveness, and my bandwidth. If you want to promote latitude in work processes, give workers flexibility to create and solve problems and select people who are ready to make decisions and embrace the associated responsibility.

Training and Development

Many organizations such as Toyota communicate the importance of developing employees, particularly leaders (Linker, 2004). Helpful national trainings such as the American Council on Education (ACE) fellowship offer aspiring leaders apprenticeships at another institution for a full year. Additionally, there are some quality training programs where people receive guidance over a prescribed period of time. However, few institutions in higher education have laudable in-house training. Unfortunately, the resources needed for the high-quality trainings are often the first items eliminated during budget reductions or reallocations that commonly occur in higher education. Therefore, if you support the idea of training, you will need to find a way to provide development opportunities in a resource-constricted environment.

To address this challenge, I chose not to fill a vacant position rather than eliminate faculty/staff training and development. The importance of this investment became clear after my supervisor encouraged me to attend a two-week Management Development Program (MDP) at Harvard University. The program was well-conceived, organized, and delivered by a series of impressive leaders across academia. The speakers illuminated wonderful principles and techniques through real-life experiences and stories. In this training, I engaged with an assigned group that included 10 attendees who were quality leaders that wanted to learn. The readings and presentations created opportunities for my group and the larger cohort to explore leadership. I found myself energized and excited to learn skills and practices to develop as a leader. It was a great experience and I decided I would rather do a training of this quality once every three years (it was quite expensive) than attend annual trainings of average quality—e.g., many professional conferences.

Based on this experience, I gave supervisees significant opportunities for quality training and development. I always stressed quality over the number of trainings attended. In some cases, it was a training like the MDP program I mentioned or a professional conference that had sessions or trainings that met their professional needs. In other cases, they were paired with an individual who would provide one-on-one training or mentoring. For example, I had a board that helped advise me on the direction and growth of the college. About half of the board members were former senior leaders in health care and the other half were still employed. I was able to match members of my leadership team with members of the advisory board who could visit one-on-one to mentor leadership skills. Some of the pairings really clicked and others were not as helpful. However, the decades of experience that the board members possessed was invaluable for my team. In fact, I regularly met with these individuals to gain insights on how I could form programs and solve problems. They were a key resource for my development as a leader. As a leader, find a way to allocate resources to support employee development. This emphasis will further positive working relationships for employees and better position your unit for success.

Worker Recognition

As a leader in higher education, there are many opportunities to speak and visit with internal and external groups. I frequently used these opportunities to acknowledge the leadership and employees who were responsible for successful efforts. Giving people credit for their contributions is essential in supporting and enriching employees' work experience (Drucker, 1990). For some, recognition has profound meaning and validation. For others, they are simply happy to see that their efforts are noticed. It also communicates to others in the unit what differentiates average outcomes and progress from exceptional outcomes and progress. As a leader, the success of your unit will likely be associated with you. However, mid-level and senior leaders are rarely intimately involved with efforts. The actual work is done by others in the unit. Since your success is the collective contributions of your employees, be sure and recognize each person's or group's contributions frequently and through many distribution channels.

Failing Is Part of Succeeding

In addition to recognizing good work, I also publicly admit to individuals and groups when my efforts or decisions may have hindered an effort. This was always genuine, so I did not make something up to lessen the spotlight on a struggling effort. However, I did share when my actions hindered an effort or something I was involved in just did not work out. Sometimes the idea is good and the execution is spot-on and the effort still fails. For instance, we developed a wonderful award-winning population health management program. The program had a forward-looking curriculum, unique recruitment potential, and innovative, world-class staff. Additionally, we had a talented leader who was a powerful and capable force behind the program. Unfortunately, the students did not show up, despite significant recruitment efforts. I was very involved and supportive of the effort and it just did not prosper through multiple efforts over several years. Putting myself as a key player in this discussion helped divert some of the focus from the individual(s) involved in the struggling effort. It also allowed me to show that efforts can fail despite adequate support, planning, and execution. To this day, I am not entirely sure why it didn't work, given the quality of the faculty and staff and the timeliness of the programming.

Communicating that trying, struggling, or not succeeding is invaluable. To be sure, failing is not the desired outcome, but showing that struggling and failing are part of the process of succeeding is important. If people cannot fail, they will not take risks and stretch themselves. Without calculated risk-taking, your unit and university will not be distinctive and people often seek places where they are more comfortable taking chances. As a leader you want employees who will think outside the box and try something that may not succeed. Speaking with individuals and groups about your errors or failures is one way you can promote risk-taking. The one thing that was unacceptable was failure due to a lack of effort or execution. As Colin Powell stated, "Don't punish failure... just do better next time," (Harari, 2002). A straightforward message like this has remarkable application for leaders who want to foster a progressive organization that counts risk-taking as one of its strengths. You may find this important organizational attribute to be helpful in attracting and retaining some of your most valuable employees. Therefore, do not punish failure, or you may deter employees from efforts that could make your unit distinctive.

People Over Plans

I am a big proponent of planning significant efforts. Later in the book I will discuss this process and applications associated with planning. However, on the flip side of planning is actually doing the work to get the job done. As Colin Powell has plainly stated, "People over plans," (Harari, 2002). What Powell is referring to is the fact that a group can produce a wonderful plan, but at the end of the day, people get things done. Consequently, he is all about people-centered organizations. If you want to get things done, you must focus on the people. While I am a fan of planning, I also believe that a dedicated person or a galvanized group are ultimately the key ingredients needed to do great things. I've witnessed that if faculty—especially new faculty—can find just one person to connect with through community engagement, research, or teaching, their contributions grow exponentially. In fact, many opportunities I have seen as a leader emerged when an individual or a few employees discussed an idea with me or someone on the leadership team. The fact that they initiated the meeting disclosed their commitment and desire (typically). Few resources are often needed to listen and conduct a preliminary inquiry. Oftentimes, I would ask for additional information or introductory work to be conducted and let them move ahead. This leadership approach was effective and did not originate through a structured planning process. It is also something faculty and staff appreciated because they knew that their idea would be heard and given a fair review.

An example of people over plans was the genetic counseling program initiated at Boise State University through the College of Health Sciences. The individual who became director reached out and visited with me to discuss the idea of starting a graduate program. I offered support after her pitch. I knew genetic counseling was a growing and important part of health care delivery, even though we had no faculty with expertise in this area. I could also see that she was a very capable professional and really had passion for genetic counseling. I also considered the fact that an online program was not available to anyone wanting to major in this degree and online education was something our college excelled at. After some preliminary work, I hired her to develop the programming and gain accreditation. After 18 months, the program was approved and underway. Boise State and the College of Health Sciences had started the first *online* genetic counseling program in the world, and it was not part of our strategic plan. The program started because it related directly to our mission (health education) and there was a dedicated individual with passion, drive and a good idea. This degree is something that has helped make the college more distinctive.

Similarly, the respiratory care program at Boise State had a committed group of faculty, supported by strong leadership. It became the largest respiratory care program in the world, known for their quality programming, diverse delivery platforms, and graduate offerings—graduate programming in respiratory therapy is uncommon. There was never a plan to be the largest program in the world, but the group's cohesion, drive, and dedication to excellence was the engine that created this outcome. The role of a leader in these circumstances is to be open to feasible mission-centric ideas that are not planned, provide needed resources, and support employees' self-directed engagement. Taking this approach can produce meaningful and unforeseen outcomes.

University Benefits

Another way leaders can communicate care for employees is by communicating and delivering benefits that support employees' work and personal priorities. One powerful benefit that supports employees' busy lives is flexible work hours and remote/hybrid work options. Faculty have benefited from these arrangements for years, but the ability to apply these approaches to staff is much more acceptable since the COVID epidemic. Basically, the need to create alternatives to onsite work was forced by COVID and for most institutions these options worked with little planning or training. While some positions require people to be on campus during business hours five days a week, many can be done remotely or at least in a hybrid arrangement that divides time on-and off-site. Alternative work arrangements allow people to more easily engage in other parts of their life such as being home when children return from school, caring for a pet, or substituting commute time for personal wellbeing activities.

Having flexible, non-traditional work options does pose some supervisory challenges for leaders who have never operated this way. Nevertheless, remote work has been done successfully across a host of industries. For instance, Yvon Chouinard, the founder of Patagonia, describes in his book *Let My People Go Surfing,* his approach to hiring people with passion for the industry and letting them flourish outside of their business efforts, typically through outdoor adventure (Chouinard, 2006). His company also supported families with onsite baby rooms, high-end childcare and creative flextime policies. This type of organizational level care and flexibility is the future of work life across the United States. If this approach is new to a unit, training can ready the group. Some adjustments and learning need to take place and it may not work for some employees. However, people will typically be more satisfied and choose to work for an employer who has flexible scheduling versus a unit that is unwilling to make these accommodations. For many, COVID showed what life could be like if they were not at a distant worksite 8 a.m. – 5 p.m., Monday -Friday. Many employees are unwilling to go back to a traditional work life and gravitate to employers who offer work-life flexibility and other benefits that support their interests. Institutions that provide this level of flexibility have a strategic advantage over other institutions and will be able to better recruit and retain high-performing employees.

When I worked at Montana State University (MSU), the Early Childhood Development Center was housed in the department I lead and provided childcare for approximately 60 children. This service ensured that employees' children were receiving high-quality care while enabling parents to see their children during the workday. As department head, I enjoyed offering a real-life experience for students while providing a valuable service to employees. The employee wellness program was also run out of our department. The exercise, nutrition programming and health screenings were conveniently located on campus so people could minimize travel and efficiently accommodate time for health-enhancement activities. In the summer, the department also offered sports camps for local children. These were all meaningful benefits and something universities have the capacity and resources to offer their employees, even at the department level. Universities are uniquely positioned to offer wonderful enrichment programs (sports, music, theater, etc.) and many offer affordable access to education for employees and family members, via free or discounted tuition.

Universities also tend to have robust retirement programs that allow people to effectively plan for their future with institutional matches of 6 to 12%, depending on the benefit package. This tends to be much more robust than the retirement packages offered through private industries. For instance, I worked in health, which is a large industry making up over 18% of the U.S. gross domestic product (GDP). My employees commonly mentioned they could make more money working in the health system than for university wages. This was true, especially for faculty who were clinicians. However, I was quick to let them know, their current job at the university was much more flexible and the benefits offered by health systems were not nearly as robust as the university system. All of this communicates to employees that we care about you and your family and support your ability to prosper, now and into the future.

Hold Employees Accountable

In the care of employees I've discussed supporting them by finding out what they have passion for and giving them the resources, freedom and autonomy to grow personally, and contribute to the mission of the university. The counter-balance to this tactic is to hold people accountable for their work. This is not a new idea and requiring accountability is supported by a number of experts in leadership and organizational effectiveness (Crowley, 2022; Wakeman, 2013; Drucker, 1990). Accountability is generated by making milestones and endpoints clear to the person or people engaged in an initiative. For instance, if someone is supported to grow their research agenda through summer financial support, they should increase the productivity and quality of their research output over an agreed upon period. Tangible outcomes such as manuscript submissions/publications, enhanced rigor in their publication venues, and evidence of seeking/obtaining external funding should be established. If outcomes are not demonstrated, then their under-performance needs to be communicated during annual reviews and promotion and tenure reviews.

The accountability considerations I have just described may seem very tangible and straightforward. You might think all you need to do is determine outcomes, dates, and have a plan for follow-through. However, holding people accountable, especially faculty, can be daunting in higher education. I am referring to a minority of employees with these problems, so it is a low numbers game. However, it is a game that can require significant time and resources. For instance, there are multiple levels of examination in a tenure and promotion review that may not be supportive of your decision as a leader. While having multiple levels of review may make for a more democratic process, the decision could take months to finalize and there is almost always a policy that will allow for additional appeals and review if the employee is not satisfied with your decision.

I have had decisions appealed and reviewed over a 30-month period and had my decision overturned. The resources associated with these blotted processes are staggering. Similarly, I once visited with a faculty member at a university that was part of a committee that created a document for post-tenure review. Essentially post-tenure review is used to ensure that tenured faculty continue to perform at an acceptable level. The committee secretly called the policy they created "When Pigs Fly." They called it this because they had created a policy that prevented disciplinary action for poor performance. At best, they would be sent to counseling for not meeting expectations. Hence, the policy was called When Pigs Fly because there was a better chance of pigs flying than a faculty member being disciplined through this process. In addition to these policy challenges, trying to act through existing review processes such as promotion and tenure or annual reviews can be difficult because these assessments have their own policies and processes that make addressing accountability challenging. Higher education would benefit from cleaning up policies and processes that don't support enforcement of performance standards. As a leader, take the time to clearly connect accountability to existing assessment processes before giving support and document progress regularly. Most people will meet your expectations. However, some will abuse the support, so consider how to effectively hold these faculty accountable.

When you encounter an employee who has difficulty meeting deadlines, producing work, and/or their quality of work is unacceptable, be sure and document this problematic behavior. As part of this documentation you need to give the employee written and verbal feedback and track when the feedback was given and keep copies of any written communication. I start with one-on-one conversations so the employee is clearly aware of the problem. If they are not my direct report, I also inform their direct supervisor. This may solve the problem. If problem behaviors continue, written feedback and documentation through emails and memos is preferable because problem employees can dispute verbal conversations. Written correspondence especially in official documents such as annual reviews provides more tangible evidence of poor performance. If the poor performance continues, include members of human resources so they are aware of the behavior. In some cases performance improvement plans may be needed which often involves the engagement of human resource professionals. Often keeping records is not necessary because performance improves. However, in the cases where poor performance is ongoing, documentation is invaluable.

Larger efforts such as starting a new academic degree requires different outcomes such as completing feasibility studies, curriculum development, faculty recruitment, student recruitment, and revenue generation milestones. While there needs to be sufficient time to demonstrate tangible outcomes, employees need to be held accountable for attaining predetermined targets. If their idea or approach doesn't work, then they need to correct their errors or leave their effort for other opportunities. Occasionally, you will encounter an employee who fails because they do not try. I have experienced this unfortunate situation but it occurs infrequently, especially if the unit hires quality employees. When this happens, I have often adopted the sage advice of leadership authorities who clearly say, don't waste your time on people who do not try (Drucker, 1990; Wakeman, 2010). In some cases, trying to hold someone accountable was not worth the effort. Instead of taking disciplinary action I followed Drucker's advice... I did not support these individuals again unless there was evidence that things had changed. There are too many employees who have great ideas and are willing to extend the effort to be successful. As much as possible, spend time nurturing these individuals. Accountability is critical but not always easy to enforce. As a leader you need to care about and support your employees, but make sure it is balanced with accountability.

Chapter Summary

1. Leadership is the ability to influence. Caring leaders can be especially effective in influencing employees.

2. Effective leaders are authentic and use leadership skills that suit their unique style to effectively influence employees. Find and develop new skills that match your leadership style by observing, visiting with other leaders, and reading about other leaders' skills.

3. Care for employees by developing their strengths and listening to their needs, desires, and aspirational goals and do not micro-manage their day-to-day work responsibilities. Also, extending latitude in assigning work to supervisees and to address their responsibilities exemplifies a caring orientation.

4. Publicly recognize employees' work, effort, and success and create an environment where individuals are not punished or minimized because an effort did not flourish (Not giving an adequate effort is another matter and is problematic). If people are punished for failure, they will not stretch themselves to take on challenging efforts.

5. As a leader it is your responsibility to train and develop your employees.

6. Planning is an important activity. However, people, not work plans, ultimately get things done within an organization. Never underestimate the power and ability of an individual or group to do great things that were not part of a plan.

7. Promote and use organizational benefits such as remote work, flexible work hours, and the promotion of traditional benefits (vacation, sick leave, etc.) to show support and care for employees.

8. Caring for employees is important, however, it does not free them from the responsibility of performing well and being accountable. Employees need to be held accountable for the effective execution of their work responsibilities.

Chapter 5
Developing Civil and Fruitful
Work Environments

Relationship Boundaries

When thinking about work environments, the word "work" is key. Many people describe their department's culture by saying "we are family" or "we are all friends" who work well together. For me, work relationships are not the same as family or friend relations. Friendships are certainly made through work, but this is not the essence of a positive work environment. This is especially the case when considering supervisee and supervisor relationships. Moreover, for people in supervisory roles who have subordinates as friends, the relationships can be awkward and counter to addressing the university's mission. I have seen leaders proclaim that they can effectively separate friendships between work and non-work interactions... kind of like a light switch that can be turned on and off. My observation is that eventually familial or friendship-type relationships cause problems for leaders, especially with subordinates.

The key for a leader is to be approachable, caring, and open, but to also have demarcation to indicate that this is a professional relationship dedicated to doing good work. I was not a friend or family member to the people in my work unit. I cared about them, supported their efforts and with many, I sincerely enjoyed their company. But the relationship was professional. While it is very common and appropriate for people from other units to develop friendships with co-workers, it is more complex if you are in a leadership position and the employees are a part of your work unit. For me, this was a downside to being a leader because I met people I liked and could envision developing a friendship with. Nevertheless, this is one of the sacrifices that I made as a leader. As one advances through the leadership ranks, the ramifications for these relationships become more and more problematic as authority and influence broadens. Therefore, reflect carefully on your position and create boundaries that help you be a successful leader.

Addressing Problem Behavior

As a leader, you are a role model for how to engage in a professional manner. If you are going to lead, you need to take this role seriously because you set the tone for appropriate work behaviors. One of the mistakes I made as a leader was to delay my involvement in dealing with problem behaviors. I would see something happen and I would just hope that it would not happen again. As a mentor of mine once said, hope is never a good plan, and he was correct. In my many years of work, I have never seen problem behavior just go away. The opportunity for ignoring problems is endless but could include poor performance, bad attitude, someone overstepping their boundaries, or over-the-top reactions to decisions.

Problem behavior needs to be communicated to the individual or group because they are not clairvoyant and are unaware of your concerns, no matter how much their behavior exasperates you. This issue was also briefly discussed in Chapter 4 related to the topic of accountability. Cy Wakeman, who consults widely in leadership, articulates the gravity of non-communication when she states that as leaders, we become the problem when we do not quickly address problematic behaviors (Wakeman, 2010). In the area of performance, she states that every time you ignore poor performance you set a new standard. She has similar hard-liner positions around creating drama in the workplace. In her book entitled *The Reality-Based Rules of a Workplace,* she describes an individual's value through the following equations: An employee's value is their current performance plus their future potential, minus the drama they create times three (Wakeman, 2013). The key message communicated by Wakeman is that as a leader you intensely influence what is and is not acceptable in a work environment. Employees want to work in a cordial, engaging environment that lacks drama. If you are unwilling to take responsibility as a leader for addressing problem behaviors, expect the problem to grow and undermine the work environment.

Think of the problems in your current workplace. Are they being effectively addressed in a timely manner? Does leadership set a positive tone through their behaviors? When I did not address issues in a timely manner, the problems only grew. I struggled with timely interventions because I wanted to be liked by everyone. For part of my career this underlying desire I had as a leader created problems for me and the work environment. From this experience, I can tell you that the aspirations of being liked by everyone and being an effective leader are not compatible. The issues I was not addressing would continue and my frustration escalated. By the time I addressed the issue, I had wasted time and energy thinking and bickering about the problem, which only made the situation more frustrating.

I remember an instance where two faculty in the same department were publicly fighting over a disagreement. By publicly fighting I mean they were copying the entire department during their email battle, which documented their differences and distaste for one another. I watched the interactions for about a week and finally sent out an email to them with the entire department cc'd that said, "Stop this silly public brawl now! No more emails to each other or the department about your differences." I followed up with separate emails saying we needed to have a conversation about their behaviors. Maybe I should not have emulated their approach of copying the entire department, but I did. Had I contacted them when the fight first started, I may have been more composed and effective and the rest of the department would have seen that the behavior was addressed immediately. As a leader, I let the fight go on too long and since I was copied on the emails, I set a standard that has no place in any work setting. Specifically, I tolerated unprofessional behavior that was distracting others from their important work for days before I took action. Do better than I did in this instance. Be thoughtful about avoiding and how you communicate problem behaviors; your action or inaction will influence your unit's environment.

Setting Conduct Expectations

Most workplaces have a code of conduct or a set of core values designed to communicate appropriate ways of conducting oneself within and outside the campus community. Through these documents, leadership is plainly stating that they expect certain types of conduct from all of their employees. Unfortunately, this important tool is not well communicated and infrequently used to create a positive work environment. I know that in some institutions, these documents are quite old and were created long before many current employees started their employment with the institution. Over time, they become hidden in strategic plans or buried in a website only to be used when a significant problem arises at the university. However, they can also be used as a blueprint for creating common understanding and expectations for employees.

As a leader, I took conduct expectations seriously and had the entire unit engage in the development of core values. Essential to this effort was using a process that resulted in buy-in and alignment across the unit. Without collective agreement, behavior expectations are of little value. In the movie *Cider House Rules,* the apple pickers live in a common area known as the cider house. Within the living area there is a list of rules that the workers are to follow. One of the workers clearly breaks a rule (smoking inside the building) while standing next to the list. When one of the actors calls him out and makes him aware of his infraction, he simply states that those are not his rules and walks away. The scene plainly reveals the need for participation, buy-in and alignment when it comes to codes of conduct.

The process I used seemed to create buy-in and alignment with employees and involved a four-step process. It may have applications within your work setting.

STEP 1: Understanding: As part of this unit-wide exercise, I first made sure that everyone was aware of the institutional values. We had the flexibility to create our own values, but they could not contradict the values of the university. For many individuals, this was the first time they had even seen the university values, so it was time well spent.

STEP 2: Dialogue and Discussion: To generate buy-in and alignment, faculty and staff were given the opportunity to engage in dialogue and discussion of what was most important and why. In the unit-wide exercise, I would typically start the session off by sending a message to everyone about the need to develop or update a set of core values through a scheduled meeting. This was facilitated through a mandatory meeting (most meetings were not required). During the meeting, I would explain why developing core values was important and something we all needed to take seriously. I was careful about how often I did something like this (bring the entire group together) to help convey the importance of the message to the unit. I then introduced the facilitator, which I highly recommend using. I was careful to select a facilitator who was good at engaging large groups and giving everyone a chance to be heard.

STEP 3: Bring Life to Values: We were able to collectively take these values and give them life through labels that we all understood and captured the intent of the value. To get an accurate label required robust conversation and the development of a succinct definition. The values were categorized under headings such as professionalism, civility, trust, tolerance, caring or collegiality. It is helpful to keep the list short since the intent is to identify the most critical items needed to guide employee behavior. If it is too long the usefulness is diminished, and people have a hard time remembering the essence of the document. A good facilitator can also be very helpful in this process.

STEP 4: Communicating the Values: Values were communicated through tabletops distributed throughout our buildings, framed posters on each floor and in the leadership offices, articles in our newsletter and a document on the website. These efforts made visible to all the values we collectively agreed to follow. To remind people of the values, we shared examples of people who embraced the values and complimented these individuals for their actions during meetings. Additionally, when individuals violated a core value, this often had disciplinary ramifications, which helped demonstrate the seriousness. The corrective feedback was obviously not a public event, but individually communicating problem behavior reinforced the values and helped create a more positive environment.

Values or codes of conduct exist in any organization. If you are new to leadership, take advantage of this blueprint to prevent problems down the road. If this does not exist in your organization, create your own blueprint. If you are not a new leader but have never engaged in this activity, a well-timed introduction of this process can also help. Even if you do not create your own values training, a leader should at the very least state the university core values and communicate that everyone is expected to work under these guidelines. However you go about this process, finding ways to communicate and reinforce values to employees is a key responsibility as a leader.

Supporting Workers in a Bureaucracy

Most colleges and universities run as a bureaucracy where the enterprises use rules and procedures to manage the systems and processes—often through centralized hierarchical governance structures. Examples include decision-making processes nested in departments, colleges, and through the provost or president's office. These decisions may also include the involvement of faculty senate or other ad hoc committees who are used to inform decisions which are written and placed in a policy document that is often thicker than Tolstoy's *War and Peace*. Dense bureaucracies are particularly apparent in state colleges and universities where state processes and systems are overlaid with university processes and systems. As I will share later, there is a need for good systems and processes in any organization composed of hundreds, and in larger universities, even thousands of employees. This is essential for a variety of reasons. However, the most central work that is done at a university or college is the work of the faculty. Faculty engagement does not flourish in an overly bureaucratic environment. *Therefore, one of your key roles as a leader is to support the bureaucratic processes needed for a smooth functioning university, while freeing the faculty and staff to do their creative entrepreneurial work.*

Hillman and Breen in their book *The Future of Management,* discusses the challenges of working within a bureaucracy in today's work environments (Hamel & Breen, 2007).

They point out that modern traditional management takes creative, free-spirited people, and asks them to conform to standards and rules which stifle imagination and initiative. They go on to explain that we have problems innovating because modern management was designed to increase efficiency and productivity, which often leads to increases in bureaucracy. This approach creates a vicious cycle around productivity/efficiency and bureaucratic growth. One idea they offer is for individuals to be able to manage themselves, underpinned by the sincere belief that every employee can help solve complex problems. They support the idea that we should not try to hire perfect leaders but instead build a work setting where employees thrive with less than perfect leaders. This is counter to what most organizations believe. In fact, there is a common belief that a search will result in the hiring of a talented leader. However, it is more common to hire an average leader and the likelihood of developing or hiring a talented leader is about the same as hiring a poor leader. Therefore, I believe their statement holds truth and offers a possible solution to addressing quality leadership issues. If higher education does not make some meaningful changes to building and finding leaders, this is another path that may need to be taken. However, I still hold hope that higher education can grow and recruit and develop high quality leaders. Having good leaders and self-directed, innovative employees combines the strength of both options and best serves higher education in the long run.

Hamel and Breen had other insights that were highly applicable to higher education (Hamel & Breen, 2007). For instance, many institutions in higher education have recently moved to incentive-based budgeting or responsibility center management (RCM) models that focus on outcomes, such as growing student credit-hour production or producing graduates in exchange for financial support (Curry et al., 2013). These models have been helpful in moving institutions of higher education that employed historical-based funding models (units get what they received the year before plus funds for salary raises) that do not effectively encourage financial stewardship through student recruitment/retention. However, as the insatiable need for additional revenue grows in higher education, leaders will likely continue to focus on efficiency and productivity for revenue growth, which will deepen the bureaucracy and the risk of stifled innovation. As a leader, the use and implementation of new approaches such as RCM budget models needs to be carefully considered and implemented within the context of what higher education in the United States must do to be a world leader. Specifically, a dense bureaucracy that is overly focused on revenue generation will not allow for innovation and entrepreneurial activities. Without innovation and an entrepreneurial spirit, our coveted position in the world will certainly fall.

Leadership in a Bureaucracy

Unless you work in a very unique educational setting, you are a leader who works within a bureaucracy. A necessary balance is achieved by creating support systems, processes and policies that are necessary for a large enterprise, while shielding your faculty and some staff from the soul-sucking force of a bureaucracy. As previously mentioned, Tichy and Bennis in their book, *Judgement; How Winning Leaders Make Great Calls,* describe the impact of an overly bureaucratized work force when they state, "Bureaucracy frustrates people, distorts priorities, limits their dreams, and turns the face of the entire enterprise inward" (Tichy & Bennis, 2007). Over-reliance on this system is not compatible with the aspiration of being a high-functioning, contemporary college or university. As stated by Herb Kelleher, the former CEO of Southwest Airlines, "It is good to have a light-hearted irreverence for bureaucracy and titles" (Pandya & Shell, 2006). If you want your faculty and students to enhance communities, solve relevant problems, become great Theoreticians, writers, and philosophers, you cannot have them concerned about arriving on campus Monday-Friday at 8 a.m. As soon as a leader's primary focus is on how faculty fill out travel forms and if they completed the human resource satisfaction survey, you will have entombed the faculty within the bureaucratic dungeon of higher education and you will fail as a leader.

Gordon Mackenzie wrote a very unique book on leadership entitled *Orbiting the Giant Hairball* (Mackenzie, 1995). He worked for Hallmark Greeting Cards and was an artist who moved into leadership and management. If there was ever a place that needs creativity and imagination for its workers, it is in the greeting card business where people need to use artistic creativity, humor, wit, wisdom, and emotion to create an impactful message. His examples of protecting the artist from the Hallmark gray-suited bureaucrats is wonderful. He describes the drive for productivity and the bureaucracy of his corporation as a giant hairball that most people get sucked into. To allow employees to be successful, the leader needs to pull employees out of the hairball so they have the vision and space to create and problem solve. He cautions employees and leaders from straying too far from the ethos of the hairball. He makes this point because working too far away from the bureaucratic engine may draw suspicion and lead management to question an individual's "fit" within the enterprise. I envisioned his hairball analogy as gravitational pull and if you or your employees get too far from the pull, you fly uncontrollably into outer space. If this happens, your flight in outer space could be a terminal contract or no longer being supported within the institution. Moving out of the hairball is essential, but you need to be careful about how you do it and how far from the center you and your employees travel.

At a university there are many people working deep in the hairball, doing the work that is needed to keep the enterprise running. Their work is critical and needs to be valued because they are doing the hairball work so others have the indulgence of working outside the hairball. However, many in these positions lose sight of the mission of the university and believe that doing internal audits, creating weekly productivity reports, conducting annual reviews, and attending parents' weekend are the mission of a university. That is simply not the case. Yes, these business management and public relations tasks need to be addressed, but this is not how you want your best people devoting their time and psychic energy. As a leader, your job is to have your faculty and unit leaders spending as little time as possible in the hairball and give them the ability to do the creative work that only they can do. Creative work also requires giving faculty and unit leaders time in their schedule to be creative. You are not giving someone what they need to contribute to the university mission by giving them unreasonable teaching loads coupled with unrealistic research expectations. In fact, this simply means that you are lost in the giant hair ball and are trying to feed the bureaucratic engine. Teaching great classes, producing creative works, engaging meaningfully in communities and producing ground-breaking research requires time for thought, reflection, focus and work implementation. If faculty are in the hairball and given unreasonable workloads, their special contributions will not be actualized and you will be unsuccessful as a leader.

How To Free People From the Giant Hairball

As a new faculty member in higher education, I was in one of my first department meetings and the dean of the college was there. The dean spoke about the work of the college and contributions made by faculty. The areas he addressed aligned with the tripartite mission of teaching, research, and service. My naive but sincere question to him was to understand what part of the tripartite mission was most important for me to focus my energy on as new faculty. His politically correct response was less than helpful. He said they are all equally important. My concern was how I could excel and make a significant contribution in one area, let alone all three. During my decades of work in higher education, I have observed that very few people truly excel in multiple areas. My assessment is that it is challenging to excel in one area and be satisfactory in the other tripartite spaces. Quality is difficult to define, but actually excelling and demonstrating excellence in three areas is a daunting task that few can ever achieve. As a leader, I was pleased if faculty demonstrated excellence in one area and were satisfactory in the others. Therefore, I looked at allocating workloads that would allow employees to meet the target of excellence in one area and satisfactory performance in the other areas. I did this by creating more professional hires, more diverse faculty appointments and start-up packages that supported this three-area balance.

Professional Staff

One of the personnel decisions I made throughout my time as a leader was to hire professional staff to cover functions that faculty historically addressed. For instance, the units in my areas took advantage of business staffing who addressed budget, payroll, and human resource needs to minimize faculty engagement in these areas. Additionally, professional staff helped build/support courses, especially online courses, advertise academic programs, and implement and support technologies. This allowed faculty to focus more on the art of teaching through streamlined processes that supported them. Professionals in the areas of securing, managing, and closing grants were recruited and organized through a department or the Office of Research. Faculty could then maximize their time working on the creative and scientific aspects of a grant proposal. The professional staff supported many of the significant administrative tasks (budgets, bio-sketches, submitting governmental documents, etc.). The same approach worked during grant execution, where the offices could help with hires, budget monitoring, payroll, monthly reporting, and other important but time-consuming administrative tasks. Hiring professional writers meant that faculty were not asked to write as many articles for internal and external communications. Professional staff also provided expertise to navigate the bureaucracy of the university, state, or federal government and better allowed faculty to devote time to activities only they could conduct.

Diverse Faculty Appointments

One of the significant changes in higher education over the past 25 years has been the use of more diverse faculty appointments. While there is a large variance in workload distribution across colleges and universities, historically the most common faculty position was a tenure track position or line. As a leader, I found that we needed more part-time faculty (adjunct faculty) or full-time teaching faculty, often referred to as clinical faculty or lecturers. In fact, I would cannibalize a tenure-track line to hire more adjunct or clinical faculty so these employees could do more teaching and create space for tenure-track faculty to conduct research. These hires and position conversions allowed tenure track faculty to have the necessary time needed to develop and support an active research agenda while the clinical and adjunct faculty took on larger teaching loads. Similarly, I allowed tenure-track individuals who excelled in teaching to move into clinical positions (higher teaching loads) so they could dramatically reduce their research responsibilities and focus on teaching excellence.

Ultimately, the use of adjunct faculty teaching one or two classes a year grew significantly to allow others to spend more time in service and research. In an area like health, employing adjuncts was helpful because we recruited professionals who were working in health occupations where our students hoped to gain employment. The real-life examples and applications shared by adjuncts with students genuinely enriched curriculums. Faculty often start their academic career with notions of how they want to distribute their work efforts. However, as they engage in these activities, they frequently find they have interest or aptitude in other areas. Whenever possible, allowing people to follow their interests and strengths is good leadership. Diverse faculty appointments allow flexibility for where faculty spend their time. Trying to fit a round peg in a square hole is not good leadership. Therefore, create appointments that align with faculty strengths and interests and apply workloads so people can succeed. Focusing faculty psychic energy into an area of excellence through workload redesign increased the chances for the whole work unit to truly flourish.

Start-up Packages

When I started my academic career, my start-up package included a used 286 Zenith computer and an office. That was it. I went to the used on-campus furniture warehouse and found a desk, bookcase, and had to ask for a phone. I actually attached the bookcase to the wall so it did not fall over on me. I was given a one-class reduction my first semester so I could organize my research and prepare for the six classes I would be teaching each year. During the first semester class reduction, I taught two new classes and in my second semester I had three new classes added to my teaching load. Anyone who has worked in higher education would likely say I didn't do a very good job of negotiating my start-up package. However, when I started, substantial start-up packages were less common and I was not mentored to negotiate. I just assumed the institution was going to set me up for success and all the support would be worked out once I arrived, which was a naive assumption.

Once I left the faculty ranks to work as an administrator, I worked diligently to create start-up packages that set faculty up for success so they could develop excellence in one of the three areas of teaching, research, or service. In addition to creating professional positions that supported faculty, I worked to create time to allow them to prosper in their endeavors. I increased start-up packages that gave faculty reduced teaching loads so they could develop courses, start their research agenda, and engage with the university and communities across the state. For instance, some faculty received summer financial support for three years to have time to engage in programming with the state department of health and welfare. Similarly, research faculty, depending on their needs, received labs, equipment, graduate student support, and reduced teaching loads of one to two classes a semester for three to five years. This may seem commonplace, but when a college has almost nothing in the way of start-up packages, regularly allocating resources for this support requires a major change in college resource generation and allocation. It also requires faculty and staff to adapt to the many changes associated with this alteration. Ultimately, this support aligned with the university's strategic efforts and better enabled faculty to contribute to the university's mission.

Leaders Assign Workload

In most colleges or universities, there is a general workload allocation given to faculty, depending on the position. The workload allocates a percentage of time to teaching, research, and service. Some institutions will also allow part of a faculty workload to be allocated to administrative tasks. Workload is always assigned by leadership and can be an effective, low-cost mechanism to help faculty develop their area of excellence and deepen their expertise. For instance, if a partnership is made within a community to address a critical health issue, a faculty member's time in teaching or research can be changed so they can focus more time on community service. Similarly, they could be relieved of a class responsibility to spend more time in community service. Or if a grant opportunity becomes available, summer appointments with additional compensation could allow for grant preparation and development.

I once supervised a department that had done a wonderful job of growing their undergraduate programming. Because of this growth the faculty were teaching in an overloaded capacity. To accommodate the elevated teaching loads, I changed their appointments from nine months to 10 months and added another month (11th month) for research. Because the budget model diverted resources back to units that grew, additional compensation (two months' salary) was given to faculty. This adjustment gave people time to focus on an expanded teaching effort, which was their area of excellence. As a leader, you will typically have considerable discretion on workload allocation, which can help produce additional excellence within your work unit. One situation where this can be more complex is within unionized environments. If the faculty are unionized, this approach will have more restrictions and processes associated with changing someone's workload. In these environments, having flexibility to assign variable workload may need to be negotiated. If the negotiated policy does not allow for this flexibility, you need to renegotiate the bargaining agreements or find other ways to support faculty growth and development.

Being an Effective Communicator

I had a realtor who told me that the three most important considerations in real estate are location, location and location. Applying his memorable statement to higher education, I would say that three of the most important traits of an effective leader are communication, communication and communication. The larger your enterprise, the more sophisticated the communication skills and processes need to be. I break communication efforts into individual and small groups as well as macro-level internal and external communication. If these areas are not adequately addressed, people become unsure of their role, uncertain about the efficacy of their contributions and disengaged and frustrated with their work. The blame typically is directed at leadership, who are labeled as "poor communicators," which is often accurate. Communication across these areas is not an event, but a process that needs to be repeated and updated consistently.

Individuals and Small Groups

Earlier in this chapter, I discussed the need to swiftly address problem workplace behaviors. This is ideally done via one-on-one communication (face-to-face, if possible). Problematic behavior is sensitive and needs to be carefully communicated. Emails and even a phone call lack the feedback of face-to-face communication. Susan Scott, in her book entitled *Fierce Conversations,* discusses different types of conversation related to teams, delegation, coaching, and confrontations (Scott, 2002). I found that through classifying a conversation, I gain clarity on what and how to communicate. For instance, if I am trying to get departments to work together as a unit, I would talk to the leaders individually and then bring them together for a three-way conversation. My first visit is to gauge receptivity and bandwidth with each group and then collectively discuss how they could come together and execute my request. I use the meetings to share an opportunity, find common ground, and identify what resources are needed for the partnership. My collective goal would be to generate interest and identify a path forward. In a confrontational conversation, I would usually have a one-on-one conversation that is used to clarify what happened, make clear what changes are needed, which is then often paired with a follow-up meeting to evaluate progress. Because every conversation is different, using these classifications or your own system can help in the preparation and execution of the interaction.

Listening

Many leadership experts convey the importance of listening (Harari, 2002; Gunsalus, 2006). Listening was critical for me because I needed to represent an amalgamation of viewpoints that aligned with the mission of the university. By amalgamating ideas, you can find areas where there is traction and common ground to change current efforts or explore new initiatives. This approach allowed my college to create an Office of Research to support research growth and build and implement three new doctoral programs. The research support and doctoral programming were all new and supported the university's desire to become a metropolitan research institution of distinction. These enhancements occurred in part because I listened to the faculty, staff, and our community partners who were interested in these advancements. In meetings when we discussed these initiatives, I gave a brief overview of the idea or enhancement and then kept my comments short to engage potential partners as soon as possible. Remember, communication is a two-way process and if one person or group is doing most of the talking, communication is likely not taking place (there are exceptions to this such as a termination discussion which is a very one-sided event). If you really embrace the concept of listening, know that what you have prepared to share will likely change and require you to be ready to do an about-face and follow the direction of the conversation. Communication requires two or more people listening and sharing based on the information provided. As a leader, you need to develop quality listening skills or you could miss opportunities and ultimately follow a path that is more difficult.

Another approach I used was to get out of my office and be seen by people across the college. I typically had no agenda but wanted to be able to visit with members of the college and discuss what was on their mind and how work was going. I also wanted to create a persona that made me more approachable so I was not seen as a figure head in an ivory tower. Additionally, I had my senior staff (senior associate dean, associate deans, etc.) meet and visit with people and groups across the college on my behalf. I wanted people to know that any of my staff could speak on behalf of the dean's office and had my full support to act in this capacity. This arrangement really expanded my ability to engage across the college and my staff enjoyed acting as my representative during their interactions. If you have a quality staff, this approach can be a very effective way to magnify your reach and connectivity within your unit.

Honesty and Feedback

Another important factor in successful communication is the need to provide honesty and frank feedback (Harari, 2002; Pandya & Shell, 2006). I especially appreciate Susan Scott's conceptualization of honesty: "Full disclosure to myself and others with good intent (Scott, 2002)." I would add that the full disclosure is done with respect and empathy for the person on the receiving end. It is relatively easy to be honest when something has gone well or someone has performed at a high level. However, when a program is failing, a key partnership has been damaged, or someone's performance is unacceptable, being honest takes courage and thoughtful execution. These conversations tend to be more complex and require consideration to ensure you have an accurate understanding of the issue. In complicated situations, there are often multiple interpretations, so the need to listen to these perspectives and dig deeper is essential. Toyota has a technique for gaining clarity by asking "Why?" five times (Linker, 2004). This process helps leaders get to the root cause of an issue and avoid focusing on some of the downstream consequences. Once you are certain of the issue, *then* engage in an accurate and frank conversation.

Don't Piss the Wrong People Off

While listening and honesty are critical in effective communication, being aware and respectful of an audience is also critical. Colin Powell provides clear and direct advice that has served me well: "Don't piss off the wrong people" (Harari, 2002). This advice is commonsensical and valuable, but many regularly ignore this message. By not pissing off the wrong people, he was referring to the key people in your organization. Be very vigilant in these situations because there may be a need to challenge people, but there may also be a need to retain your standing and support within the organization. You need to be able to disagree, but be thoughtful about when, with whom, and how you engage in these communications.

By utilizing Colin Powell's advice, I can better decide how, when, and where to communicate information. There are instances where keeping your mouth shut is in your best interest and the interest of your unit. Unfortunately, I have not always followed this sage approach. I once was in a meeting with the provost and the vice president of research with all of the university department heads. I was also a department head at that time. The two senior leaders described a financial problem that had five possible solutions and in their estimation, four of the solutions would not work. Consequently, the fifth solution was the only choice. For some unknown reason I felt compelled to offer another solution. This was the wrong time, place, and not in my best interest (if you're counting, that is three strikes). If you make a list of people not to piss off at a university, these senior administrators would most certainly be on the list. In this instance, if I had a good idea, I should have aired my thoughts through an email or in a one-on-one meeting after their presentation. As I said earlier, be thoughtful in these situations and avoid pissing off the wrong people. As a leader you will undoubtedly piss people off, just try and be mindful about when and why you are doing this.

Seek Advice From People You Trust

These techniques and approaches helped my communication. However, the faculty and staff feedback I received on internal communication was average. It wasn't bad, but it also wasn't good. I told my supervisor during my annual review that my scores were strong in other areas but communication was an area that could use improvement. He had the survey results from the college faculty and staff reviews and he could see my assessment was accurate. He suggested having lunch with the college faculty and staff in small groups. The idea he proposed was *not* to invite people by intact work groups, but rather mix people up across job classifications, departments and schools. Attendance was optional. I started each lunch in the same way. We have a big college and coming off COVID and the associated shutdowns, I started by saying, "I feel like I do not know many of you as well as I should." I went on to say we could talk about whatever they wanted (work or non-work related). I then shared some information about myself that few people knew. I asked if they had heard the term "military brat" (someone who lived or traveled all over the world because they were affiliated with the military). "Well, I am a park brat," I said, "and I lived in 15 different national parks growing up." Then other people introduced themselves and shared something unique about their lives. The lunch was simple family-style and the conversations varied. Acting on this advice really helped me connect and open communication with people in the college. In fact, it was one of the best things I did to improve internal communication during my time as dean. I would suggest finding something like this to help you get to know your team, especially if you have a large number of employees. Check with your supervisor, they may also have ideas on how to enhance communication.

Additional Communication Techniques

Miguel Ruiz wrote a book about how to live life based on the teachings of an ancient Toltec civilization located in southern Mexico. The people were known for their wisdom and knowledge for living an unencumbered life. He resurrects the teachings in his book *The Four Agreements* (Ruiz & Mills, 1997). While the work has many applications, I have found it helpful in developing effective communication. I will share three of the agreements as they relate to my efforts to improve communication. Readers who are interested in more information related to these teachings should view his other thought-provoking publications including *The Fifth Agreement* (Ruiz et al, 2010) and *The Mastery of Love* (Ruiz, 1999).

The first and most essential agreement is to *be impeccable with your words* (Ruiz & Mills, 1997). Ruiz discusses the power of words and the ability they have to lift or hurt another human being. As a leader, this understanding is vital! I have had people cite verbatim something I said a year ago and mentioned how my statement guided their actions. In some cases, I don't remember making the statement. My point is that as a leader you may make comments that do not seem important. However, your employees may take profound meaning from your words. The general weight given to what a leader has to say makes sense because people look to leadership for insights, wisdom, problem solving, strength, and inspiration. Employees often take the words of a leader to heart. With this knowledge comes a responsibility to be very thoughtful about what and how you say things.

Ruiz discusses the origin of the word impeccable and describes how blaming or judging not only hurts others, but also hurts the person delivering this communication. When you gossip it is an unfortunate reflection on your character and spreads poison to yourself and others. Cy Wakeman, like Ruiz, is very critical about judging, blaming, and gossip, and says that when you are judging you are *not leading* (Wakeman, 2010). She encourages leaders to check their egos and not let issues stew in blame and judgement; to instead have candid, productive conversations. Gossiping with others about problem employees intensifies the situation. The desire to share your struggles with others is strong, but typically not productive. So, whenever you speak, avoid gossip and be very careful to choose words that clearly and succinctly communicate your truth. Also, consider not only the words you use but also the intent behind them. A thoughtless statement or inadvertent communication can cause significant damage.

The second agreement is *don't take things personally* (Ruiz & Mills, 1997). I have found this agreement especially helpful when I hear others blaming, judging, or gossiping about me. I now see it more as a reflection on that person rather than an accurate evaluation of who I am or how I have performed. As Ruiz points out, once you agree with people who spread hurtful messages, you will be poisoned by them. Unfortunately, our upbringing often forces us to take things personally and care too much about what others say. Remember, no person has the power to make you feel poorly about yourself unless you allow them to. Also, their messages (blame, judgement, etc.) are very different from words used to help you as a leader through truth and insight. This type of communication is certainly worth listening to and should be applied to help you be a better leader. Listening to words with malintent will not help you as a leader. Less than impeccable use of words by others should not cause you to change who you are or how you work. The key is to realize what the words are intended to do to you and avoid the trap of being harmed by cruel communication.

The third agreement is *don't make assumptions* (Ruiz & Mills, 1997). I have mentioned this topic in other sections of this book, but it deserves mention again. Ongoing effective communication in a workplace is vital. In the absence of accurate, timely information, employees will make up their own story to fill in missing pieces. The assumptions that fill in the missing pieces are often inaccurate and laden with judgement and blame. Leaders and subordinates are often too busy or afraid to probe and dig deeper to fully understand a situation or issue. Essentially, they lack the time and/or courage to find the truth. As a leader you need to demonstrate not making assumptions, both for you and the people that work with you. This takes time and effort; however, it makes for better communication and relations in the workplace. Once you adopt this approach others will also engage in this behavior, especially with your example. The work setting will be a healthier place because of your dedication to not making assumptions and finding truth.

Individual and Small Group Communication Summary

A variety of tips have been offered to promote effective communication with individuals and small groups. Consider your own communication strengths and weaknesses. Some of your weaknesses can be filled in by other people, like a communication professional creating written communications on your behalf. However, if you find yourself struggling with communications that only you can conduct, this might be a signal for you to secure the use of a coach or at the very least, to seek out self-directed study to improve your communications. If a coach is not available and you desire support, check with your human resources department. These individuals have many complex and tense conversations with employees related to performance issues, illegal activities, human rights violations, bullying, and problematic conduct. People experienced in this type of communication can be helpful in assisting you in the habit of more effective communication. Also, counselors make a living by asking people honest and intense questions that require deep thought, reflection, and a subsequent revealing of emotions —their techniques may be helpful to you as a leader. Most universities have Employee Assistance Programs (EAP) that are typically used for personal counseling needs. However, these individuals can also be very helpful in improving your professional communication skills. Normally, the services are offered at no costs and are always confidential. Individual and small group communication is an essential skill as a leader. If communication is a strength, utilize this aptitude to your advantage. If it is something you struggle with, work to develop skills that allow for more effective communication. While the tips I have just shared are helpful with individuals and small group communication, they are also aligned well with macro-level internal and external communications. These areas will be explored in the subsequent section.

Macro-Level Communication Inside
and Outside Your Unit

A real challenge that I have encountered with macro-level communication is keeping people informed while still being respectful of their time. Organizational experts who embrace systems thinking do not typically view individuals as the problem in communication breakdowns but see poor systems and processes as the usual culprit (Senge, 1990; Deming, 2000). In fact, they are very critical of leaders who blame individuals for problematic systems and processes that leadership is responsible for. Therefore, as a leader you need to build effective systems and processes that support communication and are consumable for your co-workers. At all costs, avoid blaming your employees for not taking the initiative to examine communications. While faculty and staff can be a weak link in the communication process, this should be the last place you look for the source of your unit's communication breakdowns.

Probably the wisest thing I did around macro-level internal communication was to take formal and informal employee feedback seriously and use that feedback to improve communication. It would have been easy for me to defensively point out the efforts by myself and my office to communicate with my unit. This would have been a polite way of saying to the employees, it is not me, you are the problem. Instead, I asked about what I had gotten wrong and what needed to be added to our communication efforts. Some of the feedback I received in this effort was less than helpful. For instance, a few people said, "Your meetings suck." I didn't take this type of feedback personally because of the harmful intent, so these comments were not considered. However, much of the information my office gathered through informal conversations and yearly employee survey data (about 250 individuals) was helpful and used to enhance communication. One piece of advice I took as a department chair was to create a budget committee composed of faculty members from each unit and the department budget administrator. The committee was created because some faculty had suspicions about how departmental resources were being used. After meeting regularly for 18 months, the representatives asked to dissolve the committee because in their estimation the department had good oversight and funds were being effectively allocated. They also found that the detailed oversight of expenditures, review of the monthly expenditures, yearly summary evaluations, and budget planning was a time-consuming effort. They felt their time could be spent more effectively in other areas and communicated this to department members. The apprehensions around the budget and departmental expenditures were addressed and the committee was discontinued. Based on this experience, I always provided budget and expenditure summaries to my units two to three times a year to prevent budget anxiety.

I also shared with staff the mediocre feedback I had received from them about my communication efforts. They had a number of great ideas to address this issue, which they implemented! For instance, they produced weekly communications from the dean's office that gave succinct information-based summaries. People really liked this communication. Similarly, they developed newsletters and social media feeds. Not only did this work help with internal communication, but it helped us communicate with donors, community partners, and graduates who were interested in the college. Additionally, we chronicled our progress for employees and our community partners by publishing annual magazines. This was useful for showcasing all of the wonderful work that had been done over the past year. Talented writers were hired to write articles and it offered a platform for regular messages from the dean's office. After implementing their improvements, the college sent out some type of internal or external communication nearly every day of the year. At the end of my tenure as dean, my yearly communication scores were strong thanks to the problem-solving of my boss and staff. If you are struggling with some aspect of your job like communication, be open with your supervisor and leadership team; they can be an invaluable source of support.

Large Group Meetings

One common mode of communication in higher education is to schedule meetings. In 35 years of working in higher education, I have never heard anyone ask for more meetings. Maybe that is because many find meetings a waste of time. In fact, I've heard meetings referred to as improvisational garbage cans... a place for managers looking for something to do (Bolman & Deal, 1991). However, I have had many employees request more and better communication, which can be enhanced through effective meetings. Michael Doyle and David Straus offer a number of beneficial tips for making meetings work (Doyle & Strauss, 1976). They cover preparation, facilitation, role definitions, member responsibilities, and much more. People in higher education assume they understand meetings because they spend so much time in them. However, time in meetings is not necessarily a good model of how to organize, run, and engage in effective meetings, especially if people work within a system where poor meeting practices are commonplace. Taking time to read a book like this can be invaluable, because many of us never have any formal training on how to conduct effective meetings.

When I arrived at Boise State, I held four-hour meetings at the start of each semester. I thought this was reasonable because we only got together as an entire group twice a year, but faculty and staff requested that we make the meetings shorter. When I stepped down from the deanship, we were having one-and-a-half hour meetings each semester. Attendance improved and shortening these meetings allowed me and my leadership team to focus on topics and activities of the most value. Faculty and staff were freed up to work on urgent issues that they needed to address at the start of the semester such as advising, class preparation and student orientations. This is an example of listening to employees and making simple changes that improve communication. As a leader, you set standards, so do a good job with the meetings you run and expect others to do the same. Nothing is as precious as peoples' time. Make sure your meetings are a good use of everyone's time.

Large-Scale Initiatives

For large transformations such as changing a college's direction to increase research productivity or building a new strategic plan, I followed a process that was effective with most employees I worked with. As you embark on any large-scale initiative, consider these steps and modify the process to best meet the needs of your work setting. At the very least, have a plan for how you will implement your large-scale effort.

STEP 1: Meet With Your Unit: Meetings could include unit-wide events that occur infrequently or through your attendance at unit meetings within departments or schools. Make yourself and your leadership team available to the entire unit. Your leadership team could also attend unit meetings to give updates and answer questions on behalf of your office. Additionally, consider scheduling time for anyone in the unit who wants to gain further understanding or has questions related to the initiative. When I did this, the meetings were generally online (that is what faculty/staff preferred) and offered every month or two. We found that through the technology afforded through online meeting platforms, people can ask questions or make comments throughout the meeting. For those who are not comfortable sharing or speaking within a large group, I always offered the opportunity to email me, my staff, or set up a one-on-visit after the meeting. Use meeting formats and follow-up communication methods that are commonly used and perform well in your work setting.

STEP 2: Engage the Community: Universities and colleges are often an important part of the community where their services are delivered. Therefore, it is important to include community partners in planning and communicating progress made on large-scale initiatives. To facilitate this process, I engaged community partners through a group called the Board of Ambassadors (BOA). The BOA was a group of senior leaders in both the public and private sectors who were involved in the delivery of healthcare and preventative services, primarily within Idaho. Members included CEOs of health systems, senior management from health insurance companies, current and former directors of health and welfare, past and current presidents of the Idaho Hospital Association, physician leaders and other key partners. To recruit such a high-quality group of leaders requires time to cultivate working relationships with each individual and discuss how their involvement with your unit would benefit their organization and the state. In my case, the BOA was used to help the college produce programming, research, and strategic planning that was needed for the state of Idaho. Their advice and guidance were taken seriously and incorporated into our planning and programming. The BOA had very little turnover in part because these insights were recognized and used to better the college. As the relationships evolved, I also was invited to be on the boards and advisory groups for major health care entities in the state. If you and your leadership are on their boards and they are on your boards, a clear understanding of the collective missions develops, as well as partnerships. These relationships can be a powerful tool for communicating externally about the activities of the college with key health entities across the state. I strongly recommend fostering these relationships to elevate relevance, support, and understanding about your unit's efforts.

Step 3: Communication: For daunting or complicated initiatives met with resistance, I generated college magazines (hard and virtual copies) that described our decision-making processes and our plans for addressing the initiatives. This approach was helpful in describing where the college was, where we would be going, and how we would get there. The document also served to solidify why and what we were doing and chronicled that decisions were made with the involvement of the entire college and key health entities across the state. You can use a publication to record broad participation, key decisions, and agreement on a plan moving forward. A widely distributed publication reduced the desire to question what we were doing.

It is worth mentioning that efforts such as creating a 20- to 30-page magazine requires professionals dedicated to delivering effective communication within and outside the university. With something like a magazine, there is a need for graphic designers, editors, and writers to help tell a compelling and impactful story. Communication is important, so hiring professionals to actualize desired outcomes in an engaging, timely, high-quality fashion is essential. If you do not have the necessary support and expertise, be careful about which communication efforts you take on. Quality communication can easily be the full-time job of several people. If you are the communications team and have other responsibilities, design a strategy that reflects this level of staffing.

Communication Is a Shared Responsibility

Earlier in this chapter I mentioned that issues such as poor communication are typically not caused by employees, but rather systems and process problems. However, communication is not a passive process and requires engagement from the individuals and groups involved. There will also always be people critical of communication who do not attend college or unit meetings, miss question-and-answer sessions, and do not review weekly updates, yearly reports, budget summaries, or the college magazines. In short, they are not taking responsibility for their role in the communication process. In these instances, I asked why they were not taking part in the communication process and if they didn't engage, I didn't waste time worrying about them. So, my final piece of advice is to make sure that your employees understand that communication is a two-way process and everyone has a responsibility in successful communication.

Chapter Summary

1. As a leader it is important to differentiate work relationships from other types of relationships, such as friends or family. A professional relationship becomes especially important when you need to address problematic behavior.

2. Creating and upholding formal codes of conduct can be effective in fostering a positive work environment with common understanding and expectations for all employees. Finding effective ways of creating and/or gaining employee commitment to core values is essential for success.

3. One of your key roles as a leader is to support the bureaucratic processes needed for a smooth-functioning university, while freeing faculty to do their creative entrepreneurial work. If faculty get sucked too far into the hairball of bureaucracy, their ability to make exceptional

contributions will be stifled. Strive to create a balance in your unit that works within required systems and processes but does not consume your most talented contributors.

4. As a leader you have the power to make decisions that allow faculty to engage in activities only they can execute. These actions include using professional staff to navigate the logistics and bureaucracy of the university, as well as state or federal entities. Also, consider attractive start-up packages, progressive workforce configurations and supportive work assignments so that faculty have resources and bandwidth to be stellar contributors.

5. High-functioning work environments need effective communication approaches and strategies that are purposeful and based on honesty and respect. To be an effective leader your communication needs to be initiated at individual, group, and macro-levels. Do not underestimate the diverse skills needed for each level of communication and be sure you acquire and apply them in your leadership position. At all levels of communication, demonstrate and practice the ability to listen and thoughtfully respond so that clarity and truth is exemplified for everyone involved.

6. Continuously work to improve communication and ensure that employees understand that it is a two-way process and everyone has a responsibility to participate for successful communication to occur.

Chapter 6
Strategic Planning

Introduction

All units and institutions in higher education benefit greatly from conducting quality strategic planning and implementation processes. Strategic planning and implementation are key leadership responsibilities and a primary way of producing desired outcomes within a unit or institution. It doesn't matter if the unit is academic, human resources, facility services, or information technology, they all will more effectively contribute to the mission of an institution through effective planning and implementation processes.

Many institutions do not take this responsibility seriously and fail to identify strengths, weaknesses, distinctiveness, purpose, priorities, and investment opportunities. Effective strategic planning and implementation helps leaders make decisions, generate employee buy-in, gauge progress, and guide employees in their day-to-day work activities. It also helps with employee recruitment and retention because employees better understand the mission of the enterprise and their role in addressing the mission. If done properly, these outcomes are reassuring and act as a map for leaders and employees.

However, if done poorly it will have just the opposite effect and create doubt and a lack of confidence with employees and partners. Strategic planning development and implementation comes with challenges. As Mike Tyson the famous boxer once said, "Everyone has a plan until they get punched in the mouth." When developing or implementing a strategic plan, leaders will likely experience the equivalent of a punch in the mouth and need to navigate these adversities. Consequently, this process needs to be a priority that receives much of your time, attention, creativity, and resources. Some common challenges include working in a promotion and tenure environment, poorly articulated plans, failure to implement plans, and an inability to make demanding decisions that focus strategic efforts.

Promotion and Tenure

Higher education uses a promotion and tenure process focused on individual productivity. This custom and the associated challenges was discussed in the second chapter of this book. In most institutions, candidates for tenure or promotion are evaluated on tangible outcomes through their teaching, research, and creative activities. Service to the university, profession, and community is part of the review process, but in my 35 years in higher education, I have never seen anyone denied tenure because of their service performance and I know of only one person promoted using service as their area of excellence. Therefore, teaching and research/ creative activities are the main drivers in this process.

Promotion and tenure processes need to be considered when motivating faculty to engage in strategic planning or work teams because these activities are classified as service and not central to the promotion and tenure process. Therefore, it is in tenure track faculty members' professional interests to spend *as little time* as possible in service activities such as strategic planning, community engagement, or contributing in work teams. This creates a problem with strategic planning and implementation because this is time away from activities that visibly reward faculty. As a leader, you will need to address this challenge because faculty will want to focus on efforts relevant to their success but will frequently be dissatisfied if the strategic plan does not fit into their agenda and interests. This can be problematic because after the planning is done, disengaged faculty may come back and request modifications. So compelling faculty to participate in planning in a time-sensitive manner is key.

Poorly Articulated Plans

Engagement in strategic planning can be a challenge for all job classifications at a university when leaders develop flowery, grandiose aspirations that are not practical or achievable. Moreover, when the plan is paired with half-baked strategies and tactics, employees are left wondering what the unit or university is trying to do. Ultimately, the flawed approach leaves individuals pondering how they fit into the plan. This outcome is common and created through a blurred vision and mission statements and/or bad strategy (Rumelt, 2011). Ineffective strategic planning and implementation is often compounded if there is frequent turnover of key leaders that results in frustratingly repeated planning and implementation processes. The constant change in direction and focus leaves a sour taste in employees' mouths every time they hear the phrase "strategic planning." In these situations, employees come to accurately believe that strategic planning results in no discernable outcomes and is a waste of their precious time. As a leader, it is your responsibility to avoid these pitfalls. Poorly articulated and grandiose plans void of practical strategies will erode faculty and staff's trust.

As a faculty member, I was actively involved in my college's strategic planning process, which was initiated by the new college dean. The effort was facilitated by a series of large and small meetings and through the creation of many ad hoc committees. It took over two years to finalize our plan. One troubling outcome was that some plans seemed disconnected from the preliminary data we collected. Specifically, the data would indicate one direction, and the dean would sometimes push for another path. I never missed a meeting because I felt this was something the college needed for growth and development. The plan was published in late spring and by mid-summer of the same year the dean had taken a new position as provost at another university. An interim dean was appointed and the entire plan was filed on a shelf and never used. It literally just sat and collected dust. I recall thinking that so much work was committed to this project, and we never did anything with the plan. It was just a stepping stone for the dean and a waste of time for everyone involved.

Be certain that your plan is clear, action-oriented, and that you monitor engagement and progress from members of the entire unit.

Inability To Make Demanding Decisions

Author Richard Rumelt reminds leaders that using a strategic plan to focus and prioritize the work within a unit or organization requires them to make difficult decisions (Rumelt, 2011). His guidance in this process is to avoid democratic-style decisions through group voting and ranking activities. This is indispensable advice. His insight is especially relevant within higher education because many in this setting gravitate to group decision-making processes. For example, approaches such as nominal group techniques are common. In this approach, everyone is allowed to distribute a limited number of votes across potential options. The votes are tallied and the option with the most votes wins. These processes are in part problematic because of the tribal nature of units, conflicting values, and individual desires and aspirations. I made it clear when making a decision to communicate that I wanted input from my leaders and key stakeholders so I could make an informed decision to avoid these pitfalls. During these sessions I would preface the meeting by saying, "I need your input to help me make a decision on an important topic." This preamble clearly set the stage and communicated that I did not want to engage in a vote or any process that would generate a majority rule for decision making. It did however communicate that I needed their collective insights and perspective so I could make the best decision.

There is a theory developed by Ken Arrow, who won the Nobel Prize for his work demonstrating the irrationality of democratic voting. In the Arrow's Paradox he focuses on ranking-based decisions and rational choice theory. In rational choice theory voting problems occur when individuals perform a cost-benefit analysis and determine if the choice is right for *them*. Sadly, what is right for the individual may not be right for the unit or institution. While voting and ranking approaches are inclusive, they are flawed and therefore the decision may be flawed. Input from a variety of sources is critical, but decision-making through voting or ranking is not advised for these reasons. Ultimately, feedback from those who are knowledgeable and/or involved with a decision needs to inform leadership (unit leaders and potentially senior management) who then make the final choice.

As a leader you need to make difficult choices that align with strategic plans and decide where to allocate limited resources. The longer that voting and ranking techniques have been used in a unit, the harder it is to move to a system of input with leadership making the final decision. Be leery of using democratic processes just because voting and ranking provide a path of least resistance. In the end, your job as a leader is to make the correct or best choice—not to follow an easy path that makes people comfortable and happy.

Some of the most important decisions I have been involved with as a leader occurred when faculty support was split or there was strong resistance. For instance, the director of nursing in my unit supported adding online programming, even though support was split across the department. It is not easy to make a decision that may upset half of your employees. In the end, the decision to implement this strategy proved to be a strategic decision and a powerful educational tool for the college and state. Similarly, directing a college that was excellent in undergraduate education to develop more graduate programming and a stronger research agenda was also a good choice. While the decision may have been accurate, deciding to grow graduate programming is a significant decision because staffing and resources needed to engage in graduate programming is very different from an undergraduate-focused curriculum. Specifically, the depth of study, complexity, and the ability to deliver small courses that often lead to original research is fundamentally different from educating an undergraduate student. When I made this choice members of my leadership team initially disapproved and thought this was the wrong direction in part because of the enormity of the task. Nevertheless, over a seven-year period the decision proved effective and created needed research capacity and educational opportunities for students.

Despite these two successes, decisions by a leader do not always have a happy ending. Therefore, know that you will not always make the best choice. In the subsequent chapter, I will provide an example where I made the decision to have the college faculty work in integrated teams to support interprofessional education (IPE). IPE is a process whereby students learn together across health disciplines so that they collaborate more effectively once in the workforce. We worked to implement this strategic effort for six years and it completely failed. In this instance, after some helpful feedback from my leadership team, I announced that the implementation was a failure, and we needed to reallocate the resources to other initiatives. Some decisions pan out and others do not. However, having capable leadership amalgamating input to make choices is a better approach than voting or ranking.

Purpose of Strategic Planning

Now let's examine three fundamental questions that help elucidate strategic planning (Tichy & Bennis, 2007):

1. Where are we now?
2. Where are we going?
3. How will we get there?

Additional probing questions can be useful in generating dialogue around these three fundamental strategic questions. The probing questions are provided in a series of three tables (Tables 1-3), generated by management experts including Peter Drucker (Drucker, et al. 2008; Ducker, 1990) and Hamel and Breen (Hamel & Breen, 2007). I have also included questions that have helped me answer these questions. The probing questions have been divided under each of the three fundamental questions to generate dialogue and gain understanding when engaging relevant internal and external individuals and groups. It is important to generate a comfortable level of understanding with key individuals and groups (dialogue) before moving to action (discussion) (Senge, 1990). Once the dialogue is complete, then discussion can take place to operationalize the actual doing or action connected with the strategic plan.

Where Are We Now?

To answer the first question on where we are now, it is important to engage faculty, staff, students, institutional leadership, and community partners in reflective and quantitative data collecting of achievements and failures. How this is done is up to you. Allowing people to share what they think is significant should be encouraged because compiling this work validates past and current efforts and provides a chance to recognize people for their contributions. Employees within different parts of your unit will share a particular lens but additional insights can be gained from institutional databases, senior management, students, community partners, and employers. These efforts are typically focused on a time period after the last strategic planning process or after the departure of a major leader such as a dean or president. The focus is on the most recent history, but valuable information can be identified over decades. For instance, the culture of a unit or institution may have existed for decades and recognizing this could provide important information to be included in the strategic plan. Culture always trumps plans, so considering this in your approach could work in your favor. Every organization is different, but valuable sources of information regarding the first fundamental question can be obtained through:

- Quality of graduating students, evaluated through the eyes of employers
- Senior management or board perceptions of quality and productivity
- Applicability of degrees for employers
- Benchmarking with comparable institutions of higher education
- Comparisons with other institutional units such as other colleges or departments
- Student perceptions for employment readiness
- Employer and student satisfaction measures
- Student retention and graduation statistics
- Student numbers

- Recent revision and creation of degrees
- Research productivity such as number of publications, grant funding, and student involvement in research

Take advantage of data already collected whenever possible. Universities tend to collect valuable information for accreditation, federal and state reporting requirements, and for student recruitment. Do not reinvent the wheel... look around and use quality data that already exists. Fill in gaps with new data collection efforts once you have compiled existing data.

Data Collection

Collect data in ways that make the most sense for your university and community. Often a university's equivalent of institutional research will have available data on student recruitment, retention, graduation rates, demographics, and satisfaction scores over time. While the depth and quality of information varies across institutions, this is a source to check on before doing a lot of work on your own. This information is objective and in some cases the results are surprising even for leadership. For instance, while doing comparisons with benchmark institutions in my college, one of the units in the college had student credit hour production that was 156% of benchmark institutions, while another department was 90% of its benchmark institutions. This information was surprising and useful to understand capacity and our ability to take on new initiatives. Without it, I would have been left to dialogue with units about their workload and ability to take on initiatives. Dialogue without data may or may not be accurate since everyone feels like they are working hard. Data helps focus and direct the discussion accurately. Objective data is necessary when trying to lucidly understand where you are now.

Another effective place to obtain data is through academic programs that require accreditations such as nursing, engineering, education, social work, or public health. As part of the accreditation process, unit staff need to conduct student exit surveys, report graduation rates as well as the demographics of their students. Unfortunately, the process varies across accrediting bodies so you may or may not have comparable data across units.

Visiting With University Leaders

An effective approach to engage key senior management members is to invite them to visit with a unit such as an entire college in face-to-face meetings. During this time, university leaders can share perceived strengths and ways the unit could continue to grow and better contribute to the university in the future. The senior management members need to be selected by you to best inform and share their insights about your unit. Often their feedback is followed by a question-and-answer session. These events take some time to orchestrate but you can collect significant information in a one-hour session. Furthermore, having senior management speak directly with the unit conveys the importance of planning and is more effective than the unit leader relaying a message of what senior management thinks or desires. In short, having senior leaders interact directly with the unit most impactfully communicates their position and insights.

Engaging the Community

If you have not already engaged relevant community members and potential employers into your units and the university as a whole, seek and engage this group. Often university leaders are surprised by the level of interest individuals and organizations outside the university have in engaging with a university. As an employee within a university, giving a lecture or working with students and faculty is a common occurrence that is often taken for granted. For people outside of academia, it is exciting to engage with a university... unfortunately, universities are large and complicated enterprises to navigate. As a leader, your simple invitation can give people access and provide introductions so they can partner with the university.

I once had a senior leader comment that after 15 years as a president of one of the largest companies in the state, I was the first person to ever invite him to speak at the university. He gave a talk, met with faculty and students and became a wonderful source for feedback about our programming as well as the future needs of the industry he represented. Use techniques to recruit relevant community and industry members so they can help you evaluate your current efforts and create needed programming and research for the future.

Table 1. Engaging questions to help answer the strategic questions... Where are we now?

Question
[H]How easy is it for people to get experimental funding?
[H]What are the frustrating incompetencies, e.g. payroll or budget forecasting, that plague the university?
[H]Do we have an environment conducive for innovation? Explain.
[D]How would you define ourselves as a specific and important niche?
[D]Are your best people working on big issues and innovations or are they dealing with yesterday's stuff?
[D]Do we systematically seek opportunities?
[D]Do we have a disciplined process for generating solutions and ideas?
[D]Does our innovation strategy work with our business strategy?
[A]What objective data sources exist that would evaluate our performance over a 3 -5-year period?
[A]How can we parsimoniously compile the data in a clear, user-friendly format?
[A]What comparative data can we obtain (tuition costs, graduation rates, salaries, research expenditures, cost of instruction, etc.) from like universities/programs to help evaluate our unit(s)?
[A] During the past 3 -5 years, what successes do you most want to celebrate?
[A] During the past 5 years, what capacities and skills make us distinctive?
[A] How do students view our unit(s)?
[A] How do comparable institutions of higher education view our programming?
[A] How would partners and potential student employers evaluate the quality and relevance of our work?
[A] How does senior management view our unit(s)?
Table notes: [D] *Questions taken or modified from Peter Drucker (Edersheim, 2007)*   [H] *Questions taken or modified from Hamel & Breen (Hamel & Breen, 2007)*   [A] *Author generated questions*

Review the questions in Table 1 to identify what will produce the most essential information for your planning process. While a number of questions are offered in the table, you may have other ideas for engaging employees, stakeholders, and graduates, which make perfect sense since you will know what is best for the individuals or groups you are meeting with. Typically, a few quality questions or a targeted presentation designed to generate dialogue will contribute to answering the question, "Where are we now?" To focus the effort, consider meeting with leaders across your units and institution to gain understanding about what information is most helpful for them in this process.

Documenting and Summarizing

The time spent in qualitative and quantitative data collection is critical to gain a common and honest understanding of where you are now. It is helpful to have individuals across units, including students, involved in the data collection effort because their discoveries will be more firmly embedded in their memory and shared with multiple people in the unit(s). Often data can be shared in bits and pieces to relevant groups and individuals as it is obtained throughout the collection process. This allows people and groups to slowly answer the question of where we are now. This approach helps keep members of the unit engaged through a process that may take months to finalize. A big mistake is for leadership to collect the data and then present it to the unit members. It may be more time efficient, but it is riddled with problems (people question the results, ownership in outcomes is not obtained, results are thought to be part of leadership's agenda, an opportunity for buy-in is lost, etc.). Therefore, include a diverse and creditable group in this process and use their findings for the final reporting.

Create a Summary

Because of the variety of sources and the volume of data collected while answering the fundamental question of where we are now, a summary of the work should be created. There are many ways to compile the information but it should be honest, cohesive, parsimonious and clear. Fortunately, there tend to be a lot of people within a university who are very skilled at taking data from multiple sources and compiling a report or presentation for audiences that are within and outside the university. A helpful approach is to create the first draft summary of findings and deliver the preliminary results through reports and presentations. Strategic planning is important enough that leaders should be intimately involved in the reporting process and understand how conclusions were obtained through the various data sources.

Check for Accuracy

Once a draft report is created, check to see if the information makes sense to the various audiences you are working with. For instance, do the faculty seem to agree with student satisfaction scores and related comments or are they disconnected? Are the student numbers from institutional data congruent with the numbers found through your advising center? If any of the findings are problematic, do additional work to confirm or refute what has been compiled.

Confirm results also by having people review sections of the analysis or the entire analysis. Both of these approaches work. What is critical is that people have the opportunity to review data that is relevant to them and any questionable findings are exposed for further examination. For instance, questionable qualitative data may be reviewed by another person or additional information can be obtained to clarify how data were generated to help the reviewer(s) understand findings. In some cases, findings may be modified based on reexamination. In other cases, the findings may not change but people are more comfortable because they understand the limitations and sources of the data used in the analysis. Remember, people trying to understand results or making sure that data is reliable is a *good thing*. This shows they are engaged, thinking about the findings, and care that the results are accurate. Avoid getting upset by questions and feedback. Use critical reviews as an opportunity to validate concerns and further generate buy-in with reviewers.

Finalizing and Distributing the Findings

Finalize findings only after conducting a review and addressing concerns. The final work needs to be generated for a variety of audiences via long and short presentations, conversations, documents, electronic formats, and other methods to communicate the information. Strategic planning can be a long and involved process so having documentation of what was found needs to be memorialized to help answer the next two fundamental questions: Where are we going and how will we get there?

Where Are We Going?

Use the questions shown in Table 2 with a variety of internal and external groups and individual stakeholders. Also, use the questions to help faculty, staff, and leadership seek and obtain needed information. You will notice that the orientation of the questions in Table 2 is designed to help you start considering the future and how the unit(s) might engage over a defined time period. Strategic planning terms and concepts vary dramatically across facilitators, authors, and organizations, so create labels and definitions to ensure common understanding within and outside the university. The areas applicable to the second question (Where are we going?) include vision, mission, goals, strategies, and key performance indicators as outlined in Diagram 1.

These planning items are essential. Many organizations use a more involved planning process which is not necessarily a bad approach. However, these areas at a minimum must be addressed. Be careful not to make the planning too dense and cumbersome or the planning process can hinder engaging in strategic activities that actually move the organization toward desired outcomes.

Table 2. Engaging and probing questions to help answer the strategic questions: Where are we going?

Questions
[H]What tomorrow problems need to be solved today?
[H]What is the espoused idea, e.g., shared governance that you would like to turn into an embedded reality?
[D]If we were not doing what we were doing today, would we go about it the same way?
[D]Who are our customers? Who is our primary customer? How will our customer change?
[D]What does the customer value... support services, stackable certifications, flexibility, etc.?
[D]What is our plan? Should our mission be changed? What are our goals? What's our strategy?
[A]What opportunities are available because of our geographic location?
[A]What macro-level changes (health care reform, AI, Chips Act, new administration, etc.) do we need to consider in our future planning?
[A]What opportunities exist if novel partnerships are created across our units?
[A]What do our students need to meet potential employer needs?
[A]How do we create a strategic document that guides all of our units in executing our work?
[A]How can we best support the institution or our university governing body's strategic needs?
Table notes: [D] *Questions taken or modified from Peter Drucker (Drucker et al., 2008; Edersheim, 2007)*   [H]*Questions taken or modified from Hamel and Breen (Hamel & Breen, 2007)*   [A]*Author generated questions*

Diagram 1. Vision, Mission, Goals, Key Performance Indicators (KPI) and Strategy

Definition	Term
Future aspiration	Vision
What we do	Mission
3 -5 aims that embrace our vision	Goals
Actions to address goals	Strategy
Barometer of success	KPIs

Vision... What Are Your Aspirations?

Most organizations have a vision statement. Therefore, the question becomes does the institution need to update its vision? Similarly, a unit such as a college may be working within an institutional vision and desire to create or update a vision for the college. No matter the situation, the purpose of a vision statement is to clearly and succinctly describe a future aspirational place for an institution or unit (see Diagram 1). Ideally, the brief statement should be memorable and inspiring. While a vision statement should reflect core values and represent the desires of employees, it cannot meet the needs and desires of all employees, partners, and students. In short, you need to decide what the organization or unit will be in the future, and it cannot be all things to all people. Examples of some quality vision statements outside higher education include:

Google... to provide access to the world's information in one click.

Disney... to be the leading entertainment company in the world, creating magical experiences for audiences of all ages.

Walmart... to be the destination for customers to save money, no matter how they want to shop.

Most people are familiar with these companies, and they fit the description of what a vision should be. The creators convey a clear idea of what it is they want to be, and all this is done through a quick glance that creates a concrete image in a matter of seconds. Regrettably, this is not the case with all vision statements. For instance, review this vision statement from a prominent university:

Our university will be perceived and acknowledged as the outstanding public university in the nation—a world class university. It will be a community of scholars and a center for learning where individuals can develop their intellectual capabilities throughout their lives in an environment that promotes academic achievement and research excellence. Each individual's responsibility to one's self and obligation to society will be nurtured. It will be a diverse community where the highest moral and ethical values will prevail with a dual purpose, an inward focus on learning and an outward focus on service. It will be the embodiment of the land grant, sea grant, and public research university dedicated to excellence. It will provide outstanding educational programs having a global perspective with a foundation based on knowledge, compassion, and understanding.

Now this is a very full vision statement and an inspiring vision, but it is problematic. It is too long, overly grandiose, and one gets the sense that they want to become everything and this simply isn't possible. Also, it is unclear what is of most value in this aspirational statement. Compare this to two university vision statements which are more understandable, concise, and focused:

We envision a world without barriers to student access and success in higher education, and we strive to make that happen.

We will become a metropolitan research university of distinction.

When one reads the first vision statement, it is clear that they want to make higher education accessible within a student success-focused educational environment. Given the rising costs of education and the difficulty associated with obtaining a college degree, this vision is relevant and exciting. The second statement articulates the desire to nurture and grow research as a distinctive characteristic of the university. Both are quality vision statements that succinctly articulate a distant ambition that describes their priority and destination. The work in developing a vision statement is to prioritize the *essence* of where you hope to be in the future. Often if the vision is long and drawn out, this work has not been done, or the developers have tried to appease too many groups with multiple visions included in one statement.

Avoid Isomorphism

Another consideration for vision statement architects is to avoid trying to be like another university. The common desire to be like Harvard or Yale is an isomorphic process whereby one institution attempts to be like another. However, this orientation ignores essential elements such as an organization's strengths, distinctive qualities, brand recognition, endowments, and a host of other important factors. In many instances, if they deeply examine their aspirational institutions and identify what they are all about, they might quickly abandon this desire. The strength of the vision statement comes from identifying the unique essence of what your organization is about and reflects something your organization or unit can do to improve the world. Saying that you work at a place like Harvard will not engage and inspire your employees, students, or community partners. However, saying you will make quality education accessible to students, particularly the underserved in your state... this will engage and inspire.

Failure by Wordsmithing
and Adding One More Item

Vision statements can also get bogged down in wordsmithing and the creep of adding just one more idea or descriptor. A good facilitator can help you avoid these pitfalls and save you time. If you do it on your own or hire a facilitator, set the stage by outlining some boundaries before starting. Boundaries could be where you want to be over a prescribed time period such as five years, the length of the statement, the need to prioritize and the need to develop something that is understandable and speaks to multiple groups. Many facilitators want no restrictions or limitations when starting a visioning process. However, without restrictions time can be lost and a dense rambling statement is often the outcome. You are then left with the unenviable position of removing items that stakeholders found important. The vision is only the start of the strategic process and needs to be paired with more action-oriented efforts such as goals and strategy. As Bolman and Deal accurately point out, a vision without a strategy is an illusion (Bolman & Deal, 1991). Take care that your vision statement does not become an illusion.

Mission... What Do We Do?

A mission statement flows from the vision statement and broadly describes what employees do and elucidates the unit or institution's purpose. It is not a list of tasks that people engage in on a day-to-day basis but a statement that describes the purpose of the entity and embodies what is being accomplished. It is crafted in a way that connects what people are doing with the vision and outcomes of the unit or university. In short, it explains in broad terms why you exist. For many great leaders such as Colin Powell, mission is central in being successful and producing clarity around what needs to be done (Harari, 2002). Mission connects individuals to the enterprise and guides their work to collectively address desired outcomes. It tells people what they should do (Ducker, 1990).

In higher education, colleges and universities are in the business of creating and disseminating creative works and knowledge. Target groups can be diverse but students are the individuals who are typically most targeted for this growth and development. Exceptions to this singular focus include the work of extension services in land grant universities that provide education and problem-solving to communities throughout the state. Other service efforts fall into this broader category. Ultimately, the work that is done contributes to a better and more robust society. The way you go about creating desired outcomes is guided by values and codes of conduct which help direct the mission and will be discussed later in this chapter.

Mission statements should be developed for institutions and significant units within the institution such as student affairs, colleges, or auxiliary units such as athletics. They should provide an anchoring so people can align what they do on a day-to-day basis around the mission. Therefore, even if you are making copies of a report or cleaning floors, you know how this work is part of the effort that educates students, produces creative works, or solves important problems. Examples of strong mission statements taken from three universities include:

Our primary purpose as a public research university is the creation, dissemination, preservation, and application of knowledge for the betterment of our global society.

Our school of business mission is to develop analytical, communicative, ethical, and globally competitive business leaders through high quality teaching, research, and service.

These statements are concise and clear and describe action and what the institution or unit is about. As with a vision statement, mission statements can become long and rambling because there is a lot of work and effort that goes into teaching, research/creative activities, and services. However, even if an employee within a university or unit is in a support role, they should be able to connect that having good food, healthcare, recreation opportunities, adequate facilities, etc. as being important components of achieving the mission. Higher education mission is fulfilled through teaching, research/creative activities, and service, and the mission statement should clearly convey some or all of these areas.

Core Values

Organizational and/or unit values were discussed earlier and are helpful in communicating codes of conduct. They are also helpful in crafting a mission in that they help guide how people go about engaging in the unit or organizational mission. In short, values help individuals know what approaches, actions, and orientations are acceptable or prohibited. For instance, professionalism could be a value, and this determines appropriate ways of working with students in the delivery of their education. If faculty and staff are professional, they are available to work with students during working hours, prepared for classes, help students and visitors navigate the university and ensure they get needed support, etc. Faculty do not belittle students in a class setting or miss an appointment because they were busy with research. This type of behavior simply would not be professional. There are many ways one can go about teaching or engaging in research/creative activities and service, which are the core components of what we do (the mission) in higher education. A short and clearly defined list of values and beliefs helps guide the way employees engage in their mission on a daily basis. Values can be included in the mission statement but typically are provided in a different section of the strategic plan. Regardless of how you decide to include this in your plan, it needs to be clear that the two are linked in your planning and implementation efforts.

Goals

A vision statement describes where you want to be in the future. The mission broadly identifies what it is that you will do. Goals focus the planning effort by describing a few broadly stated outcomes, to be addressed over a specific time period. Typically, no more than five broad goals are developed and approved by the university board or vice president. As Peter Drucker clearly states, if you have more than five goals then you have nothing (Drucker et al., 2008). The goals should be created through the lens of what makes you unique, capable, and represent your distinctive niche (Drucker, 1990). While working at Boise State University, senior leadership did a good job of creating five strategic goals, developed and crafted in a way that allowed university units to contribute to these goals.

An Example of Effective Goal Development

At Boise State, goals were developed with extensive input across the university through town hall meetings, focus groups, interviews, and survey data. The larger statewide community was also included in this process. The goals connected with the vision of becoming "a top research university that focuses on student success and has global impact." The goals were stated in a way that diverse units could contribute to some or all of them, highlighting their capabilities and uniqueness. As a leader of a college, I identified ways our unit could contribute to achieving these goals in measurable ways, and we were given the latitude to make plans based on our opportunities and strengths. The same was true of other units across the university.

For instance, one of the goals was to advance research and creative activities. Specifically, the university wanted to address this goal by positively impacting lives and breaking down traditional barriers to address big problems that face the world. Within our college, we initiated a major effort to establish additional graduate programming and deliver faculty resources to grow their research agendas. We also started a new doctoral program in public health and provided funding to support the curriculum, student assistantships, and associated research activities. Furthermore, we offered $600,000 of research support to college units so faculty and students could collect preliminary data for larger research efforts, purchase equipment, and support summer salaries directed at research that would help grow the college and subsequently the university research agenda. Therefore, the college was able to invest and engage in ways that directly addressed the university goal of advancing research and creative activities. These are only examples related to one goal. In total, the plan was helpful in allowing the college to create these tangible and university aligned outcomes. Momentum happens when many units implement their own plans and collectively contribute to the university vision and related goals.

One of the things that the president and provost at Boise State University did to ensure progress and *accountability* was to require yearly reporting on progress related to a units' strategic plans, which are tied to the university plan. This was done in a variety of ways through yearly written reporting, detailed spreadsheets that document unit progress on goals and initiatives, and yearly face-to-face college meetings with senior management and work units. During meetings the president and provost briefly shared progress they had made on university-wide strategic efforts. Unit leaders would then present progress made through their strategic efforts. Having the entire college present during these meetings helped convey the importance of this work and the seriousness associated with the strategic efforts. Similarly, budget processes were tied into the strategic plan and units could request one-time or recurring monies to help support strategic initiatives. Collectively, the reporting and funding helped keep units on track and fund strategic efforts. The importance of accountability will be touched on again later in this chapter.

How Do We Get There?

Often goals and strategies can become entangled. To avoid this confusion, it is helpful to think of goals at a macro-level and strategies as the efforts and investments that go into addressing a goal. Therefore, there may be multiple strategies used, particularly for a unit to contribute to a university-level goal. Additionally, the university may devise high-level strategies that help guide units as they attempt to contribute to university goals. For instance, in the example given around the goal of advancing research and creative activities, a university strategy might be to enhance technology across the university to support faculty engaged in research and creative activities. A unit might address this university goal by creating a unit goal to start a PhD program. This goal for starting a PhD program could involve a number of strategies including creating a curriculum, conducting an external review by content experts, obtaining funding for graduate assistantships, and seeking board approval for a new academic program. Therefore, it is important to consider the level or unit involved with this strategic process because what seems like a goal at one level could be a strategy at another level.

Strategy and Resources

The purpose of strategy is to align and allocate resources to achieve strategic goals. It takes resources to put the strategic plan into action (Edersheim, 2007). Strategy should be a cohesive response to important challenges because the challenges are often dense and convoluted, requiring multiple coordinated efforts for success (Rumelt, 2011). Resources come in many forms and include financial support, space, equipment, partnerships, people, location, sports programs, and the list goes on. As a leader, it is important that your resources and strengths are used to address strategic challenges. Peter Drucker captured this approach when he communicated the need to staff your best people on strategic initiatives; not relegating them to yesterday's problems (Edersheim, 2007). As a leader you have the ability to ensure that your most valuable resources are used to address strategic priorities. When you choose a strategy, you are making a critical decision as a leader because it also means you are saying no to other options. Therefore, strategy is something that requires resources, coordination and the ability to make a decision that optimizes for success.

Strategy and Risk-Taking

As a strategic leader you also need to find a balance that incorporates appropriate levels of risk in your strategies. Remember, not stretching yourself or only taking on initiatives that have low potential for failure will not likely move an organization towards aspirational goals that ultimately advance the institution or unit. Conversely, taking on too much or too many risks can also be problematic and over-stretch and over-commit the unit or institution's resources. As a leader, striking a balance with risk and challenge should be key in your decision making. Some reallocation approaches and pros and cons that leaders can take are summarized in Table 3.

Table 3. Generating resources for strategic planning priorities.

Approach	Pros and Cons
Letting something go... Allocating vacant positions to high priority initiatives.	Employee positions are kept but the timing of openings is hard to predict.
Letting something go... Redeploy current faculty and staffing from failing programs to strategic priorities.	Employee positions are kept but matching interests and skills from failing programs to strategic efforts can be challenging.
Letting something go... Close a program down and sweep all of the lines, equipment and space for priority efforts.	This creates resources quickly in a predictable manner but the loss of jobs can destabilize the workforce.
Generate additional resources... Develop or grow new programs, increase existing offerings including research or grow consulting and community services.	This does not disrupt the workforce but requires incentive budgeting and faculty and staff who have an entrepreneurial spirit.
Ask for support... Ask for resources (money, space, equipment, staffing) internally and externally to support strategic priorities.	This has the advantage of not needing to change the staffing or structure of a unit but it can be difficult to obtain resources in a financially constrained environment.

Let Something Go Today To Prepare for Tomorrow

Strategies are a major leadership responsibility. Collectively, input is generated around a goal, but strategy defines how this espoused effort becomes reality. While others should provide valuable input, leadership ultimately makes resource allocation decisions. Table 4 shows a number of questions that can be helpful in identifying "how we will get there" and ultimately what strategies will be employed to address the goal(s). As mentioned in a previous chapter, Peter Drucker proposes a thoughtful question that addresses this point: Are we expending resources to keep a corpse from stinking (Edersheim, 2007)? Hamel and Breen offered a similar examination with, "What do we need to let go of so we can innovate? (Hamel & Breen, 2007)." These questions converge on something that higher education has struggled to embrace. Specifically, higher education is challenged with the idea of letting something go so resources can be allocated to address what is of most value.

From a strategy standpoint, letting things go can be a quick way to generate capacity and resources for new investment. Depending on the approach adopted by an institution, these resources can typically be reinvested back into a unit. However, eliminating a program (a degree, minor, badge, or service supported through the university) or restructuring a unit is typically met with fierce resistance even when there is overwhelming evidence that the program or structure has failed. People desperately want to avoid change and work to keep things the way they are into perpetuity. Even if a unit says they are open to change, the reality typically is that they will resist meaningful change. In fact, many come to higher education because of the stability and predictability associated with their jobs. Change does not fit well with this orientation.

One way to minimize resistance is to redeploy resources by assigning people to other efforts or through different structures. The idea behind this approach is to assign people from failing areas or areas that are no longer central to the strategic plan to areas that are central. Similarly, if administrative structures related to faculty support are no longer working, the current workforce can be reassigned to a different structure that meets the contemporized needs of the organization. For instance, a common approach within departments is to take administrative staff from individual units and create a pool of staff who have a narrowed set of responsibilities across more units. This can be helpful as systems become more complex and require higher levels of expertise to operate. In some instances, the number of people needed to do the work as a pool is less than the previous structure. At the very least, the restructuring should be more responsive and effective. For some this level of change is fine but for others they will insist that their current job is the only type of work they can do... This is especially true for some faculty. Evaluate these types of concerns and decide if the juice is worth the squeeze.

Another tactic is to sweep lines when people leave for other opportunities or retire. The obvious downfall with this approach is that it could be years before someone leaves their position. However, it has the advantage of not eliminating occupied positions which could destabilize the sense of job security and could cause valued employees to leave. Finally, it may be necessary to eliminate an entire unit or program, including associated positions. This has the advantage of creating resources to reinvest relatively fast but will send ripples of fear and unrest across the entire institution because the unthinkable has occurred... a group of faculty and/ or staff all lost their jobs.

Table 4. Engaging questions to help answer the strategic question... How will we get there?

Questions
[H]How do we generate processes that produce hundreds of strategic options?
[H]How do we accelerate the reallocation of funds from dying initiatives and put this into growth potential?
[H]How do we accelerate the redeployment of resources such as faculty, staff, space, and money?
[D]What do we let go of (programs, divisions, support services, etc.) so these people can innovate?
[D]Are we expending resources by trying to keep a corpse from stinking?
[D]Given our services, mission and strategies, what core capabilities do we want to invest in?
[D]How do we need to invest to attract and develop the needed employee knowledge base?
[D]What do we have to abandon to create tomorrow?
[D]What must we strengthen or abandon?
[A]How do we prioritize the investment of resources?
[A]How do we assign strategic priorities and hold individuals and groups accountable for these efforts?
[A]How do we differentiate movement from progress?
[A]How do we obtain the resources necessary to address our strategic imperatives?
[A]How can we best support the institution or our university governing body's strategic needs?
Table notes: [D] *Questions taken or modified from Peter Drucker (Drucker et al., 2008; Edersheim, 2007)* [H]*Questions taken or modified from Hamel and Breen (Hamel & Breen, 2007)* [A]*Author generated questions*

I worked at one institution where eight tenure track faculty delivered a graduate program (masters level) to a total of seven students. That is correct, the program had more faculty than students. When the university did an analysis across all programs, it was obvious that this program after several decision to eliminate it. While some individuals were reassigned, many were let go. This was the right decision and freed up recurring dollars through salary savings. It also created a negative outcry from faculty governance groups at the institution and through trade magazines such as the *Journal of Higher Education*. There are many ways to obtain resources; be sure and think through the methods you use because altering employment status can be an uneven landscape to navigate.

Generate Additional Resources

If an institution works under an incentive budget model, growth and revenue production through enhanced or new programming, consulting services, research activities, community projects, etc. can often generate additional revenue. Typically, generating additional revenue is supported by leadership, faculty, and staff. However, how the resources should be used may vary across groups. One effective approach is for the institution and unit to keep a small portion of new revenue generation for centralized investments. The bulk of the revenue goes to programmatic expenses and any profits can be used by the unit generating the resources for reinvestment into strategic initiatives. For instance, one institution gave a portion of online education revenue to the university (12%) and college (6%). The distribution to the university started immediately with the program's inception based on expenditures and college funds were collected once the program was profitable, and their portion was based on gross revenues. The program generated $15M a year and this created recurring dollars for the institution, college, and units that implemented the programs. Other universities have adopted similar approaches, but the institution takes 60% -80% of the total revenue and the remainder is used for programming. Taking such a large portion of the revenue is out of balance and can cause resentment from the units and compromise the quality of the programming. Examine the distribution of revenue before embarking in a venture where splits are necessary, and make sure the arrangement is one that supports all entities involved.

Another tactic for obtaining resources is to find a way to generate revenue through current program growth, research growth, or consulting/programmatic services to the community. This has the advantage of creating new resources without changing or eliminating programming. This approach requires that faculty and staff have an entrepreneurial spirit and the ability to grow profitable programs, compete nationally for grant awards, and provide services that are needed in the community. This opportunity also needs to be paired with a budget model that allows for adequate distribution of funds to the unit generating the resources.

Ask for Resources

Typically, resources are earmarked for strategic initiatives that can be requested through units, institutions, or state and federal coffers. One common way to request these funds is through some type of yearly budgeting process where these entities and levels of organization provide an opportunity for units to make prioritized requests. The funding is provided for one-time or recurring financial requests based on criteria such as likelihood of success, need, available funds, ability to contribute to the strategic plan, amount of the request, and matching contributions. Within any organization, there are many legitimate needs that units make eloquent justifications for why they should be funded. Depending on the institution or unit, the process can be surprisingly competitive. The process is somewhat like going to Las Vegas and you can only place two bets, and it is important that you win... How and where do you place your bet? What gambling venues are you most comfortable with? What risks are you willing to take? How big of a win do you need?

At the end of the day, making requests for money is often a low odds game and you may get some small win(s) to keep you interested and coming back for more. However, obtaining a large sum of recurring dollars is difficult and tends to only work when all the stars align. In over three decades of work, I had only one opportunity to be part of a unit that received a large recurring strategic investment. The allocation made a substantial and positive impact on our programming, research, and service. However, this level of support is infrequent so other options need to be considered as part of your funding strategy. Despite the low odds associated with asking for money, resource requests are always a path to explore, especially if it is tied to strategic initiatives. One thing is certain, if you do not ask, you will almost never receive the support.

Key Performance Indicators

Key Performance Indicators (KPIs) are metrics used to gauge progress on strategic initiatives. Often information is provided on all of the *movement* being made but little *progress* is actually achieved. For instance, summaries might be provided on the advertising that has been generated for a new program, personal contacts made to recruit students, but no progress is made on student recruitment. Obviously the two are closely linked but a KPI that must be considered in starting a new program would be the number of students recruited. All of the work around advertising and personal contacts is movement... having a starting group of 20 students is progress and needs to be a KPI. Therefore, pick a KPI that demonstrates *progress* is taking place rather than how much or how hard everyone is working. KPIs are similar to going to the plate in baseball and doing lots of work to obtain a base hit. Ultimately, a base hit is what moves the team forward toward their goal, so that needs to be your KPI.

Limit the Number of KPIs

Be frugal with adopting measures, especially if you have oversight of a large operation. I was involved in a very detailed planning process that also included milestones or tasks for current operations and new strategic efforts associated with our unit. When all of the items were compiled on a spreadsheet with dates for completion, it contained more than 300 items. While the thoughtfulness associated with the effort had some value, trying to track more than 300 items was way too much work. Once the 300 items were presented to the unit leadership team, it took the wind out of their sails even before work had started because of the enormity of the effort. Based on that experience, I would suggest having a shortened list of manageable KPIs for all the efforts taking place within a unit. You can then encourage people involved in the various efforts to develop a detailed document that helps them plan in a more comprehensive fashion including important milestones, assigning responsibility to tasks, and identifying dates for completion. Also, having a limited number of KPIs helps people keep progress measures in their consciousness and better guide them in their daily activities. The details associated with the various efforts can exist within the subgroups working on the various projects. Having a few goals and targeted KPIs helps keep the important things available for you on a regular basis and items are not lost in a dense list of 300 items. Find KPIs that you can easily and accurately measure progress on and make sure that your faculty and staff are aware of and buy into these measures.

Accountability

Key performance indicators are a way to ensure that the workforce—including you as a leader—are being held accountable for your strategic responsibilities. I once heard a very successful college president refer to strategic plans as bloviated documents of little value. He saw a lot of flash with no discernible map of how the institution would do the work needed for the aspirational vision. Bloviated documents are especially problematic when an eloquent, charismatic leader creates an engaging vision with no plan for reaching the destination. This has the impact of getting people excited, but nothing seems to happen, and people are left discouraged about the leader and the process. His position might have been different had the strategic planning process been connected with KPIs, which allow leaders to quickly see if action effectively addresses the strategic plan. However, the president was correct, a strategic plan is truly a bloviated document if leadership is not purposefully aligning and allocating resources to achieve strategic goals and tracking progress through KPIs.

Transparency

Strategic planning requires significant resources to be mobilized and allocated to efforts. Consequently, leadership and employees become curious about the progress made and if coworkers are being held accountable for the resources allocated. Therefore, transparency is highly valued (Crowley 2022). Without transparency people will often fill in information gaps for themselves, which is often inaccurate and viewed with a negative slant. Consider providing regular updates on progress, how dollars were spent, and outcomes. You will likely find that this provides time for celebrating successes and also showing where progress has been slow or non-existent. Openly showing the numbers and milestones will provide support for you as a leader and encourage groups with lagging strategic efforts to up their effort or consider other strategies. The process is not designed to publicly shame anyone in front of their colleagues, but rather to describe where the various institutional or unit efforts are collectively and gauge the progress of the entire unit.

Goals, KPIs and Individual Performance

A necessary outcome of an effective planning process is for people to know their role in contributing to the mission. Goals and KPIs can be helpful in that effort. For some, making this connection is straightforward. For instance, student success is often a central outcome for institutions of higher education and faculty have the most direct role in this mission. For support service groups, the connection may not be as direct and as a leader you may need to make these connections clear for these employees.

For instance, I had oversight of Health Services at a university and helping students maintain health and wellbeing was critical to student success and fostering a thriving community, which were two of the university's five strategic goals. I simply shared this observation with the 45 employees in that unit and mentioned that they could directly impact these goals and to consider this alignment as they developed their strategic plan. Similar connections need to be made for administrative staff, information services, facility services, etc. Specifically, as a leader you need to make it clear and tangible to support staff why their work matters and how their efforts relate to university goals. Don't assume these employees have made this connection.

As part of connecting and communicating with support staff, another leadership responsibility is letting people know what they should be doing (Edersheim, 2007). It sounds simple but many employees are not certain of how they should spend their time. A clear plan and purposeful communication efforts can help make these connections. As a leader you can also make these connections by explicitly stating the essential contributions that can be made by each unit and the individuals that populate these groups.

Yearly Evaluations of Strategic Efforts

Each year, you and your employees need to stop and reflect on the progress made on your unit's strategic efforts. Discussion, annual reports, and presentations are common ways of communicating these outcomes. In addition to these types of actions, consider a simple scoring system such as a three-item scoring chart that includes achieved, some progress made, and no progress made. To complete this scoring sheet, updates will be needed from many units and workgroups. Unlike a written report or presentation, this evaluation requires relatively little work, so your staff probably will not complain about having to conduct this reporting. It also has the added benefit of requiring the various groups to visit with leadership to reflect on progress during the past year. Furthermore, it provides you with a quick progress summary. Based on the findings generated through the evaluation, modifications and changes can be made. Remember that the plan is never cast in stone and as a leader you and the unit need to be flexible as you work through the implementation process. The flexibility could be as simple as changing completion dates, to dropping an effort and replacing it with another initiative. The evaluation items are something that you should develop with your leadership team and work groups. This helps them create value in the exercise. Examples of evaluation questions are shown in Table 5.

These questions are designed to provide an opportunity to probe for additional information. For instance, if the reporting efforts helped the institution understand your value and contributions, you may want examples of how that was achieved. The examples could come from a meeting that reviews the responses, or you could request one or two items that most contributed to or prevented a successful outcome. After reviewing answers to the questions and reviewing other reporting documents, modifications can be made to create an improved course for the next year.

Table 5. Questions to help annually evaluate the efficacy of a strategic plan.

Questions	Achieved	Some Progress	No Progress
1. Did the strategic planning and implementation process help focus your efforts?			
2. Did you make meaningful progress on your goals?			
3. List each KPI and evaluate progress.			
4. Did you regularly communicate your strategic progress?			
5. Did the planning and reporting efforts help people within the institution understand your value and contributions?			
6. Is your unit able to navigate the changes associated with the strategic implementation process?			
7. During the past year, did you frequently visit the strategic plan with your work team(s)?			
8. Were the strategic efforts implemented in a high-quality fashion?			
9. Do you have updates and revisions for the strategic plan based on your year-end review of last year's performance?			

Chapter Summary

1. All units and institutions in higher education deeply benefit from conducting quality strategic planning and asso-

ciated implementation processes. Some common challenges include the promotion and tenure environment, poorly articulated plans, failure to implement plans, and an inability to make demanding decisions that focus strategic efforts.

2. Find ways to assign credit to the promotion and tenure process for engagement in strategic planning. Be certain that your plan is clear, action oriented, and that you follow through with engagement and progress from members of the entire unit.

3. Use decision-making processes in strategic planning that are made with input from employees and relevant partners but are void of voting processes. Final decisions are guided by faculty, staff, and partners, but made by leadership.

4. Ultimately, strategic planning must answer three fundamental questions that include: Where are we now? Where are we going? How will we get there?

5. In answering the question, "Where are we now?" obtain accurate, creditable data, collected from multiple sources and effectively communicate it across stakeholders.

6. In answering the question, "Where are we going?" the organization or unit must develop a clear and succinct vision, mission and goals as part of the strategic effort. It is impor-

tant that these items are developed and applied in a way to provide direction and that optimizes the allocation of resources.

7. In answering the question "How will we get there?" the use of strategies and key performance indicators (KPIs) is necessary. Strategies represent the way goals are addressed and direct the allocation of resources. KPIs are used for ongoing assessment to measure progress (as opposed to movement) and allow for necessary adjustments as strategies are implemented.

8. Be transparent and honest with faculty, staff, and key stakeholders about strategic initiatives launched and openly communicate the progress associated with these efforts (both good and bad). Ensure people are held accountable for their strategic responsibilities.

Chapter 7
When To Strategically Engage Work Teams

Work Teams and Strategic Efforts

Working as a team offers tremendous advantages for any unit or organization. As Patrick Lencioni stated in his book on teams, if you get all people in an organization to row in the same direction at the same time you can dominate any industry (Lencioni, 2002). I do not think many people would argue with this statement, especially if they've been involved with team members who exhibit high levels of trust, commitment, engage in open and critical conversations for effective decision-making, and hold themselves accountable for results. Under these circumstances, small and large groups can do remarkable things that can never be achieved through individual efforts.

However, working in an environment that has high-functioning cross-disciplinary teams that are dedicated to *university level* outcomes is rare. In order for teams to work in higher education, a number of conditions need to be in place and are outlined in Table 1.

Table 1. Conditions needed for successful work teams.

Conditions For High-Functioning Work Teams	Common Concerns and Obstacles
1. The institution is committed to training the workforce on how to work effectively in teams.	Universities typically do not invest in systematic employee training.
2. The employees have a compelling reason for why they should engage in teams.	Employees are suspicious of leaders wanting to change just for the sake of change and are averse to additional work associated with teams.
3. The university has a promotions and tenure process that includes effective participation in teamwork as a meaningful predictor of being promoted and/or tenured.	Promotion and tenure primarily evaluate candidates on individual level achievement and productivity in research and teaching.
4. Success is measured through university-level outcomes and performance.	Typically, individuals engage in teams to support their personal, unit, and/or disciplinary interests.
6. A culture exists for teams to be accountable and results-driven.	Individuals are accountable to their unit or discipline and have limited affinity outside these areas.

Few universities meet these prerequisite conditions at a level needed to create high-functioning work teams dedicated to the success and proper functioning of a university. What is much more common are behaviors that compromise the success of teams. For instance, in meetings when a cross-college group is charged with a university-level task, are people focused on this effort for the benefit of the university, or are they focused on improving themselves or their unit? Observe their behaviors. Are they answering emails or revising a paper for publication instead of engaging in the meeting? Look around the room in any meeting and see how many people are engaged. Do employees show high levels of trust so that you can share weaknesses or concerns that may emanate from your team? Do you say what needs to be said or do you hold back because you are not sure if your comments will be well received? Do people visit with you personally about issues of concern but they never voice this during the meeting? Are there people on the team that seem to never say anything of value and just take up space? Does one person always seem to dominate the floor during meetings? If good outcomes and progress are associated with a team, are members quick to share their involvement and contributions? However, when the team fails, do these same members scatter like roaches when a light is turned on? Maybe in a failed effort they say, "I was just a member of the team so don't blame me... the people in Education and Business came up with the crazy idea and I never supported it in the first place."

It is not uncommon for leadership to place people on teams or committees just to make sure a unit gets a piece of the pie. Furthermore, the university may be asking for a level of engagement that people are not prepared to address due to a lack of training. Check benchmark institutions and see how many have made significant investment in training work teams. Typically, the idea is not even considered, or the decision was made to not invest in this training. The resistance to training is common because people feel they already know how to work in teams, which is rarely the case. The institution then spends more time dealing with team dysfunction and related issues than work directed toward strategic outcomes.

Really reflect on the way you and others at your institution engage in teams and *decide where you are as an institution in the evolution of creating effective work teams.* Later in the chapter we'll examine ways to determine the level of team development within a unit or organization. Evaluating where you are in teamwork is critical before moving forward to engage teams in strategic plan implementation.

Engaging in Work Teams

As mentioned earlier, work teams can be very effective in the implementation of a strategic plan, but very difficult to create and manage. I have spoken at more than 100 disciplinary graduation ceremonies. Speaking with graduates, their families, and friends was a highlight of my time in higher education. While the talks varied, I always spoke about the hard work and sacrifices students made on their paths to becoming college graduates. Examples I shared were the many final exams, papers, and group projects they engaged in to reach this point in their academic career. Whenever I mentioned group projects, there was a collective and audible moan from students across every discipline. The audience in turn would laugh.

The moan came because group projects required the members to work as a team and many of the hallmarks of a high-functioning team were not part of their experience. The audience had similar experiences. In fact, I cannot remember ever having a student in my classes say that they had a great team and that they enjoyed the experience. In talking with students, the reasons for this reaction were that it required more work, took longer, some team members did not adhere to timelines, and often a member or members did sloppy work that required others to cover their responsibilities. Many of my students would comment that it would have been "more effective and easier to just do it on my own." Sound familiar? Not surprisingly, this is the same kind of feedback voiced in many work settings. Working in teams does not necessarily get better after college.

In higher education many incorrectly believe that they have effective work teams because the committee members are generally affable and things seem to get done. However, review the statements in Table 2 and see how many of the statements you honestly agree with and then consider the efficacy of teams in your setting.

If your unit or university seems to align with the statements on the left, then you probably work in an environment that is team-oriented and you can execute within this structure. This is good news and something you should use to your advantage. However, if this is not the case, then your unit or institution may need time, development, or training before engaging in significant team-based strategic efforts.

Table 2. Evaluating unit or institutional capacity to create effective work teams.

Area	Common Barriers
Faculty commonly share classes across majors and trust that other units can play an equal role in delivering curricula to students.	Faculty are very protective of majors and their students. They want instructors who are housed within their unit.
Part of the specific recruitment and hiring criteria is to recruit faculty and staff who work well in teams.	While this is in some job descriptions, this consideration is typically not a strong factor in determining recruiting and hiring decisions.
People are focused and engaged during team meetings.	Typically, there are no ramifications for not engaging in a team-based meetings.
Human resources are commonly shared across units without resistance to meet the needs of the institution. For example, faculty are shared across departments and colleges.	Units are very protective of the faculty and staff that are assigned to their unit and resist sharing unless significant compensation or support is part of the arrangement.
Common processes are used to facilitate and manage work teams across the institutions.	Processes and procedures vary across units, especially in the execution of teams.
Faculty and staff are open to change based on feedback given from members of other units at the university.	Faculty tend to be very insular and are resistant to hearing or acting on feedback from other units.
Team members put the needs of their unit behind the needs of the institution.	The order of importance in addressing needs is typically the individual, discipline, unit, and finally, the institution.

Successful Teams Require a Willingness To Work Together

In many settings the idea of having high-functioning teams is truly a distant vision. I have encountered academic units where members of the same unit would not speak to each other and threatened to take legal action against colleagues. Others, because of the poor work climate, have filed grievances with human resources because co-workers were and contempt for their coworkers, supervisors, and students. In some instances, faculty publicly showed disdain and questioned the credibility of a colleague's academic discipline. Depending on the situation, actions, and opinions, conclusions like these may be very appropriate and in other instances they are likely excessive in their response, remarks, and actions. Nevertheless, if there is this level of interpersonal conflict and dysfunction within units, what possible hope is there of working as effective work teams? If a leader takes a job in a new unit, it is not uncommon to run into these types of problems. Developing teams in this atmosphere is almost impossible. Therefore, be cautious and honestly evaluate your unit closely before embarking with teams to address strategic initiatives.

I want to share an example of a significant failure I experienced as a leader because of my inability to accurately estimate the unit's maturity to engage in teams. Because of my blind spot, a vital strategic initiative was never addressed. In this example, people were outwardly cordial, so there didn't seem to be many interpersonal conflicts to prevent the successful implementation of the initiative through teamwork. I later saw that this was not the case.

The initiative was to deliver our curriculum in a way that all of the students could better work in teams to address patient/client health and wellbeing concerns. Because promoting and delivering healthcare is a complex and idiosyncratic process, the goal was to provide students with the skills and insights to work in teams to better deliver care. In short, the skills and knowledge of many health professionals across diverse disciplines would be better than the current more compartmentalized delivery system. In order for this to happen, students would be trained using an approach called inter-professional education or IPE where they would be trained together so they would better collaborate once they became practitioners.

An interesting aspect of the IPE initiative was that members of the various units all agreed that this was an important and worthy initiative. Even the various accrediting bodies were requiring this approach for accreditation. Also, one of the factors that lead us to adopting this approach came from one of our board members in the community. In short, the board member said we did a wonderful job training our students within their disciplines but they were weak in working *across* disciplines. This feedback also demonstrated a need to implement IPE for the betterment of health care in our community. This information helped answer the all-important question of why we should implement IPE. Investments involved sending groups to conferences on IPE training to acquire skills and insights around IPE. Guest speakers came to campus to provide workshops and break the units into workgroups to develop IPE programming. A capstone class was created around IPE education so students could engage in IPE training with students from other disciplines to collaboratively address health issues. Additionally, travel and equipment incentives supported individuals in attending trainings and presentations. A part-time director for IPE was hired internally to promote it across the unit with key strategies outlined to grow the programming and further enhance student training. Initially it looked like the initiative was a success, until the actual work of working together was initiated.

The capstone class never really seemed to click. In fact, over time faculty had students sign up for certain sections so students from the same discipline could take the same capstone together from an instructor from their discipline. The faculty were teaching about IPE, but the common curriculum was abandoned for options that were more tailored to the needs of a given discipline. The attendance to monthly trainings and speakers dropped off and events that would attract 50 to 100 people had turnouts of 5 to 15. Other courses that had interdisciplinary foundations developed problems because the various units could not agree on the curriculum. Coverage and scheduling issues within a given discipline became more important than IPE. Within health disciplines enormous amounts of work go into developing schedules for clinical rotations that would meet the needs of students, faculty and the preceptors. IPE required a change to a Rubik's Cube that had already been solved and faculty were not interested in making a difficult task even harder.

The reasons for the units not being able to work as a team varied from poorly aligned accreditation requirements to someone from another unit not being a good partner. It seemed that everyone was willing to collaborate and partner in teams, but the other unit(s) were the problem. This ongoing effort continued for almost six years until it was abandoned. It was not abandoned because the approach wasn't needed or sound, it failed largely because the units could not work in teams across disciplines to create and implement an IPE curriculum. Ultimately, this happened because I (the leader) failed to accurately gauge the level of maturity or readiness around teams in the unit. Reflecting back on the initiative, it really had little chance for success.

Other academic entities have experienced similar struggles when trying to get different disciplines to work and teach together in a more integrated fashion. In one instance, a $170M building was constructed for a prominent medical school and the provost arranged faculty so that disciplines were mixed throughout the building instead of organizing faculty and staff by departments or academic areas. Similarly, a college of business used a new $50M dollar building to assign faculty so that they were not segregated by departments, such as marketing or economics. The approach was not without merit since environments can have a significant impact on human behavior. In both instances, it took the faculty and staff about six months to gravitate back to their tribe and be housed with their people. Yes, they just traded offices and work areas so they were organized as they were in the past. The exact reason for the failure is hard to pinpoint but obviously the faculty and staff were not ready to work in cross-disciplinary teams and went back to something that was familiar and comfortable.

To avoid a poor investment of limited strategic resources, there are ways to evaluate your unit or institution's level of readiness to engage in teamwork. The four levels include:

Level 1: Make Sure Individuals Understand What They Should be Doing

Throughout the strategic planning effort described in chapter 6, a desired outcome is for people to know how to contribute to the mission. Besides strategic planning aiding in this outcome, a competent leader should also provide guidance to clarify focus for their supervisees. This direction—what employees should be doing—is a key function of management and great progress can be made within a unit or organization when individuals are clear on what they are supposed to be doing! This sounds obvious, but many within organizations spend time trying to solve this Rubik's Cube and unfortunately some employees never receive the guidance to use their time efficiently. *If people are not clear on what they need to do in order to make meaningful contributions, they are not ready to make contributions through team-related endeavors.* Therefore, make sure people are aligned at an individual level before you engage them in teams. Significant progress can happen when employees have this clarity and execute relevant work that is supportive of the strategic plan.

Level 2: Look for Low-Lying Fruit

In any organization there are likely to be pockets of effective teamwork that have developed organically or intentionally. Because small numbers of dedicated people can increase the chances for effective teamwork, this is a logical place to start once individuals know what they are supposed to do. As a leader you will spot these pockets when, for instance, you see a research team that distributes work based on differential strengths, positive outcomes such as obtaining prominent funding, publishing in top journals, and students wanting to be a part of their research team. These are all indications of a team working effectively. There may also be units that seem to work well in teams like a department or college such as business where the science of work teams is studied, incorporated into their educational curriculum, and integrated into the unit's day-to-day operations. In other cases, the unit may have acquired the team skills and processes through practice refined over time. These units may be opportunities to strategically invest because the capabilities and skills needed to work in teams already exist and the likelihood of achieving goals and implementing strategies is more likely to happen than with a group that does not possess these skills.

Another approach is to identify individuals across units that have a disposition and approach to work that is conducive to effective operations within a team. Often, they are some of your prized employees who are respectful, candid, reflective, professional, engaging, and are known as someone who shows up and gets things done. As the comedian Woody Allen once said, half of being successful in life is simply showing up! A group of people that show up with these capabilities can be effective in harnessing the power and advantage that comes from effective work teams. If the ability for team engagement is variable across your unit, this may be an appropriate place to start.

Level 3: Focus Locally Before Addressing Organizational Efforts

Be sure that your unit has developed team skills and processes that allow them to excel as a team before you propose team initiatives across the organization. Depending on the size and complexity of your unit, this can be a significant undertaking. Often the resistance and challenge you experience within a unit will be minor compared to the resistance across the entire organization. Units in higher education normally value autonomy. It is a real success for a unit to get a few departments or schools to agree on similar processes or methods. Creating university-wide processes and methods, especially within academic units, can be very confusing and mystifying. Therefore, try working locally on team initiatives and then decide if you have an appetite for spearheading an organizational level effort.

Level 4: Commitment To Building Teams

There are few universities that have high-functioning teams that engage in strategic work throughout the organization. However, you may be fortunate and move into a unit where the groups' ability to work in teams is high. As long as you have experience and understand what it takes to create high-functioning teams, by all means move forward. If part of your units' ability to work in teams is lacking, make sure that you provide training and ensure that everyone participates. Know that making something mandatory in higher education is a card that should be played infrequently; you need to commit and communicate the seriousness of the request. Second, pick a project or initiative that is palatable for your unit and has a high chance for success. Often success breeds success and having an exemplar that exhibits the advantage of teams will be important for people to see. Finally, know that this is a long game and may take years to implement and promote, so a patient mindset from everyone involved is needed.

Developing teams is a lot like running a marathon. If you are not a runner and are in poor physical condition you will be well served to start off by walking a mile or two before you attempt running. Also, you may need help from a trainer who is knowledgeable and familiar with running and training so you can optimize your chances for success. Depending on a host of factors, it could take a couple years of training before you attempt running a marathon. It is not uncommon for someone to not finish their first marathon, so be prepared to fail and try again. With teams, adopting a similar approach is helpful so you don't overshoot the runway and reach for a level that you are not ready to obtain. Team work takes time to develop and is something that can be refined and nurtured over many years.

In this chapter we discussed the power of teams as well as the hard work that is often needed to develop high-functioning work teams. In the subsequent chapter, we will review other elements essential to effective management and administration within higher education. Specifically, we'll explore hiring practices, succession planning, and annual reviews/feedback mechanisms to help manage a unit's most precious resource... its employees. Additionally, the use of professional staff within academic units will be advanced as a valuable approach to operating the business and logistics of running an academic unit. Finally, we'll examine creating effective systems and processes with units and the university enterprise so that day-to-day operations of units can be successful and efficient.

Chapter Summary

1. Utilizing effective teams has a tremendous advantage for any unit or organization. However, few universities have

high-functioning work teams that are effective and dedicated to unit or university-level outcomes.

2. In order for universities to successfully engage cross-disciplinary teams, quality training must be present, compelling reasons for engaging teams (such as credit toward promotion and tenure) must be relayed, and a culture of accountability needs to be present in order for the team to become embedded within a unit or organization.

3. To increase the odds of implementing successful work teams, evaluate the maturity of your unit and institution in this area. Make sure individuals understand their responsibilities and that a stable work environment exists before initiating the use of teams. If you are ready to promote teams, seek out and utilize individuals and groups that already demonstrate capacity to work this way to generate a proof of concept for others to view. Provide on-going training and other support so employees can engage in progressively more complex team-based activities over time.

Chapter 8
Balanced Leadership Essentials

Introduction

Leaders within higher education regularly apply and navigate basic business systems and processes. While many academics do not like to consider the business aspects of their jobs, managing them proactively is critical for success. Consequently, a balanced leader needs to understand and apply essential business elements for effective management and administration within higher education. To this end we'll explore hiring practices, succession planning, and annual reviews/feedback mechanisms to help manage and develop a unit's most precious resource... employees. Additionally, we'll review using professional staff within academic units and forming partnerships outside the unit as valuable approaches to addressing the logistics of running a unit. We'll also take a look at centralized and decentralized management structures that can provide a number of options for assembling support within units. Finally, we'll examine creating effective systems and processes within units and the university so day-to-day operations can be more successfully and efficiently administered.

Hiring

It's important to make good hires; that's obvious. Employees make up the heart and much of the value of a university, so great care should be executed when hiring. Ideally, you want to fill vacant positions as soon as possible to help maintain continuity and cohesion within the unit and/or organization. Making good hires is also important due to the substantial and recurring costs associated with the search and productivity lost when a new candidate is brought on board (Schloss et al., 2009). Additionally, a poor hire—especially within leadership positions—is like a bad spot in an apple and can grow and add instability to the entire unit and organization. Poor hires can derail and detract from strategic efforts and halt momentum in units. Weak faculty hires can lead to compromised teaching, research, and creative activities. Therefore, poor faculty hires directly compromise the mission of the university. What is even more concerning, especially if someone is hired with tenure, is that tenured faculty members are difficult to change and almost impossible to remove. Problem hires in service units lead to frustration and inefficiencies for faculty, staff, and students and indirectly compromise the university mission. Whatever the position, the mission is compromised when the wrong person is hired. Therefore, making good hires needs to be at the top of a leader's priority list.

Within most organizations, hiring processes restrict the number of people who provide input on the candidates and protect their confidentiality throughout the search and hiring process. Conversely, in higher education, especially academic leadership appointments, there is a very public method associated with most searches and large committees to identify and select potential candidates. The open and inclusive process offers a number of advantages and weaknesses.

Advantages of University Hiring Practices

An obvious strength of the hiring practices in higher education is that people are able to engage and be a part of the selection process. Furthermore, the search committees are purposefully populated so that relevant units are represented. Great deliberation typically happens to ensure that the correct mix of units and employees are selected to the committee. Considerations involved in selecting individuals include faculty rank, mix of job classifications, gender, years at the university, and of course a desire to participate on the committee. If this work is done effectively, the members have significant involvement in selecting candidates and are able to offer their viewpoints and assessments and argue for or against potential candidates. This approach creates ownership across units and allows for future employees to interact with the people and units that they will be engaged with once they start working at the institution. In short, both the candidate and their future work associates have a chance to meet and evaluate one another and create a preliminary evaluation of the opportunity.

A large committee also has the advantage of providing multiple points of view that are used to evaluate the candidate. The voices of many typically mitigate the bias of one or two who may try to dominate the selection process. The members often bring different perspectives, expertise, and insights that allow for more comprehensive consideration of the candidates through multiple lenses. This attribute can be lost within an individual or small committee search method. Any feedback given to the hiring authority tends to be vetted with the committee through the chair. This has an advantage for the hiring authority because they receive amalgamated feedback and an understanding of the level of consensus across the group. This insight is beneficial because many positions serve a variety of constituents, and a split or weak level of support can be a concern. Ideally, a candidate should start a job with support from the units they will work with or supervise, and this search process can help gauge backing.

The hiring authority typically does not engage in the selection of candidates because the committee selects potential candidates for a visit to the university (the hiring authority often approves the final candidate pool). This instills confidence within the committee, units, and university that a friend or favored employee of the hiring authority is not placed in the position simply based on personal preference. Consequently, the hiring authority treats the hiring as a truly shared process. It is shared because the committee identifies the finalists and gives the hiring authority feedback on candidates along with feedback from across the university. The hiring authority uses this information along with their impressions generated through the interview process to make a final decision. Often the outcome results in a hire that the committee, university respondents, and the hiring authority all agree on as a viable candidate. If any of these entities voice strong resistance, the hiring authority typically considers another candidate or fails the search. It is challenging to enter a new university and successfully take on a faculty or leadership role if all groups are not supportive of the hire. This process has the advantage of bringing someone on board that is generally supported across the university.

Hiring Practice Concerns

There are advantages to hiring practices in higher education, but there are also a number of weaknesses that can compromise recruiting and hiring the best candidate for a given position. At the end of the day, the ultimate outcome should be to hire the best candidate who can benefit the unit(s) and university. Unfortunately, common higher education hiring practices do not necessarily deliver this outcome and are overly focused on traditional practices and processes.

Public Nature of Searches

One problem with university searches is their public nature, which can deter potential candidates for fear that it could compromise their standing in their current position. Imagine the questions that are generated from a candidate's supervisor, co-workers, and supervisees when they read about their candidacy at another university. Why are you leaving? Are you unhappy here? You started us down a challenging strategic effort centered on growth... how can you leave in the middle of this charge? Is our institution a poor fit? These types of questions and concerns do not instill confidence with coworkers and could compromise the candidate's current position and chances for future growth within their current institution. Therefore, many will not even consider looking at a position because of the exposure, even if the job is a good match for them and the institution.

Focus on Personal Preference and Needs

Another problem with higher education searches is that members of the search team may focus on their personal interests or the needs of their unit and disregard the needs of the institution. This was discussed in Chapter 6 and is referred to as the Arrow Paradox, which describes the irrationality of democratic voting. In short, problems occur when individuals perform a cost-benefit analysis and determine if the choice is right for them. This can create situations where committee members favor candidates from preferred institutions, disciplines, content expertise, etc. that may not be what the unit or institution actually needs. I remember one instance where a faculty member would not support a candidate because in their words "they would not help further their research agenda." Because of the committee member's cost-benefit analysis, he felt we needed to consider one of the other applicants who could potentially support their research agenda.

Many other considerations fall under this concern. For instance, many faculty and professional staff may prefer a laissez-faire management style because it gives them considerable freedom to determine how and when they will engage in professional and personal activities. Choosing a leader who tends to leave faculty and staff alone may work well at a personal level. However, it can be dysfunctional at a performance level if individuals are not held accountable and if their progress is not regularly monitored. This can be especially problematic if the previous leader used this approach and a new leadership style is needed to align the unit with the expectations of the institution.

Similar problems occur if committee members are looking for someone who is friendly, funny, and/or affable. Common feedback given by committee members focus on the candidate's affability or approachability. While this is not necessarily an unimportant consideration, it can be an issue if business and research acumen are the keys to the unit's future success. Being easy and nice does not necessarily translate to a strong hire. A similar bias is often shown if candidates come from outside higher education and people fear that they simply cannot understand or adapt to a university work environment. Often committee members feel that processes and systems from corporate America are a bad match for higher education, so they do not support these candidates. While this orientation might be correct, it can hinder progress if many of the institution's systems and processes need to be changed. Committee member biases that reflect committee member preference may sacrifice the best decision for the institution.

Time and Money

While search processes in academia are inclusive, they are very time-intensive and expensive. In fact, most searches take a year to complete. Once a position is vacated, an interim is commonly selected and a committee appointed using some type of nomination process. Depending on the search, the committee may have between 10 to 30 members. In fact, senior level searches may have a committee and several subcommittees representing the various parts of the university. Often the committee members are asked to develop a job description which is reviewed, revised, and wordsmithed. This is used to develop advertisements for the position, which is circulated for several months. Next, criteria are developed, often through a Likert Scale, which allows the hiring committee to rank candidates based on the candidate's materials. Next, the committee meets to amalgamate scores and refine the group of candidates to a group of semi-finalists. This group is selected by considering scores and related discussions that take place within the committee. Based on these results, preliminary interviews are arranged, typically over Zoom, and then finalists are selected for individual onsite interviews that take one or two days.

The onsite interviews solicit feedback from a larger portion of the institution and this data is summarized. The onsite data comes from individual meetings, group meetings, presentations, public forums, and meetings conducted during meals. All of this is summarized for the hiring authority along with a list of the candidate's strengths and weaknesses. In some instances, the candidates are ranked, but many hiring authorities prefer feedback without any ranking. The time, effort, and costs are substantial, especially if the search does not result in a hire. If the search fails, it is back to the drawing board and the process starts again and another year will pass before making a hire.

Sometimes a search firm is used for hiring leaders within academia. This is not unique to higher education and is used across many industries to find and examine quality candidates. The effectiveness varies dramatically, depending on the quality of the firm. A quality firm with seasoned employees can help organize the search process and find quality candidates that would not otherwise be found. Organization and planning provided by firms can be helpful because institutions and committee chairs may or may not have the skills, understanding, and familiarity needed to conduct a search. I have witnessed searches where candidates sat alone in a lounge for two hours because of scheduling errors, arrived for lunch where no food was served, arrived for a meeting, and the attendees missed the meeting, etc. This reflects poorly on the institution's quality and the interest in the candidate is compromised through this type of slap-dash experience. Finally, the search firm can act as a contact for questions from potential candidates. This can provide candidates with a feeling of greater confidentiality and a place to ask frank questions.

However, many search firms do not find additional candidates and instead ask people within the institution to engage in all of the organization and planning. Furthermore, they can do a poor job of answering questions for potential candidates. When conducting an interview, firms can provide some valuable guidance, but after going through the process once, people essentially have the template on how to conduct an organized and professional interview. Similarly, your institution may have superior networks for recruiting candidates to apply for an open position compared to a firm. Often search consultants have never worked in higher education and bring limited value to the effort. I remember being involved with a senior-level search where the consultants had never worked in higher education and did not understand key elements of the position or the work environment. We essentially spent a lot of time educating the staff about higher education. In this instance, they acted more like a poor realtor when you are trying to buy or sell a house. You just want to remove the realtor from the process so you can move things forward.

Depending on the search and related services, the firm could charge over $100,000 plus expenses. This is a significant investment. Therefore, if you use a firm, make sure they can bring value and you have good reasons for using their services, e.g., they specialize in filling the vacated position and have a good track record, or you simply do not have resources to conduct a professional recruitment and interviewing process. Consider the substantial organization, recruitment, and professionalism that could be created within your organization for $100,000! In fact, if an organization is large enough and has multiple searches each year, hiring someone internally to oversee these efforts may make sense.

Despite some of the concerns associated with using hiring firms, there are instances where making this investment makes sense. A number of questions are listed below in Table 1. If you answer *no* to several of these questions you may want to consider taking this route to fill the position.

Table 1. Questions to ask when considering the use of a search firm.

Does your unit or organization have the skills and knowledge (marketing, event planning, etc.) to execute a professional search?	Yes /No
Does your unit or organization have the resources (people) to organize and execute a professional search?	Yes /No
Have you been successful in making quality hires in the past?	Yes /No
Do you have the ability to recruit quality candidates from across the world (this tends to apply to researchers, endowed professorships, and senior leaders)?	Yes /No
Is a failed search something you can easily navigate?	Yes /No
Can someone within your unit or organization act as a neutral third-party intermediary for communications with potential candidates?	Yes /No

If you answered "no" to several of these questions, you may be well served to investigate the use of a search firm. If you take this route, ask probing questions about their staffing, services, and clients to ensure the firm is well-matched to your needs.

Reference Checks

A final concern with academic searches is the poor process generally used to evaluate a candidate's past performance. I have been involved with many search efforts and have never had a person from the reference list give an unfavorable recommendation. They are all positive and when asked about a weakness it is often a useless statement such as "They work too hard," or, "They care too much." This type of response is consistent no matter if the references are checked by committee members, search firm consultants, or the hiring authority. Interestingly, I have had many supervisees who have taken new positions at other universities. If I was on the reference list a representative from the search always contacted me. However, a number did not list me as a reference. In every instance when I was not listed, I was never contacted by anyone involved with the search to get feedback from their candidate's current supervisor. I simply found out from my supervisee that they were leaving and taking a new position. This may seem surprising, but it is a common practice even with internal university hires.

Background checks are universally made to insure you are not hiring someone who may have broken the law. However, I have been involved with searches where the search committee was told not to Google candidates because the information could be inaccurate and bias the search process. For one candidate a search committee member revealed that they had received a vote of "no confidence" and was going to be removed from their current position, and the committee was asked to ignore this information. Past performance is the best predictor of future performance, so make more intensive examinations of final candidates when something like this is found. While more intensive background checking may or may not reveal issues of concern, additional probing and investigation is important before making a decision. It makes absolutely no sense to ignore information found on the internet or via feedback from a reliable source. Some of this faulty technique might come from poorly conceived and executed training designed to avoid bias in the selection of candidates. Therefore, question and push back on approaches that seem counter in your ultimate goal of hiring a quality candidate.

How To Make Better Hires

Aspects of the hiring approach in higher education are unique and have distinct advantages and weaknesses. To be successful in the future, it is important to balance practices that maintain current strengths while minimizing approaches that compromise the desired outcome. What follows are modifications to consider in creating a better process.

Succession Planning

Every position at a university will be vacated. This is basic and common knowledge. While some departures may come as a surprise, many can easily be predicted. For instance, if a president has served for 15 years and is in their late 60s, there is a good chance that they will be leaving their position in the near future. Similarly, if the average time in a deanship is three to five years and most of the deans at your institution have been working for three or more years, the chances for these positions being vacated is high. In some instances, employees communicate they are looking for other opportunities and plan on moving in the next year or two. Generally, people mean what they say, so this would be key information that this position will likely be vacated. Despite this knowledge, leaders do not plan for inevitable turnover and scramble to conduct national searches multiple times every year as positions are vacated. This approach really does not make sense.

Succession planning is one way to better prepare for leadership turnover in higher education. Succession planning is a strategic process whereby an organization identifies and develops key employees to fill critical roles, especially in leadership. Most universities do not engage in succession planning and many mandate that a search be conducted for key positions. This approach does not allow vacant positions to be easily filled through internal appointments. While external searches are certainly a legitimate and needed option in filling positions, so is the process of targeting and training employees to fill vacated positions. One clear advantage of succession planning is that the year-long process used to search for a new candidate is eliminated. Not only is it more time-efficient, but hundreds of thousands of dollars are saved by not conducting a national or international search with a search firm.

One limitation of an external search is that members of the search visit and listen to a candidate for less than 20 hours. In fact, it is often limited to a presentation and one to three meetings even if someone is a member of the search committee. While this time is helpful in making a quality hire, internal candidates have often worked at the institution for years, so their strengths, weaknesses and skills are much more evident. Consequently, internal candidates take much of the speculation out of the hiring process because you essentially know what you are getting. Even though people think they can spot a quality candidate through an interview process, selecting the right person for a vacant position is difficult at best. The truth is that few can do this reliably and most overstate their ability to spot a quality candidate.

Another downside to hiring an external candidate is the time required to become familiar with their new unit, organization, and culture, as well as the systems and processes within the institution. This typically takes six months or longer. If the search process takes a year, and an additional six months is for onboarding a new hire, the unit and organization does not have an employee who can make full contributions for 18 months. This is especially concerning in leadership positions. If the position turns over every three to five years (which is not uncommon), appointed and fully operational leadership is missing 30 to 50 percent of the time. This is a striking statistic. Even though an interim is put in place, they often still keep their current duties and are not able to make significant and important decisions in an interim position. This void creates a lack of continuity in strategic efforts, and the unit is left adrift until new faculty, staff, or leadership are selected and oriented within the organization. Additionally, the employee filling the interim position becomes overloaded, resentful of the burden, and some leave administration altogether because of their ongoing interim responsibilities.

Internal candidates are also familiar with the institutional culture, strategic imperatives, and internal processes, which helps create a consistency of purpose (Deming, 2000). Many strategic efforts can take a decade or more to implement and frequently multiple leaders will be used to address these important efforts. Internal candidates have the ability to quickly step in and stay the course and address long-range strategic efforts. Examples of long-term efforts include creating international programming, growing a deeper research agenda, building out a robust online educational platform, creating a new college, or creating the healthiest learning community in the region. Often an internal candidate who is familiar and aligned with institutional and unit efforts can be an ideal replacement.

Succession planning does not come without investment. Key individuals need to be courted and groomed for the positions through training and purposeful work assignments. In some instances, the employee may leave for other opportunities, which can result in losing an employee with excellent potential and losing the training and development investment. However, many employees who are identified as having leadership potential appreciate the designation, training, and opportunity for advancement in their current location. In fact, the designation and development opportunities can act as a retention mechanism to keep employees around for internal opportunities. Take the attitude that you want to create good things for good employees and this mantra will serve you well even if the employee leaves your organization. Consequently, there are some risks with this investment, but investing in your people also offers more advantages than disadvantages.

Downside To Succession Planning

A downside to succession planning is that a committee is not engaged in the selection of the final candidates. Typically, in these situations an appointment is made by the hiring authority as part of the effort to quickly put a new leader in place. One way to offset the lack of faculty and staff involvement in the selection process is to have the hiring authority visit with the impacted unit and/or primary stakeholders before making the appointment. I once appointed a leader to run a large nursing program. Prior to making the appointment I visited with each faculty member in the department to explain why I was making the appointment and to get their feedback on this tactic. There was a small group that was not supportive of my decision, some who were neutral, and another large group that was supportive. While this approach was effective, I did run the risk of many not supporting the appointment. If this had happened, I would have had to rethink my decision because I would not want to appoint someone to a leadership position who started with most of the faculty and staff not supporting them.

How To Embed Succession Planning

One method to start succession planning is to identify people within your unit that have leadership skills and potential and start training them during your leadership tenure. The concept is very straightforward since one of your key responsibilities is to nurture and develop your supervisees. Once you identify someone with leadership potential, ask if they have interest in leadership. Remember leadership is needed in all positions and job classifications. Consequently, if an employee wants to stay in their role as a faculty member, they could maintain this position and engage in leadership through oversight of students, leading a research team, or running an academic program. If you expand the application of leadership into your thinking, there are many leadership roles for faculty and staff and students.

One position you should target for succession planning is your current position. Remember, even if you do not plan on taking another position, at some point you will leave, and a quality employee will be needed to fill your position. Who better to take on this training than the person most familiar with the position. Even if there is a policy to conduct an external search, the training, experiences, and development you provide for your potential replacement will place this internal candidate in a more competitive position for selection through an external search process. Think about the roles and experiences that are necessary to be successful in your position and ensure that the internal candidate fits and excels in these areas and they will likely become a competitive candidate.

Characteristics To Consider When Hiring

While succession planning can help fill positions, there are many valid reasons for conducting an external search. For example, despite your efforts to develop a succession plan, a position could be vacated before key employees are ready to move into a new role or you may not have a strong internal candidate for the job. Additionally, there can be issues within a unit where someone from outside the organization is needed to facilitate change. Whatever the reason, it is important to be clear about the traits you are looking for in the hiring of an internal or external hire.

Traits of the Vacated Employee

Often when a position is vacated, the common reaction is to recruit someone with skills and content expertise similar to the previous employee. I have worked at institutions that actually refer to the vacated position by the previous employees' last name, e.g., "the Evans position." Even without this actual label, this replication of previous employees transposed onto potential hires is common. Conceptualizing the position in this way can focus people to consider candidates similar to the previous employee. Anytime a position is vacated this transition should be treated as an opportunity, even if you lost a quality employee. Therefore, do not box yourself into hiring someone who can teach the same classes, or engage in the same administrative or leadership tasks and processes as the previous employee.

Drucker's Five Rules of Making a Hire

Peter Drucker outlines five rules to follow when making a hire (Edersheim, 2007) and they can be applied to internal and external candidates. First, you need to look at a number of qualified people. Higher education tends to advertise broadly and review all eligible candidates who are then pared down through a series of review processes. Therefore, higher education generally does a good job in addressing this rule. Next, think hard about what this candidate brings to the organization. When applying this rule, be sure and consider the candidates strengths, weaknesses, and gaps that exist within the unit or university. As previously mentioned, it is not uncommon for people to hire individuals who are similar to the current people in the unit, which may not be what is needed. Next, be sure and have many people meet with the candidate, especially people who will work with them so you can gain multiple perspectives about what the person can bring to the organization. Again, higher education tends to be very good at addressing this rule, so it is likely part of your organization's recruitment efforts. Finally, after the hire, make sure you follow up to inquire if the new hire understands the job. Once the hire is made you want to be sure they have the understanding and direction needed to maximize their chances for success.

Identifying What To Look For

To gain clarity about what type of hire is needed, engage faculty, staff, leadership, and key stakeholders by asking them what type of employee will best meet strategic needs during the next five years. Within this conversation identify items such as content expertise, backgrounds, skills, approaches, ability to work in teams, and needed experiences. Often the description starts out looking as if you are recruiting a person who has the combined attributes of Einstein,

Gandhi, and Mother Teresa. While this would be an outstanding hire, a more focused and reasonable description of essential and preferred characteristics and experiences needs to be generated.

Often the focus is on developing a job description that concentrates on skills and expertise. While these considerations are valid, they can carry excessive weight in the selection process. Other valid considerations include how the candidate complements the strengths of the unit (Edersheim, 2007), enthusiasm (Harari, 2002), talent (Buckingham & Coffman, 1999), passion (Chouinard, Y. 2006), affability, attitude (Maxwell, 2007), and a balanced ego (Harari, 2002), are often given insufficient weight in the decision-making process. I really worked to bring people into my leadership team that brought different perspectives, approaches, and skills to create a group that could more broadly and successfully identify problems and solutions that were critical for success. Additionally, when they were given latitude to use their unique attributes they became part of the team and were invested in our success. These characteristics are often given insufficient attention in making a hire in higher education because importance is instead given to degrees, number of publications, and external funding potential.

Maybe you have experienced hiring someone who had impressive degrees, worked at a prestigious research university, published prolifically and taught classes that were difficult to instruct. However, this person also disrupted the unit through their rough personality and made students angry and dejected because of the faculty members' insensitivity. Not considering multiple priority characteristics has been challenged by many notable leaders. For instance, Peter Schutz, the former CEO of Porsche once said, "Hire attitude and train skills" (Pandya & Shell, 2006). Herb Kelleher, the former CEO of Southwest Airlines told his employees that "we are prepared, including legally, to fire you for having a bad attitude" (Pandya & Shell, 2006). Therefore, weigh multiple characteristics and considerations when you are looking for a quality candidate within your unit or organization. Remember, any hire could last for decades, and you don't want a disruptive force created due to a deficient set of hiring criteria.

Quality

A final factor to consider when conducting an external hire is the tendency for some employees to avoid hiring highly qualified and talented candidates. Remember, your primary mandate is to hire the best employees you can afford. As Hamel and Breen once stated, you need to have a Bozo-free Zone (Hamel & Breen, 2007) in your organization. This same consideration was described by Buckingham and Coffman (Buckingham & Coffman, 1999), who discussed the resistance a "B" level employee can have towards hiring an "A" level candidate. In short, they found that Bs don't like to hire As. In fact, they may want to hire a "C" level candidate to maintain their elevated place in the organizational hierarchy. As a leader you need to make sure these candidates are not eliminated from the process, especially when a committee is charged with identifying a group of semi-finalists. This may require a conversation with the committee chair from you as the hiring authority or with the entire committee as you give them their charge. Obviously, the way you choose your words and deliver this message needs to be well thought out so people don't feel they are subpar.

Consider Modifying the External Search Process: Shorten the Search Timeline

Few industries spend a year filling a vacant position. Nevertheless, this practice is common in higher education. There are many reasons for this, including tradition. Many feel that interested candidates expect interviews in the early spring and candidates move to the university in the summer and start in the fall. There is really no strong reason for this pattern other than this is the way it has always been done. There may also be a tradition to recruit during a national conference that is in the fall, and people need time to transition from their current position/home before they move to a new location. The logic seems absurd given that most occupations fill a position in weeks or months after it's vacated. Granted, moving in the middle of a semester can cause challenges, especially for teaching schedules. However, a semester runs for a little less than four months and quarters are even shorter, so a four-month timeline is certainly feasible. If it is a professional or leadership position, a semester clock really has no bearing on the timeline.

Taking a 12-month process and turning it into a four-month timeline requires that everything run at a faster pace. Searches need to be a priority, so committee members need to accommodate the scheduling associated with the shortened time period. For instance, the committee selection can be done in a matter of days and the job description developed and finalized in two weeks. While the job description is developed, you can identify and secure advertising outlets. Many outlets advertise virtually, so ads can be placed immediately after the job description is finalized. Similarly, human resources will need to generate approvals and open the position over a two-week period. While advertisements are distributed through virtual and print avenues, employees within the organization can formally and informally recruit by posting positions on the university/unit website and through word of mouth. Approximately 45 to 60 days would be given to advertise and recruit for the position and secure applicants. Once the semi-finalists are identified by the search committee, Zoom meetings are conducted over a five-day period for committee members and the hiring authority to review. Based on the review of semi-finalists, three to four top candidates are identified. From this finalist group, the top candidate is brought to campus approximately two weeks after the Zoom interviews. If the candidate is strong and seems to be a good match, you extend an offer. If the offer is not accepted, or the candidate seems to be a questionable fit, bring the next best candidate to campus. Another approach is to create a more closed interview process with a diverse group of faculty and stakeholders and identify one individual to bring on campus for a more open visit. When this happens, the institution brings in only the top candidate for a visit. Unless something changes during the visit, the candidate is hired. Both approaches help maintain the confidentiality of the candidates' interviews.

There will be resistance to this timeline and approach because it is different from the process at many universities. Common concerns include the process not being congruent with disciplinary norms or a desire to have all four finalists come to campus so people have a choice. Furthermore, individuals may complain about the timeline being too short and meeting opportunities not working because insufficient notice is given through the abbreviated timeline. As a leader, you need to have a good response to these legitimate concerns associated with changing the traditional process. When I accelerated the search timeline, I tended to argue that quickly filling the position with a good hire was good for the unit, university, and the students. As discussed earlier, problems with continuity, progress, overload, and work quality can occur with drawn-out searches. Therefore, the new approach is a necessary and positive change. If the accelerated timeline fails, the processes can simply be extended another four to eight months to generate another pool of candidates.

Dedicated In-house Search Professionals

Unless you do not have the necessary staffing within your unit or university, assign the search coordination and oversight to a person within the university. If possible, a well-organized individual *within your unit* can be a strong choice because of the supervisee/supervisor relationship. There may be other individuals outside of a unit that can assist through entities such as human resources or through a vice president's office. If this support exists, this resource should be used to help distribute workloads and take advantage of their capabilities, expertise, insights, and availability. Ideally, the search coordinator will organize all of the logistics associated with the search. The logistics are significant and include committee and candidate scheduling, purchasing and placing advertisements, collecting applications, ensuring technical support for Zoom meetings, and arranging travel for campus visits.

Candidates often have questions related to the search and the search coordinator can often answer procedural questions or direct them to individuals who can answer questions related to the position. Give thought to who addresses the candidate questions so all applicants receive similar access and information. Additionally, space, food, and audio-visual equipment will be needed for the campus presentations/ meetings which require video capture of presentations, reservations, and meal planning. Furthermore, the coordinator needs to invite and ensure attendance at meetings, presentations, and meals. Finalize transportation for the candidate, along with a detailed agenda and related support for the critical visit. As part of the campus visit, candidates may request a car, real estate viewing, etc. All of this needs to be meticulously taken care of by the coordinator.

I can remember a department chair who never used a coordinator or any of the services on campus and took care of the logistics himself. Every candidate had dinner at Hippo's Pizza and he purchased four pizzas and two pitchers of beer for the group. It was a place where you sat on picnic tables, kids were running around, and video games blazed in the background. Decisions like this all make an impression. Ultimately, attending to the details of a search are a key indicator of the quality of the unit and institution. Remember a search is a two-way process and both parties want a good match. The coordination and the way candidates are treated throughout the process is critical to the recruitment process. Having a coordinator requires a significant commitment, but it is an essential part of a quality recruitment effort.

In-depth Reference Checks and Candidate Interactions

Reference checks are simple, do not take much time and are a critical part of the hiring process. Certainly, the names on the candidate's reference list need to be checked. If the current and possibly the previous direct supervisor are not on the reference list, one or both of these individuals need to be contacted before extending an offer. It is not hard for a candidate to have an engaging resume/cover letter, excel in Zoom interviews, have a strong campus visit, and yet be a problematic hire. Some people interview better than they perform, and some perform better than they interview, so speaking with a direct supervisor can help you evaluate what type of performer you are considering. Be sure that the person who conducts these interviews is good at follow-up questions during the reference check and can probe for concerning performance or behavior issues. Know that the quality of someone's direct supervisor can vary and that their job search could be related to dynamics with that person. If their current supervisor shares concerns, check with the previous supervisor to see if their response supports or refutes the current supervisor's feedback. The hiring process is very involved, so something like this can be easily overlooked. Visiting with the previous supervisor(s) is essential.

Red Flags

Candidates tend to be on their best behavior during an interview. If something happens during the interview that is concerning, take this seriously. I have had candidates drink five glasses of wine during an interview dinner which made for a very disjointed and rambling conversation. In another instance, the candidate made disparaging comments about overweight people by referring to them as big fat slobs and made inappropriate comments about their current employer throughout the visit. If someone can not maintain their composure over a 16-hour interview, much more will likely surface once they start working full-time in your unit. If your plan is to hope these indicators will disappear once the candidate is hired, you will be disappointed. As painful as it may be, a failed search is preferable to a questionable hire, so watch for red flags during the interview process and take them seriously.

Extending an Offer

Once you have a strong candidate, consider ways to make an attractive offer. All institutions have limitations, particularly when it comes to a base salary and compensation. There are many considerations that go into generating a salary offer such as cost and availability of housing, competitor salaries, and national availability within a particular field. For instance, positions such as nursing or informational technology may require higher salaries because of the limited availability of workers in these areas. This may require special funding requests through central administration, or it may require you to cannibalize a position within your unit to generate funds for the elevated salary costs. In areas where housing is a concern, giving someone a signing bonus of $5,000 to $10,000 to help with these costs can be helpful, especially for candidates who are new graduates and have little in the way of savings. Some universities, especially in high-costs areas such as Southern California can provide low-interest loans, but this is unique to these locations that have extremely high cost of living.

Beyond salary, there are a number of items that can encourage a candidate to work within your unit. As mentioned earlier, you never know what is of value to the candidate, so part of the interview process by the hiring authority should involve gaining insights into this important question. For some, having flexibility to work remotely part of the time can be attractive, particularly for pet owners or people with children. Others may desire reduced teaching loads initially to focus on their research agenda. Some will appreciate summer compensation until they have an opportunity to generate a summer revenue stream. Additionally, robust start-up packages related to equipment, discretionary spending, student support, computers, training, office furniture, etc. can all be a part of this effort. Also, the quality of schools or access to the arts or outdoors can be important factors. Be sure and consider these types of items to bolster the candidate's offer.

One consideration that has grown in importance is assistance with employment options for a spouse or partner. Given the salaries of most universities, it often takes two incomes to make ends meet. This consideration almost always requires institutional-level policies and support, since many units are too small to make this request feasible. If the institution is large, availability of diverse positions is more common than in smaller institutions. Connect with human resources or through a vice president's office to explore the availability of positions for the candidate's spouse or partner. Some institutions will use an incentive model whereby the university will pay one-third of a salary, the vice president will pay one-third, and the hiring unit of the spouse or partner will pay one-third of the salary for a fixed period of time, such as three to five years. This gives the unit a financial incentive and time to allocate funds to fully fund the position. Additionally, having contacts through advisory boards in the community can be a way to find employment opportunities for a candidate's partner. This became a reciprocal process for me, where I could arrange discussions for spouses or partners with community members and similar support was given to organizations when they were trying to recruit someone into their organization. Be sure and visit with human resources, your unit leader, and community members to explore current and new approaches for providing options for spouses or partners. Without these options, you could lose out on some important hires.

Annual Review and Other Forms of Feedback

Annual reviews are common across all industries. The yearly review provides an opportunity for a supervisor and their supervisee to review performance and progress during a 12-month period. Most institutions have a mandatory form and related questions that must be addressed by the supervisor and supervisee. While this part of the review process needs to be followed and likely has many attributes, other questions and reporting requirements can typically be added to improve the efficacy of the review. For instance, the questions outlined in Table 2 can provide additional insights not commonly seen on review forms. They were generated by management leaders and the author. They provide questions for reflecting more deeply about the past year to gain understanding about what facilitated success and what contributed to sub-par performance. Pick from the questions provided in Table 2 and/or create your own questions that are customized for your supervisee.

Table 2. Questions for potential inclusion during an annual review.

Question	Source
How have you changed your job?	(Harari, 2002)
What jobs have you eliminated?	(Harari, 2002)
What have you innovated?	(Harari, 2002)
How have you made things more efficient?	(Harari, 2002)
Are you given the things you need to be successful?	(Edersheim, 2007)
Do we have policies or structures that prevent you from doing your job?	(Edersheim, 2007)
As your supervisor, what things am I doing that helps and hampers your efforts?	(Edersheim, 2007)
What training, skills, or support do you need to be successful in your efforts during the next year?	Author
What are your 2 -3 biggest accomplishments and disappointments during the past year?	Author
What are your top three priorities for the next year?	Author
Have your professional aspirations changed during the past year? Can I help with your aspirations?	Author

It is important to pause, reflect, and discuss work performance at least once a year to ensure the job is still a good match and to improve effectiveness in the following year. I took time each year away from my worksite around my annual review period to consider how I performed, what was accomplished, and how I would move forward the following year. I also used this process to help me decide if I should do this for another year or move on to something else. For instance, at Boise State I was able to make a number of contributions as a dean and wanted to transition into another role before I lost my passion, drive, and temperament for the job. I brought the decision to move on to something else to my supervisor during my annual review and we generated a plan to allow this transition to happen in a way that was good for me and the university. The annual review provides a platform for these considerations on a yearly basis.

360-Degree Reviews

A very effective approach to annual reviews is a feedback process from multiple sources such as 360-degree reviews or multi-rater reviews. A drawback of only using a supervisor and supervisee to provide feedback over a year's work output is the possibility of bias or seeing the year through two very different lenses. The multi-rater review uses peers, coworkers, partners, leaders, and other appropriate sources to provide feedback on an employee's performance during the past year. There are a variety of tools that often use Likert scale type statements which are usually accompanied with open-ended questions. The responses are put into a report with themes and shared with the employee and their supervisor. This process generally creates a more neutral platform for dialogue and discussion around an employee's strengths and weaknesses and a more productive way to generate a development plan. Supervisors and supervisees can become stuck if one person feels communication is a weakness and the other feels it is a strength. Feedback from multiple sources can prevent resistance to accepting feedback and making needed changes. It also can correct a supervisor's incorrect perceptions of their supervisee. Therefore, the multi-rater feedback system can be helpful for both parties.

The multi-rater review process like any approach has some weaknesses. First, it requires additional work across the workforce. Even though being part of a multi-rater process only takes 30 to 60 minutes, this adds up if you are asked to evaluate multiple individuals at a time when you are preparing for your supervisee reviews and your personal evaluation. For this reason, many institutions collect multi-rater data every other year or every three years to help manage the workload. Additionally, if someone is asked to take on a difficult task such as increasing a unit's workload or restructuring a unit, the feedback from that unit will likely be poor. In these situations, the use of these tools may be problematic unless it is customized and uses questions that explain the leader's charge so that they are not blamed for an institutional decision. Therefore, it is important to consider someone's work responsibilities when using these tools and the feedback given from people who are impacted by mandated changes.

Honesty

Nothing is easier than giving a high-performing employee positive feedback about their performance during an annual review. Typically, these sessions are tension-free and everyone leaves feeling good. However, telling someone that their performance is not acceptable and needs to change is a very different type of discussion and is more challenging. Giving corrective feedback can also be derailed because like grade inflation in schools, supervisors tend to give inflated evaluations (Wakeman, 2013). For instance, some supervisors consider effort over outcomes, or they compare employees to other individuals in the unit. This approach is not effective because performance needs to be tied to outcomes and if the entire unit is composed of marginal producers the evaluation likely misses the mark. Others simply have a hard time giving corrective feedback and delivering an average or sub-par evaluation rating. A sure sign that a leader has problems with confronting marginal performers is seeing a unit that has average or sub-par performance while all of the employees meet or exceed expectations on reviews. This situation should be a red flag for you to address.

Another reason for not giving critical and honest feedback on evaluations are that many attribute poor performance to external circumstances that are out of their control. An example of external forces was the COVID-19 epidemic. Many supervisors and some institutions required all employees to receive satisfactory evaluations because of the stress, personal losses, and isolation they experienced during the epidemic. While COVID was a unique occurrence, many poor performing employees received positive evaluations. This is a shame because without honest feedback the entire evaluation exercise is of little use. As Pandya and Shell (2006) articulated through their interview with Jack Welch, leaders need to be candid about performance. As a leader, be careful to not be susceptible to patterns that prevent you from giving honest and candid feedback during an annual evaluation.

Yearly Evaluations Are Not Enough

While yearly reviews are needed and helpful, you are falling short as a leader if evaluation meetings only occur once a year. You never want to go into an evaluation where the supervisee receives a poor evaluation and that is the first time they have been made aware of their shortcomings. Typically, a supervisor should meet with supervisees regularly throughout the year. Depending on the structure of the organization and the position, the meetings can be weekly to every three months. Additionally, there are opportunities for informal meetings and non-planned interactions where a number of items can be addressed (both positive and corrective feedback). Most evaluation processes require employees and their supervisor to craft items that are related to their development during the next year, which should be discussed across the 12-month period.

Critical feedback is very difficult for many employees to receive because they are typically working hard and trying to do a good job. Therefore, they should have many opportunities to learn how they are performing so the evaluation meeting acts as a way to formalize what they know through many interactions throughout the year. As a supervisor, you will be well served to have a thoughtful, organized, and robust annual review process and multiple opportunities to meet with your supervisees so they generally know how they are performing throughout the year. If you are working with a particularly confrontational or difficult employee, keep a log of your sessions in case the employee decides to take action against you. Receiving corrective feedback can create an array of responses, depending on the temperament of the supervisee. Having documentation that you worked fairly and consistently with the employee can save you and the university much time and effort if the employee becomes argumentative or disgruntled and decides to take you to task on your corrective actions.

I was a unit leader at a land grant university where I had over 40 direct reports. This may sound impressive but in reality, I had too many direct reports and was not giving them the attention and time needed to foster their development. Buckingham and Coffman (1999) are important architects associated with the Gallup organization's extensive work on finding characteristics of great managers. They clearly state that if you cannot visit with each of your supervisees for at least four hours a year you have too many employees or you should not be a manager. I clearly had too many employees and felt I was doing well to just give a formal review each year and attend to my other responsibilities as a leader. However, this reporting structure was not conducive to one of my most important functions as a leader... developing my supervisees. Author Andrew Tempe accurately articulated that as a leader you teach, coach, mentor, and inspire (Temte, 2021). It is impossible to meet these standards if you are not meeting individually with your supervisees throughout the year. Therefore, make sure you have a structure, schedule, and focus that prioritizes this important responsibility.

Your Evaluation Feedback

In addition to the work you produce when evaluating your supervisees, you must also prepare and effectively engage in your own evaluation process. Make sure you are thoughtful in developing goals for your next year's work and devise ways you can address areas that need attention for your professional development. Often you can tie these areas together and keep track of milestones or actions that show your commitment to addressing goals and personal growth. When completing your annual review report for your supervisor do not share all you have done... this is a lot of work for you and laborious for your supervisor to read. Instead, provide the best examples of your work that relate to your goals or areas for improvement such as communication or budget management. Additionally, the examples should be accompanied by a high-level overview of what was done across the entire area of review. For instance, in the area of fundraising you could describe one or two gifts and also summarize the total funds generated through three to five major avenues (individual gifts, corporate sponsors, crowdsourcing, etc.) to give an overview of accomplishments and how you achieved these outcomes.

Moreover, your annual review is also an opportunity to request additional training or support you might need during the next year. You want to be prepared for your annual review, so review your work, accomplishments, and plans for the next year. Be clear and concise with your written and verbal communications and be open to feedback. You do not need to follow all recommendations from your supervisor, but you need to be *open* to their suggestions and insights and engage in conversations during your meeting. It may be helpful to think of the employees you supervise and do a quality job preparing for their annual review. You want to emulate these behaviors along with addressing any of your supervisor's special requests.

Building a Team of Professionals

In chapter five of this book we discussed the idea of using professional staff to help with effective communication. This expertise and support are invaluable in organizing, generating, and distributing needed communication within and outside of a university. Other critical areas associated with leadership positions can also benefit from the use of professional staff. Specifically, professional staff can be instrumental in the areas of financial preparation and management, human resource management, fundraising, event planning, and research support and management. Typically leaders, especially academic leaders, lack expertise in these areas and if not properly executed, can compromise the effectiveness of their unit and the university. Even if they are experienced in these areas, they may not be able to oversee the day-to-day operations because of other job responsibilities. It is therefore the responsibility of leadership to identify quality professionals within and outside the university to help spearhead these important obligations. Additionally, leaders need to have the humility to ask for support and insight from these professionals when there are gaps in expertise and follow their guidance. Given the complexities of a contemporary university environment, professionals are a necessity if leaders are to be effective in executing their work in higher education.

Professional Financial Management

If you are a leader who has financial responsibilities such as budget development, budget oversight, approval of expenditures, or revenue generation, you need to hire a professional to help manage this responsibility for you. Depending on the size and complexity of your unit, this could be a portion of a person's job allocation or it could require multiple professionals to execute this work. The financial manager needs to be a professional who is detail oriented, understands or can quickly learn the university financial system, and is fluent in building and operating shadow systems. This support will give you accurate and timely information related to expenditures, projections, and reserves so you can confidently make mission-critical decisions on a regular basis. There are few professional support positions that are as valuable as a capable financial manager.

Hiring a Financial Manager

The financial manager may have a business or accounting background, which may be very appropriate and address the needs of your unit. Hiring someone from outside the university who can excel within a university environment can be challenging and often expensive. The chances of an outside hire not making a successful transition from industry to higher education is not small. Therefore, if you take this path you should prepare for the possibility of this hire not working out. Another option is to recruit someone from within the university. Some of the best professionals I have found within universities are people who have worked within a university setting for years and learned how to build, maintain and manage budgets, generate revenue projections, and execute financial reporting *on the job.* These individuals have progressively grown in their jobs and received increasingly more complex work and higher levels of budget and financial responsibility within the university. Internal employees of this caliber will likely be obvious, and you need to actively recruit them to be on your team. Remember, without question, this individual is one of the key professionals on your staff and their effective contributions are critical to your success as a leader. There are few things that can remove you from a leadership position faster than mismanagement of funds. Therefore, put the best person you can find in this role and if that person does not exist within your unit, find someone outside your area who meets this standard as quickly as possible.

When I started my role as dean, I was familiar with budget responsibilities and oversight in higher education settings, but not for an entire college. However, each institution is different so I had a lot of new systems, processes, and practices to learn and overseeing a college produced another level of complexity for me to navigate. Unfortunately, the timing of my hire coincided with the senior budget administrator in the college retiring. To help fill the void, another person was hired to replace the budget administrator prior to my arrival. The replacement was a well-intended gesture but problematic because the person they hired was from outside the university. Therefore, two new employees (myself and the new budget manager), were given responsibility over a college budget with both of us new to the university financial systems, budgeting processes, etc.

The learning curve required significant time devoted to understanding basic processes in an environment with little formal training or orientation sessions for new hires. While there was some training for the budget manager, most of the insights were gained from other employees sharing their knowledge, practices, and information. It took a couple of years to get the budgeting processes within the college to an acceptable level, and I ultimately ended up hiring someone from within the unit to take over this key responsibility. My only regret was that I waited two years to make this change. Hiring a highly-skilled internal candidate from within my unit made a world of difference and gave me the information, control, and insight needed to better meet the financial needs of the faculty, staff, and students within the college. Again, having capable, knowledgeable professionals in this role is essential or you will struggle to effectively manage and deploy resources to address daily operations and strategic efforts.

Financial Management Is Nothing To Fear

Often leaders with little formal financial training (which is the majority of academic leaders in higher education) feel apprehension over their financial responsibilities. However, if they have a quality financial professional on their team who has the skills to record financial transactions, manage assets, liabilities, revenue, expenses and payroll, maintain a general ledger, ensure cash flow management and generate financial projections, their apprehension quickly dissipates. Even if the leader is new to responsibility over a unit's finances, much of what is done by the financial professional and what needs to be done by the leader can be acquired, assuming the leader is willing to learn. Financial considerations are not advanced sciences that only a select few can understand. Rather, financial considerations such as a budget or revenue projections are all tools to effectively plan and carry out day-to-day operations and address strategic initiatives. You simply need someone who can run with these tools.

Building a budget with your leadership team and financial manager can be an excellent way to connect and communicate the year's programming and strategic efforts to a list of key expenditures. This exercise allows for prioritization because typically there are more items to fund than resources can accommodate. In these instances, items of most value are identified, and others are modified or removed from the list so that the most important work is supported and funded. Therefore, building a budget helps leadership, faculty, and staff ensure that adequate resources are available for the most important efforts. Conversations with leadership and the budget manager about this topic are an excellent way for the entire team to justify and identify priorities.

Similarly, if your income has a variable component such as revenue generation through educational programming or grants and contracts funding, accurately projecting these revenues is essential in planning for expenditures during the year. Without mastering this skill, you can at best react once the actual revenue is placed in your accounts. Reacting once money is deposited is not ideal because it takes time to generate personnel proformas, secure space, purchase equipment, execute hires, and implement plans. Projections require the various revenue centers to communicate with leadership and the financial manager(s) to provide estimations of revenue generation based on objective data such as yearly growth over time, student inquiries, weekly registration numbers, number of website hits, new advertising and outreach efforts, numbers of quality grant submissions, or number of grant resubmissions. The conversations are valuable to understand the various efforts occurring across your unit and to create a reasonable estimate of funds for a given year. Therefore, the effort requires a series of conversations, tracking, and a consolidation of these efforts to estimate revenues over a time period. As a leader you need to be able to listen to this feedback, ask probing questions, and then meet with your financial manager to determine final estimations.

As a leader, be open and candid about your level of knowledge and understanding associated with financial responsibilities. Even if you are a seasoned veteran regarding financial matters, ask questions to become oriented to the systems and processes if you move to a new unit or institution. Usually, if you are candid about your gaps and are open to learning, many will make themselves available to provide needed skills and understanding. A key person in this effort will be your financial manager and you need to have a strong and open business relationship with this team member.

Keep It Clear and Simple

Having someone who can make financial matters transparent, clear, and simple within your unit(s) is indispensable. Some important areas to communicate are revenue generation that is reported quarterly or biannually and summaries of expenditures; particularly revenues that are strategically invested within units. One way to summarize the information is to show primary sources of revenue generation by programs across areas and sub-units, and pair this recent data with two years of historical data to show trends. Similarly, a percentage of growth or loss can be shown across revenue areas. One way to communicate this information is through college-wide meetings that include a slide deck of the summarized information or through meetings with various entities that make up your unit. Consider making the slide decks of summarized information available to anyone in your unit and allow time after budget presentations to answer questions so that people accurately understand the financial situation. If you do not share information employees become very suspicious of how monies are used. Suspicion and confusion can be avoided if financial summaries are shared in a clear and simple manner.

Common Financial Practices Across Units

In larger units, it is helpful if all areas use the same shadow systems and processes for managing and reporting financial information. The budget manager within your unit needs to have oversight of this responsibility with your full backing and involvement. If common systems and processes do not exist, create them. Once constructed, the financial manager needs the authority to ensure budget personnel in other areas consistently follow the policies and procedures of the unit. The use of consistent practices may seem simple to enforce because universities have centralized systems and practices that everyone uses to manage financial matters. While there is always a centralized system with defined policies and procedures that all units follow, most units run shadow systems to give them more up-to-date data, insight, and flexibility. It is surprising that most centralized systems are inadequate to address the growing needs of a contemporary university. While upgrading or modifying a central system may seem like a logical response to this shortfall, system changes are very expensive and take years to implement. I have never experienced or talked to anyone in higher education who reported a system change that was on budget, on time, and met their needs—even after spending millions of dollars and investing thousands of staff hours to get the financial system to operate at a reasonable level. It is more realistic to expect that the projected costs and time for full implementation will double or triple, and many will still be dissatisfied with the final product.

Because many centralized systems are inadequate and modifying or using new systems is filled with pitfalls and cost overruns, most units create their own shadow systems and utilize the centralized system when updating institutional financial information, submitting funding requests, generating reports, or reconciling budgets across the university. This approach can be effective because the costs of shadow systems are relatively low and are commonly used across the university. A universally used software program such as Excel can work as a shadow system and can be easily modified and updated to meet the needs of the unit and associated sub-units. In order for this to be most effective, all of the sub-units within a unit need to use similar shadow systems and processes so the financial status of the entire unit can be monitored and quickly summarized for the unit leader.

If all of the sub-units use a different system and their own processes, it is almost impossible for the financial manager to have oversight across all the sub-units' budgets and income streams. Furthermore, the ability to confirm that a sub-unit's bookkeeping is accurate is difficult to reconcile, which often leaves the unit manager hoping that the sub-unit's information is accurate. Other problems can arise if dissimilar systems and processes are used when a sub-unit's financial manager leaves and someone else needs to make sense of the systems they were maintaining. If the entire unit uses the same system, then multiple users of the unit shadow system can generate training and one-on-one support for the manager's replacement.

Example of Needing Common Financial Practices

The concerns associated with operating multiple shadow systems within the same unit is something I experienced as a college dean. It has been my experience that leaders within sub-units typically want extensive autonomy and control over their operations. They want their own person who deals with budgets, communications, human resources, graphic design, etc. This is understandable and often a sign of a good leader because they want to effectively manage their operations and one way to do that is to have people reporting directly into sub-unit leadership. However, this flexible approach is problematic for two primary reasons. First, you do not have a quick and easy way to confirm the accuracy of a group's shadow system. As a leader in this structure, it is your responsibility to make sure the sub-unit's finances are accurate and you do not have an easy way to do this with different shadow systems.

In one instance, I had a unit that conducted a search and found a strong candidate. However, this candidate had a partner who also needed a position within the same unit. The question then became, can we afford to hire the candidate's partner? I worked closely with my budget manager and the sub-unit's leadership for days trying to understand the unit's shadow system, which was like learning algebra in a foreign language. We could not keep the candidate waiting indefinitely, so I made the decision to also hire the candidate's partner. Unfortunately, this resulted in errors and the college spent the next three years reallocating resources to cover the shortfall caused by this decision.

In an ideal world, a university-based centralized system would be user-friendly for all on campus and there would not be a need for shadow systems. Most institutions of higher education are not at this place. Therefore, having sub-units that use a common shadow system is likely the solution for many institutions, despite what software salespeople tell you. There will likely be strong resistance from sub-units to use a common shadow system and related processes. However, it is in the best interest of the unit to adopt this path. As a leader you need to be careful about requiring something of your entire unit that is met with strong resistance. As will be discussed later in this chapter, attempts to centralize efforts are often met with strong resistance. Nevertheless, common financial systems and processes should be required. In fact, it may be worth considering a structure whereby subunits can retain control of budget decisions within their area which is typically the primary concern, however, they are required to use a common system that is managed by them or managed through your office as the unit leader. This approach is a compromise and will generate the consistency needed across your unit. The tactic of having the unit office maintain the subunit's financial system will also help avoid the staffing dilemma of having too many financial managers within the same unit. Again, centralizing the bookkeeping and shadow systems will likely be met with strong resistance but this will promote consistency, accuracy, timely reporting, and potentially reduce payroll costs that can be diverted to other strategic priorities. The benefits of a common system and processes may be enough of a compelling reason for unit leaders to embrace a centralized or common structure across the unit.

Office of Research

The emphasis on research and creative activities varies dramatically across universities. However, if your university expects faculty to publish in refereed journals and generate a funded research agenda, an office of research can provide invaluable support. Most research institutions have a university-level entity that supports and helps manage externally-funded projects. Typically, this unit is led by a senior administrator such as a vice president and they support grant development and submissions, compliance—especially when federal or state monies are involved—reporting, budgetary support, and grant management. There is great variability in scope of work and the level of support provided through this university-level entity. Many universities that are dedicated to growing research and creative activities also dedicate staffing to support this work within large units such as colleges, centers, institutes, schools and/or departments, which is the focus of this approach.

While university-level units provide helpful support and oversight, most units require additional staffing to provide faculty with the full attention and support that is required to engage in funded research. Essentially, units generate an office of research to engage in the similar services that are provided at the university level but in a deeper, more comprehensive, and customized level of service. Specifically, employees within a unit-level office of research can help with writing and editing proposals, generating budgets and budget narratives, creating bio sketches, negotiating/developing contracts with legal counsel, providing detailed oversight of budgets, brokering hires with human resource representatives, and ensuring that researchers and the unit are in compliance with federal, state, and university policies. This unit-level support is needed because obtaining funded research is very competitive, complex, and labor intensive. To address this reality, unit and university-level professional staffing need to partner to maximize chances of successful programming. A partnership is needed because the university research division supports the entire university, which ranges widely across disciplines such as music and art, education, material sciences, human health, business, and political sciences. While the university oversight and expertise are needed, it is very challenging to have staff that can work across all of these areas with the flexibility and depth of knowledge needed to be successful. The unit-level office of research allows for the needed flexibility and depth of understanding and content knowledge necessary to support the faculty and staff who work within specific disciplines.

There are instances where unit-level support needed for funded grants and contracts can be acquired through an institutional unit. However, most units such as colleges, institutes, or centers require content expertise and a deep level of support that is not commonly provided centrally. In this situation, an office of research should be created and staffed with people who can support faculty and staff in a comprehensive manner. This support allows scientists and artists to focus on their scientific and creative work while the office staff supports important logistics, compliance issues, business, and reporting requirements. This arrangement encourages faculty and staff to engage in funded projects and increases the chances of the timely successful submissions and execution of the funded project.

Unit-level Human Resource Expertise

As with the research and creative activities, human resources (HR) functions can be enhanced by having a university HR department that is led by a senior manager and HR professional(s) within university units. Depending on the size of the unit, this could be a portion of a person's job responsibility or there could be multiple individuals assigned to this task. Similar to an office of research, this person or group of individuals works with the central-level university HR department to make sure complicated and important HR activities are effectively executed in a timely manner. For instance, the types of hires within a university are varied and require an understanding of how and under what type of classification someone should be hired. Universities also have many faculty classifications such as research, tenure/ tenure track, clinical, instructors, lecturers, and adjunct faculty. Knowing what classification to use and how to execute the hire is something the unit's assigned human resource person can support. Additionally, students are hired at universities as part-time workers as coaches, athletic trainers, researchers, and teaching assistants. Similarly, there are a variety of hires related to staff including professional staff, classified staff, temporary hires, temporary hires with benefits, and many others. The unit HR person can be the subject matter expert who can support leadership in navigating hires in concert with the central HR office.

In addition to selecting and navigating systems and processes associated with hires, a HR professional can support efforts that ensure employees and contractors are paid correctly and on time. They can organize annual review processes by ensuring they are conducted according to policy, completed in accordance with university deadlines, and confirm that the reviews are connected to merit and cost of living adjustments. Human Resource professionals can also verify that employees complete required training, manage faculty contract renewals, maintain promotion and tenure documentation, manage sabbaticals and execute separations from the university. This support becomes especially important as the number of employees within a unit increases and the programming grows and requires extensive student, part-time, and contract employee hires. Again, hiring professional staff to support these functions will help streamline HR processes and ensure that employees receive the services they need and that your unit is known for its competency in this area.

Partnering With Professionals Outside Your Unit

Much of this chapter has focused on the value of strategically placing professional workers within your unit to support increasingly complex and demanding work functions. However, there are many other work groups within a university that provide services that do not exist within your unit. It is vital to have partnerships and strong working relationships with these professional groups. Examples of professional groups *not* commonly found within work units include legal, compliance, information technology, health services, employee assistance programming, event and catering services, teaching and learning development, facility services, architectural planning, and student affairs. Moreover, as demonstrated earlier, there are professionals housed in units that need to partner with university-level professionals in areas such as human resources, payroll and budget, strategic planning, research/grants and contracts, curriculum development, community services, and distance learning. Across all of these and other areas your unit will be able to more effectively address the mission of the university by creating strong and meaningful business relationships with these partners.

Examples of how effective partnerships support a thriving university are ubiquitous. For instance, almost any grant or contract work will require significant guidance and interaction with legal, the research office (unit and university level), compliance, facility services if additional space is needed, human resources (HR) for hires (unit and university levels), and event and catering services for events that may be associated. Depending on the scope of work, many more partners may be included. A unit simply cannot effectively engage in the execution of their work if there is not a positive working relationship and synergy across these other university areas.

Often, employees focus on the efficacy of their supervisees and unit, which makes sense. However, not focusing on nurturing partnerships will compromise your ability to achieve work goals—a reality often missed by leaders. In fact, leaders often complain and criticize partners when work is not completed in an effective and timely manner. When challenges arise with partners, a leader should always try to first work with them and understand the issues through their eyes. Often this approach can help both parties develop a mutually agreeable understanding and determine levels of service and timeliness that work for both parties. This may require you extending a timeline because your partner has low staffing or heavy workloads. If you work with them to extend their timeline, they may be able to shorten it for your benefit in the future. If your approach is to complain and contact their supervisor when something does not go your way, their desire to support your needs in the future will likely be diminished. Being a valued partner who works to maintain strong working relationships goes a long way to support your success as a leader.

Being a Good Partner

As dean I needed accurate and timely institutional data about the college's students, and this information was available through the university Office for Instructional Research. At this time, there was the equivalent of 1.5 employees supporting this work for the entire university. They were skilled and hard working. However, the volume of university reporting functions and unit-level data analysis was essentially overwhelming the small operation and things were not getting done. I could have complained and put the blame on the office. However, as I considered the situation, I decided to advocate on their behalf for additional personnel support so they could effectively address the volume and complexity of the work they needed to address. I did this by getting other deans on board, talking with the provost, and sharing how these delays were impacting the work of all colleges—and in some cases—our ability to address outcomes the provost had given to the entire academic community to address.

Today, this unit has six full-time employees that are supervised by an associate vice president. My work was not the only factor that helped increase their staffing. However, my advocacy helped, and it facilitated a strong and more trusting partnership between our units. Had I just complained, the partnership would have been compromised, and their needed changes delayed. As a leader, always consider how you can be a trusted partner who looks at the entire enterprise and needs beyond your unit.

Do not confuse this example of being a good partner as a reason to accept poor service and support. That is not partnering, it is enabling poor behavior. In a true partnership, both entities expect value in what they provide and receive. Beware entities that say they want to partner but bring little in the way of value and are not committed to improvement. In one university, I observed a negotiated university cleaning contract with the university unionized cleaning staff that set a level of cleanliness to be "a reasonable level of dinginess." This was the agreed upon quality standard. In this instance, I did complain because I could not have our facilities looking dingy if we were to recruit and retain students and meet donors and community partners on our worksite. A partner who provides poor quality services is of little value and other approaches or arrangements need to be made if the recurring level of performance is sub-par.

Pooling Professional and Administrative Support Across Sub-Units

An approach that organizations look to implement to improve efficiency and control costs is centralizing efforts. The concept is straightforward and common-sensical. Many sub-units such as departments have staffing redundancies within their areas that exist at unit levels. In these instances, a single unit manager may be able to provide direction, leadership, and coordination of staffing within sub-units and eliminate the need for multiple managers. For example, financial responsibilities within the sub-units could include staff that input data, facilitate purchases, and input employee hours for payroll. Quality control, consistency across units, choice of shadow systems and supervision could all be the responsibility of one manager. If a unit were composed of five sub-units, the reclassification could save $15,000 across each position for a total savings of $75,000. The same logic has been used within large university systems where important functions such as human resources, legal, or information technology could be centralized by a Board of Education or Board of Regents. If the system had five universities, the need for five directors or vice presidents would be eliminated and hundreds of thousands of dollars could theoretically be saved. Given the logic of centralizing efforts, it is surprising this approach is not widely adopted. It is even more surprising that almost all entities intensely resist the idea of centralizing services.

Problems With Centralization

While there are many reasons why there is a distaste for centralization, control and work quality are two powerful reasons commonly given. In many instances, these reasons are valid and represent a good rationale *not* to centralize. For instance, entities such as human resources (HR) within a university system are asked to customize systems and processes to meet the unique needs of the university. If the human resource functions are centralized, the centralized entity needs to ensure customizations across five institutions. Invariably, the central unit will resist customizations across the five universities and the universities will receive fewer services than they had when they ran their own HR division. Not only do they receive less, but the centralized units are often slower and have more problems (at least for the first two to three years), than their university-centered HR group. Moreover, because the reporting lines in a centralized unit have HR reporting into a system-level board, accountability for poor or slow performance can be more difficult to correct and manage. If these problems transpire and commonly occur, the financial savings are negated, and employees are upset with their president and board because of the inferior services they are receiving through the centralized model.

These problems can be found when centralization is attempted within and across institutions.

Therefore, if you are going to centralize efforts, make sure there is an *obvious and compelling reason*. Be certain the effort will create quality and timely services and result in meaningful resource savings. Know that once the program or service is moved from an institution's management, many employees may be hypercritical of the new system and set a high bar for success. Consequently, be thoughtful in how and when you engage in centralization efforts. Some examples follow to describe when and when not to centralize, and how to address concerns.

Example 1: Compelling Reason

When I started my deanship at Boise State, we were a small college and had one person taking care of most of our information technology (IT) needs. At this time, our IT person made updates to our classroom and faculty/staff computers, and they would manually insert a disc into the PC to update the systems. With almost 250 computers this was a significant effort. Additionally, if someone had a problem with their computer or needed help connecting a printer to a computer, they called this employee. If there was a computer malfunction and a faculty member had a deadline for a manuscript, they called this person in the evening or on the weekend. Even when the IT person was on vacation, people would reach out for support. Our college and university were growing and so was the need for more IT services.

During this time, the university president hired a new IT director who pushed to centralize IT services. As part of the centralization, we would give the professional position to IT and in turn they would address our needs. Because many lines across the university were centralized through this change, the number of employees in IT grew dramatically and the various areas of IT expertise were now housed under one unit. As part of the centralization effort, resources were allocated to a helpline that had a triage system to address faculty, staff, and student issues 24/7. Given the level of service, the centralization effort could provide our unit at no additional costs, it was easy for me to visit with my leadership and move ahead with the IT centralization. The change provided us with more expertise, 24/7 coverage, faster response times, and created a much healthier work environment for our current IT employee. In this new configuration the college IT person would have uninterrupted time off in the evenings and weekends and more flexibility to take vacations. Additionally, the employee now had supervisors and coworkers with content expertise who were better able to supervise and develop the employee. This centralization change was positive for everyone involved. Therefore, if the centralized effort clearly creates more expertise, faster response time, better coverage, and better working conditions with minimal or no new costs, the obvious benefits make it easy to follow this path.

Example 2: Is the Juice Worth the Squeeze?

I once considered pooling all of the administrative positions across four sub-groups to create a pool of staff who
would take on the various administrative functions within
the unit. Instead of a limited number of people taking on all
of the administrative tasks generated within a sub-unit, tasks
and skills would be distributed across the pool and sub-units
would receive individuals who were focused in a given area
and could engage in these tasks in a more responsive high-
quality fashion. Furthermore, one classified position could
be eliminated for a recurring salary savings of approximately
$45,000.

While the leaders within the sub-units wanted administrative tasks addressed effectively and quickly, they most
valued the flexibility of a supervisee they could deploy as
needed. They also wanted systems and processes that func-
tioned well within their sub-unit and the idea of adapting to
a new unit-wide system and procedures concerned them.
Additionally, one of the things that all sub-units had at this
institution was at least one administrative assistant. For
some, they would lose their only administrative assistant.
These assistants typically kept the business functions of the
unit running, and without their support the leaders worried
that things would not get done, or they would need to take on
clerical functions. Finally, as one leader communicated, if all
the other sub-units at the university had this current struc-

ture and support, why were we disrupting something that worked across campus?

When I proposed pooling the positions a visceral response from the leadership team was clear and strong and had the energy of a mushroom cloud. The comments were direct and included, "My administrative assistant is an integral part of our program and if they go, I am gone." And, "We are different, and the pooled staff will not fit into a system we have worked hard to develop." Also, "Why would you change someone's job just before they retire, has this place lost all sensitivity toward the people who work here?" And finally, "This will not work, and it will compromise the functioning of our unit!" There were some advantages to this change, but the loud and clear responses convinced me that it would not be supported, I could harm working relationships, and there was not enough of a *compelling reason* in their minds to make a move to centralized administrative staffing. The juice simply was not worth the squeeze, so I abandoned the idea. Really evaluate and consider the resistance to centralization and if you move down this path be certain it is worth the effort.

Example 3: Centralize When Resources Are Insufficient

There are many services that a unit may need, but the volume of work may be insufficient to warrant hiring a person to take on this responsibility. One example mentioned earlier was having one financial manager and having sub-units hired for data entry, processing, etc. Other examples include graphic designers, marketing professionals, community relations experts, or fundraisers. Given that many universities are using incentive-based budgets, recruitment and retention of students has become more important if programs are to be sustained. Maintaining or increasing student numbers requires program-specific efforts that necessitate the expertise of marketers, advertisers, graphic designers, community outreach experts, and other forms of exposure and communication that are provided by a team of professionals. The problem is that most departments may only have one or two academic offerings that need this support, which would not warrant hiring a full-time professional. However, a college can have many program offerings that need support and if the effort were centralized the hire would make sense. Even though the schools and departments would rather have their own staff, a quick analysis of costs and workload makes the choice of centralizing a logical and prudent avenue to follow. In this instance, the sub-units essentially have two choices, centralize the effort and receive a portion of someone's time, or pass on the opportunity. This creates a strong position for centralization.

The key in this approach is to find skills and support that sub-units need but cannot justify or afford primarily because of costs and work volume. Sometimes this can be addressed through contracted services outside the university, but this can be expensive and the services somewhat disjointed. In order to make an addition feasible, resources may need to be taken from each sub-unit. This will require serious discussion and some tradeoffs across the unit. Considering cash flows, strategic priorities, and other considerations will likely play a role in this decision-making process.

If the hire is made centrally, it is important that the individual is housed and supervised by a unit leader or someone in their office. Having these professionals housed and supervised by a sub-unit causes problems around ownership, sub-unit dedication and the ability for the professional(s) to work across areas. This approach may be easier to execute than taking staff from sub-units and pooling them for centralized tasks. As mentioned earlier, taking staff away from a group is often met with hard resistance. Starting something new that is needed by all is an easier sell, even if it requires sub-units to allocate a relatively small level of resources for the centralized position.

While centralizing functions can save resources and streamline processes, be thoughtful and cautious when considering this move. If you do centralize functions, make sure the idea is sound and the reasons are compelling. You do not want to harm essential relations because the idea was just not worth the effort.

Building Good Systems and Processes

Management and leadership authorities emphasize the need for effective systems and processes (Deming, 2000;

Linker, 2004; Senge, 1990). In fact, many consider systems and processes essential in developing a high-functioning enterprise. Much of the literature on this subject comes from the manufacturing industry such as Toyota Automotive Company, where they put considerable effort into effective systems and processes to produce high-quality automobiles with minimal errors and omissions. Higher education has not embraced these approaches and commonly shows disdain for these practices because they seem too business-like and counter to the free thinking and innovative ethos of higher education.

Higher Education Is a Business

Contrary to many academics' views, higher education has many business processes that are essential to the day-to-day operations of running a university. When poor processes and systems exist, time, energy, and money are wasted trying to accommodate basic processes that are essential for success. For instance, if a contract that spans six months needs to be finalized in 30 days and the internal process takes 90 days, the workers have lost 33% of the time (60 days) they needed to execute the contract. This delay frustrates workers because they are ready to start but cannot because the contract is not finalized. This requires the workers to fit six months of work into a four-month period, which results in working nights and weekends. If this pattern is repeated over multiple contracts, workers are always lacking the necessary time to do a quality job because internal systems and processes are flawed. Poor processes such as this result in low job satisfaction and retention problems for leaders.

Poor systems and processes not only impact employees but can also have negative ramifications with funding sources because they are concerned by the institution's inability to execute a relatively simple contract. Consequently, they may decide to work with other vendors in the future. This is only one example of what can happen with poor systems and processes. Poor systems and processes tend to compound when they occur across many areas. Not only is it difficult to generate contracts, but delays occur in employee hires and obtaining needed equipment such as lab equipment or computers. These are common symptoms of poor systems and processes. Access is delayed to promised start-up funds, purchasing basic supplies becomes onerous and convoluted, and errors regularly occur on paychecks and travel reimbursements. When many basic business practices are slow and flawed, the enterprise can come to a standstill and people leave the organization or just accept the flawed environment and resign themselves to the fact that they work within a broken organization. In this situation a loss of institutional control occurs and the university is left behind and positioned for failure.

However, if a university is empowered to address these issues, a very different environment is created. In this situation, unnecessary processes are eliminated, customer and employees' needs are evaluated, and systems are put in place to address these needs. W. Edwards Deming and Toyota (Deming, 2000; Liker, 2004;) have developed helpful approaches for instilling consistency of purpose around quality and continuous improvement efforts. The interested reader should explore Jeffrey Liker's book that explores the 14 management principles associated with "The Toyota Way," which are heavily influenced by the work of Deming. Liker and Convis (2012) subsequently expanded their work with Toyota to include lean leadership. At the heart of their approach is the need for all employees to expose problems and solve them within the organization. This orientation is different from many organizations where it's more common to complain or ignore problems and move on to more pressing matters. One particularly effective technique is to get to the root of a problem by asking "Why?" five times.

In the delayed contracting example given earlier, asking "Why?" five times allows the problem to be exposed in depth and detail. Here's an example of what that process could look like in action:

Question: "Why did it take 90 days to execute a contract?"
Answer: "Because it sits in legal for months without any progress."

Question: "Why did it sit in legal for months?"
Answer: "They are understaffed and the state contracting laws make a simple contract challenging because of

mandated indemnification wording that is required in all state contracts."

Given that state requirements cannot easily be changed, two questions are then asked...

Question: "Why was this not communicated to funders earlier in the process?"
Answer: "Well, we weren't aware of the indemnification laws, but we can bring this into initial discussions earlier from now on."

Question: "Why are we understaffed in legal?"
Answer: "We're adequately staffed with attorneys, but the use of more paralegals is needed to support the volume of grants and contracts, which are growing rapidly at our university."

Question: "Would it make sense for us to house our own paralegal within our unit?"
Answer: "I hadn't thought of that, but we are growing so rapidly we could really use a paralegal or half a position to support the volume of grants and contracts we deal with. I could see that really streamlining the process."

As you can see from this exchange, asking "Why?" five times requires some commitment to the process, but if you and your team see it through, it can illuminate key information and solutions that are unlikely to be revealed through brief exchanges.

Example of Better Processes
in Higher Education

I once worked with a divisional dean of nursing who was a Lean Six Sigma Black Belt (individuals trained in waste reduction to enhance efficiency and quality) and did a wonderful job of getting everyone in her unit to focus on continuous improvement by asking employees to find how they could improve processes by making things better, faster, and cheaper. I was impressed by the way she included faculty and staff (classified and professional positions) in this process and publicly celebrated these accomplishments to recognize their insights and the importance of this work. Their work received several awards through the university, and they were seen as a model for creating positive change to enhance organizational effectiveness. Examples of their accomplishments were big and small and ranged from streamlining enrollment processes, improving student clinical placements, and improving simulation lab scheduling.

One effort that helped increase enrollments and required partnerships across the university involved a revision in student entrance into an online baccalaureate program. The School of Nursing was losing students to for-profit colleges because of the prolonged and convoluted application and review process used in the college and university. To address this problem, the faculty and staff created a "one stop shop" for online students who were associate degree Registered Nurses (RN) and wanted to enter programming to receive their baccalaureate degree. This required working across multiple business units at the university so that they would all attend the free online application day. The groups included student advisors, financial aid, and the registrar's office to be available and enroll students during the interactive Zoom session. This process saved time and money and provided a positive and caring student experience. However, because the university had not adopted Lean Six Sigma training across the university, it was only implemented within the school of nursing. Therefore, the school benefited (local optimization), but the innovation was not adopted across other programs at the university.

Caution Related To Process Improvement

As dean at Boise State University, I worked with the College of Business and Economics to contract with their faculty to train our college employees (faculty, staff, and leadership) in the principles of waste reduction to enhance efficiency and quality through Lean Six Sigma training. We were able to use these skills to improve processes and workflow on a number of unit-level business activities and within our unit-level curriculum approval processes. However, we quickly noticed that many of the waste and system issues related to both unit *and* university-level processes, which required the entire university to be dedicated to process improvement and Lean Six Sigma principles to optimize university outcomes. As dean, I could have our unit engage in this training and apply what was learned. However, having the university adopt the approach required much more work and considerable persuading. In Chapter 7 we discussed the challenges associated with creating university-wide work teams and a similar problem existed in creating university-wide approaches to reduce waste and improve quality.

At first glance, the idea seemed compelling and something that should be a priority and an easy sell... after all, who does not want to eliminate waste and improve quality? With this somewhat naive schema, I worked with another dean to pitch this idea to the university's senior management. After several months of intensive work, we were able to have all the senior staff at the university attend a meeting with a consultant who understood Lean Six Sigma. I was able to share the positive response that was received within my unit and that the training could be done in-house by the faculty in the College of Business and Economics. The facilitator had the group identify waste and process problems, which turned out to be an extensive list that covered many university systems and processes. This generated interest and energy, and the group left the meeting open to the idea of university-wide training.

However, one key leader did not attend the meeting and that was the college president. The president felt that there were other pressing matters that were higher priorities than improved internal processes and waste reduction. This was an error on my part to try to move something forward without such a key person committed to the effort. Additionally, before we could consider a university-wide initiative like Lean Six Sigma training, leadership needed to admit to long-standing problems with our systems and processes that had never been addressed. As you might guess, the idea was never adopted. As with work teams (Chapter 7), creating a university-wide effort requires strong support from leadership across the university, especially the most senior leadership. If you are going to implement process improvement across the institution, make sure you have senior-level support, and a willingness to embrace and solve problems. If this group does not see this as a priority, a university-wide change will not happen.

Without sufficient institutional commitment in system and process improvements, you will be limited to unit-level efforts. The unit changes will help, but many of the critical issues will remain unaddressed because only a small portion of the enterprise's employees will have the skills and mandate to work in a unified manner and solve institutional problems. Without university leadership on board, you will likely work with university-level processes in a manner that will better optimize processes within your unit. These efforts may or may not result in institutional-level changes. The local optimization may work and improve your unit's quality and reduce some waste, but the enterprise will not typically benefit from these efforts. While many universities provide this preparation as a robust part of a student's educational training, I am not aware of a university that has adopted this approach across the enterprise and trained employees to reduce waste and enhance the quality of the university's operations. If a leader were able to pull this off, it would be a model that could be replicated across higher education.

Many of the leadership essentials reviewed in this chapter are basic block and tackle business systems and processes that are critical for day-to-day operations within a university. While it may be tempting to work on more exciting efforts such as creating new degrees or applying for multi-million-dollar grants, these aspirations are hobbled if these basic operations, systems, and processes are not working adequately. In fact, having your university day-to-day operations in good order is best to address before moving ahead with growth initiatives across the university.

Chapter Summary

1. Leaders within higher education regularly use basic business systems, processes, and practices that are critical to being a successful, balanced leader in higher education. However, many do not have these skills and do not devote time to develop these competencies. This omission can seriously compromise the functioning of units and the entire institution.

2. Higher education has unique hiring traditions that are helpful in that they may generate inclusivity, input, and ownership through the hiring effort. However, the traditions are also problematic because of their public nature, time, costs, and frequent inability to produce the best hire. To avoid these problems, consider creating the equivalent of an in-house search firm, employ succession planning, consider personal characteristics in addition to technical skills, shorten the duration of searches, conduct in-depth and probing reference checks, and create a culture focused on hiring the best candidate.

3. When extending a job offer do not assume what is of most value to the candidate, i.e., salary. It is your responsibility to probe for this information during the interview to formulate an offer that best meets the candidate's needs and desires.

4. As a leader you need to engage with your supervisees frequently through regular meetings, informal interactions, as well as annual performance appraisals and multi-rater reviews such as a 360-review process. A supervisee should never be surprised by feedback during a formal review, so regular interaction and honest feedback is essential to avoid this pitfall. In addition to conducting engaging and reflective reviews with supervisees, make sure you prepare for your own annual reviews by giving your supervisor meaningful

and concise summaries of your activities and accomplishments that include your candid feedback of your performance and job satisfaction.

5. The use of professional staff within academic units and partnerships outside the unit are essential considerations for effectively operating the business of education and addressing the logistics of running a unit. Areas addressed in this chapter include:

Financial Management-If you are a leader who has financial responsibility such as budget development, budget oversight, approval of expenditures or revenue generation, you need to hire a professional to help manage this responsibility. This individual is one of the key professionals on your staff and their effective contributions are critical to your success as a leader. Therefore, hire the best and most competent person you can find to help you install common financial practices across your unit, and generate clear and simple reporting for groups and individuals to use.

Office of Research-If your university expects faculty to publish in refereed journals and generate a funded research agenda, an office of research can provide invaluable support. These professionals can take on a number of tasks including helping researchers with proposal development (bio sketches, budget development, etc.), post-award support (grant budget support and/or oversight, purchases, hires, etc.) and support to close out funded projects. This support allows faculty to better focus on the creative and scientific aspects of a project and ensures smooth and compliant operations during the funding periods.

Unit-Level Human Resource Support-The human resource activity within a large and busy unit requires hiring many full and part-time employees. These hires require that state and federal laws are followed and that the employees receive their correct and timely pay, which can be facilitated through this position. Additionally, they can coordinate mandatory HR training, annual review submissions, processing and tracking of sabbaticals, conduct promotion and tenure documentation, etc.

6. In order to be successful within a university you need to have strong partnerships with professionals across campus. There are many entities such as legal, compliance, information technology, health services, employee assistance programming, event and catering services, communications, teaching and learning for faculty development, facility services, architectural planning, and the list goes on. These entities are invaluable in executing your work, which can most effectively happen through strong partnerships that grow by your being a trusted and reciprocal partner.

7. There is a common notion that centralizing functions and services within a unit, university or system will standardize efforts, increase efficiency, and lower operating costs. However, efforts to centralize are strongly resisted and often result in poor service and little in the way of cost sav-

ings. If you are going to centralize services, be sure there is a clear and compelling reason for this structural change. Be certain it is cost-conscious and better organizes and deploys expertise, creates faster response times, enhances coverage, and improves working conditions.

8. Creating effective systems and processes with units and the university enterprise can create significant efficiencies and improvements surrounding the flow and execution of work. This is an area that has been largely ignored or addressed on an ad-hoc basis across higher education. Employing industry practices such as Lean Six Sigma can help improve systems and processes across units and universities. However, to get the most out of these efforts the entire university needs to commit to this effort, which can be challenging given that "better systems and processes" is not a very compelling or glamorous sell for many university administrators.

Chapter 9
Community Engagement

Introduction

Universities are uniquely positioned to impact communities at multiple levels through their employees and students. In this chapter, we explore how universities can better support communities and improve the functioning of society.

Community Engagement

Communities are formed when groups of people share common characteristics and goals that unify them and create affinity and belonging. Therefore, a community could be a city or neighborhoods within cities. Similarly, communities can form based on common ideologies or issues, such as health and safety within communities, or clean air or water within a geographic region. Communities can also converge around economic viability through supporting success in small business start-ups or increasing yields through agricultural training and support. In some instances, communities are forged by addressing global issues such as global warming or hunger, and people in these communities may work on an international stage to address large scale problems. Colleges and universities, especially comprehensive institutions, are in a unique position to engage and support communities in these efforts because of the unique faculty expertise and mission associated with most institutions of higher education.

Land Grant Extension Services

A robust example of community engagement through universities can be found in extension service programming that is found within land grant universities. Extension services engage in statewide communities to act as a bridge between knowledge found in universities that can support communities. Much of the education is done through non-credit educational programming dedicated to improving individuals and the communities they live in. Some of the more high-profile programming has been in agriculture, but many other topics are addressed including health, nutrition, natural resources, business development, and youth development and programming, under the umbrella of family consumer sciences.

Resources for extension services were initially allocated to state land grant universities through the Morrill Act of 1860. Over time, programming expanded beyond agriculture and additional resources were committed to support other programming. Land grants therefore have significant resources to address local and state needs and improve communities. When resident faculty and students combine forces with extension workers, the ability to facilitate needed programming can grow exponentially in scope and sophistication. With the ongoing concerns commonly voiced about the usefulness of universities, extension services through land grant universities represent an intact, powerful way to improve states by addressing a host of community needs.

One way to magnify the impact of extension services is to embed extension faculty within academic units. This structural decision is not without challenges. For instance, these arrangements often require some type of split appointment where a faculty member is jointly housed in a department and extension services. This arrangement can prove stressful for employees if the supervision across two areas is not effectively managed. Additionally, the type of instruction or training conducted is different for community programs than the formal educational training associated with the curricula of associate, baccalaureate, or advanced degrees. Also, because the scope of work is different from traditional faculty positions, modifications are needed for promotion and tenure criteria to accommodate extension faculty. Nevertheless, the ability for faculty and other professionals such as extension agents to partner in funded projects, program development, program implementation, and research is far-reaching. The partnerships are not only between extension services and academic faculty and staff, but with university students.

An example of this synergy was a federally-funded effort to provide families receiving welfare assistance training and support to enhance family resources and ultimately move them off the support of the federal and state governments. The funding was uniquely available through extension services and required an analysis of the client needs, programming to address the identified needs, and support mechanisms to ensure success. The specific areas included nutrition and health, individual and family development, resource management, community development, and housing access and maintenance (Duncan et al., 2001). For instance, many of the clients needed job training that would translate to local employment. In order to engage in the training, families needed child support services and transportation that was provided through the programming. Furthermore, many families wanted help raising children and affordable, high-quality nutrition for their families. Skills and tactics were developed and offered through the effort to empower individuals to improve their futures.

One of the program requirements was to measure outcomes to evaluate if the program was effective in facilitating desired changes. In this example, the extension faculty was the lead on the funded project and they partnered with extension and department faculty to develop and deliver programming through extension agents. University faculty were integrated to develop and execute the evaluation of the muti-year intervention. This portion of the project supported graduate students who helped with interviews and other data collection efforts. The award-winning program was recognized for its practicality, innovation, and effectiveness. Therefore, the talents of many across the university were recruited to deliver community-based services across many state counties. This effort improved the quality of life for many and helped reduce their reliance on welfare assistance.

Community Programming and Interventions

At the heart of any community engagement is the ability to connect and partner with groups in the community. Partnerships (primarily internal partnerships) were discussed in chapters 7 and 8 and were critical to successful work through university business systems and processes. In this instance, the ability to partner within communities is the fundamental skill that must be supported across the university if meaningful progress is to be made. The partnerships take time to forge but can be significant if faculty and staff are given the responsibility and time to engage with the community. Additionally, structures such as centers, institutes, and community -facing committees can help grow community engagement through faculty and staff partnerships with community members.

How To Create Community Partnerships

Creating partnership to address the needs of communities is something that takes time, sincerity, humility, and a caring attitude. Throughout my tenure in higher education, I invested *significant* time and energy to create *meaningful* partnerships. This often required me taking a day or two out of my schedule to attend meetings, be on their boards, make them members of my boards, meet regularly for coffee or lunch, and attend events and other activities that allowed us to regularly connect. Community partnerships require work and as a leader you need to invest the real time and energy required to make a partnership a reality.

A common mistake made by leadership, faculty, and staff within a university is to set up a meeting with a community-focused group and during the initial meetings, outline their problems and offer to solve them through a grant. This is akin to going on a first date and outlining plans for the wedding, home construction, and retirement strategies. As a new person who is trying to gain access into a community, much time needs to be spent getting to know people. As a person new to their particular circumstances, dedicated time must be delivered to understanding their interests, aspirations, fears, and collective story. The time up front allows people to really know the members of the community and the members get to know the university players (Lachapelle et al., 2011). This is a process that communicates respect and care for the community. To accomplish this connection, people may need to invest months or years of work connecting with the group. If others before them did not follow through with promises, the duration for gaining support can be considerably longer.

As time is spent getting to know the community, sincerity and humility can go a long way in forging connections. Remember, the community members do not care how much you know until they see how much you care. This can be challenging for some individuals, especially if they have studied, practiced, and have expertise within an area that is of concern to the community. Being able to sincerely hear perspectives, stories, and personal issues creates connection. Explaining what the community is going through or sharing special insights into their reality before connections are made typically drives a wedge between the university and the community. Once the wedge is in place the ability to connect and start effective work may never happen. While these skills can be taught, many people simply do not have the ability to connect and partner. As a leader, you can save time and resources by finding people who possess characteristics that naturally allow them to engage through these essential traits. Table 1 offers actions that can support or hinder community engagement.

What follows are some examples of partnerships formed with faculty, staff, and community members. Again, as long as faculty and leaders see this as part of the service and/or research responsibility and understand the significant time commitment needed for community-based engagement, important work can be done in communities while generating additional respect for universities.

Table 1. Actions and activities that can support or hinder community engagement.

Supportive Activities and Actions	Hindering Activities and Actions
Listening fully to the needs of the community.	Moving too quickly to solve problems before needs are understood.
Respecting the wisdom and insights of community members to solve their problems.	As an authority, pushing your insights and solutions onto the community.
Becoming a board member who supports businesses and community efforts.	Avoiding engaging in the community beyond your formal role as a university employee.
Helping a community find ways to continue needed work after grant funding runs out.	Leaving a community once grant funding runs out.
Meeting regularly with community leaders to stay abreast of the community happenings.	Only meeting with community leaders when you need something for your efforts.
Including community members in presentations/publications that describe the community work.	Only including university employees and co-researchers in presentations and publications that describe the community work.
Acting as a conduit for other community groups to connect with university employees/students.	Limiting your community engagement to your individual project
Allowing the community to take control and ownership of a community project or intervention.	Keeping control of a community project or intervention to maintain funding and acclaim.

Centers and Institutes

Not all centers and institutes focus on community partnerships, but many have this as part of their mission or as a process embedded in their operations. I once worked with a fellow dean to form an institute designed to address wicked problems. Wicked problems are complex, almost unsolvable problems, that plague society such as sustainability, health, or literacy. We worked closely with members of the university and city communities to identify issues that would qualify as a wicked problem within the community. Over a five-year period, the institute addressed three issues which included mental health, basic needs for students during the COVID pandemic, and diversity, equity, and inclusion issues within the community.

The institute's approach was to act as a neutral convener and authentic partner to help create capacity and address issues critical to community wellbeing. To this end the community members identified these needs through a variety of approaches that are beyond the scope of this chapter. However, the issues were significant and had strong community and university backing.

The first initiative was to find a way to care for people in mental health crises. At the time there were inadequate facilities for people to receive care during a mental health crisis and many were incarcerated because there was nowhere to place them. There was a groundswell of support to address the issue and the presidents of two large health systems and the director of health and welfare for the state agreed to meet and discuss solutions. The three entities decided to build a hospital that could provide psychiatric care for people in crisis within the city and surrounding areas. While the idea never came to fruition because of litigation between the two health systems, the initiative is a good example of how members of an institute can broker important work in the community.

The second effort was targeted at addressing basic needs of students during the COVID pandemic. During this period of isolation many students struggled to find affordable housing, food, access to health care, and other basic needs. Consequently, this was an issue for the city and the university. Through this effort, students were surveyed to obtain a baseline of their needs. Apartment and hotel vouchers for students and their families provided 228 safe nights (safe lodging during homeless periods) and the institute distributed COVID emergency federal funds to 12,300 students. Additionally, the student food pantry was expanded to better meet the nutritional needs of students. Even though students were members of the university community, they also were part of the city community, so this joint effort helped address needs across two interrelated communities.

The third effort addressed diversity, equity, and inclusion (DEI) in the workplace. While the topic has received disdain from the Trump administration, it was initiated because of a clear and urgent need from employers across the region. This effort was very successful and had over 300 organizations participating in DEI training and development over a five-year period. The organizations represented a variety of business sectors such as banking, food production and distribution, lumber production, chip manufacturing, education, and healthcare. The programming was initiated because employers realized that they were working within global markets and providing goods and services for diverse groups of individuals and communities. Therefore, they needed a workforce, policies, and work environments that embraced DEI principles. The effort was coordinated and directed through the institute. Funding came from many organizations to support training, and a DEI Conference Summit reached more than 3,000 people over a five-year period. Moreover, employees of the institute provided and facilitated training and forums for business professionals, networking across businesses, and public entities across the state.

Collectively these examples give insight into what a university center or institute can do to provide needed facilitation, support, and expertise to address critical issues within a community. As a leader, you need to hire and supervise individuals who create a vision for the institute that aligns with helping communities. The employees within the center or institute must be able to listen and act as neutral conveners and authentic partners in addressing critical community problems and needs.

Using Boards and Students
to Address Community Needs

As dean, I created a board made up of senior leaders and former leaders of health entities across Idaho. The board included a number of current and past CEOs, vice presidents, and directors from private and public settings, which took years to create. In recruiting these leaders, I made it clear that I was not recruiting them to obtain financial contributions. I was recruiting them for their knowledge and insights about healthcare across the state and nation. The board created a unique place for these leaders to meet and discuss health issues through a non-competitive lens. As leaders in healthcare for the state they were often competitors but were dealing with the same issues. The neutral ground and focus on common problems created an environment that existed nowhere else and helped them in their partnerships by providing valuable insights, information, and knowledge. They helped me with my efforts at the university and I in turn supported them through consultation and being a member of their boards and committees. Again, to generate these valuable partnerships I put forth significant time to meet with each member between meetings and in some cases I met with them on a monthly basis. This partnership created deep working relationships that lasted over a decade, and the board experienced almost no turnover.

One way I was able to use their expertise was in developing new educational programs and updating current curricula. Through their input, we were able to take their advice and match it with faculty insights and skills to create and update educational programming. Additionally, leaders from the various health disciplines became board members for academic units such as respiratory care, imaging sciences, and nursing. Many of the college leadership also participated on boards and committees of the professional areas they led. Through this structure, degree completion programs (programming that allows associate degree students to receive bachelor's degrees) were created, which helped medical providers enhance their status and level of accreditation while better preparing students to work within these organizations. In other cases, we grew enrollment or created educational opportunities to meet staffing shortages across the state in nursing, genetic counseling, public health, and social work. Through the advocacy of the board and the hard work of the faculty, the students were able to engage in relevant curricula, internship experiences, and our graduates became highly sought after employees who provided critical services. The partnership was good for the state because graduates filled needs, and it was good for students who received excellent jobs. This effort helped make our college a go-to place for addressing health needs across the state.

Graduate Students Working in Communities

In most universities, the number of graduate assistantships (work opportunities designed to support students financially during their educational pursuits) has declined for decades. The reasons vary and are related to not having a way to increase needed adjustments associated with cost of living, budget cuts, and reallocation of internal funds. One way to offset these shortfalls is to create community partnerships where graduate students can provide part-time employment for public and private organizations. The arrangements give students needed income, research topics/access to research data, and the organizations receive services and a pipeline to hire students after they graduate.

The partnerships are typically formed by faculty and leadership within the various academic unit(s) networking with community partners. For example, one-off support for graduate students was created through the department of kinesiology where they addressed fitness programming for soldiers on an air force base. Through this arrangement, a graduate stipend funded a graduate student so they could conduct testing and create exercise programs for the soldiers. Similarly, another kinesiology department partnered with a Nordic ski club and a graduate student coached youth as part of their graduate assistantship. Through another school, ten scholarships were created through the State Department of Health and Welfare in the area of child protective services. This is an area that has high turnover and has difficulty recruiting qualified applicants. This program supported many students, provided an essential workforce for the state, created a pipeline for hiring future full-time employees, and gave students financial support and valuable work experience.

The possibilities for creating connections with diverse employers to support graduate students is tremendous. Not only does it help students and the community, it also can create circumstances for conducting valuable applied research. The partnerships help students fulfill their research requirements for graduation, contribute to a body of research, and assist employers in obtaining needed information to run an effective organization.

Community-Based Research

Many universities, especially those with strong research agendas, can engage in community-based research to help communities in an assortment of ways. Funding from these efforts can come from foundations, corporations, local, state, and federal entities. Often the funding is designed to enhance communities and their residents through work directed toward health, human services, agriculture, workforce development, public policy, and economic development. Through this mechanism, partnerships are formed with the collective goal of finding answers to questions relevant to the community while also gaining knowledge on how the work can assist similar communities across the state or nation.

Some disciplines naturally engage in community partnerships and are interested in community needs as part of their research agenda. For instance, in public and community health, researchers commonly work with communities to identify health-related problems and work to co-develop interventions that address those issues within the community. Researchers work to address community issues dealing with chronic diseases, substance abuse, cancer prevention, nutrition, suicide interventions, fetal alcohol syndrome, effective parenting, and other important topics. Similarly, research within business can lead to increased productivity and lower costs which expands the viability of business and economic growth within a community. When each contribution is considered across the university, hundreds of research efforts can take place through faculty and students that support the well-being and vitality of communities. For communities, this work is generally welcomed because it addresses a need and is externally funded. A common reason for not embracing many community needs is insufficient funding. Consequently, research-funded interventions are often a solution to unfunded problems in communities.

Part of being a responsible partner is to work with communities after the grant funding expires. If a university abandons work once the money dries up, friction can result between the community and university. In this case, the project tarnishes the perception of the university and potentially worsens the relationship between state citizens and the university. To avoid this pitfall, a sustainability plan should be developed and initiated throughout the funding period. This work is the responsibility of both groups (university and community) and is often difficult and complex and requires using the entire funding period to identify solutions. If this reality becomes obvious six months before funding runs out, it is typically too late to find a solution. Promoting sustainability around funded community programming is something you should support and promote as a leader.

As a leader you can incentivize faculty and students to engage in community-based research. This can be done through college-funded mini grants, faculty start-up packages, and brokering partnerships across your state. In some units, a community development person can be hired to create and promote these efforts and increase faculty/community engagement. Once a meaningful portion of faculty and students are engaging in community work as part of their service/research requirements, the work should be communicated within and outside the institution. As discussed earlier in this book, the importance of communicating what your unit or university accomplishes is necessary to relay the value of higher education to employees and citizens. This is a responsibility that you must execute as a leader within the university.

Chapter Summary

1. Universities, especially comprehensive universities, can make significant and meaningful contributions by engaging in work that evaluates, strengthens, and supports communities across diverse topics including agriculture, business, health, policy, and human development. Land grant universities are especially poised to make these contributions through extension services, university faculty, and students.

2. Creating partnerships to address the needs of communities is something that takes time, sincerity, humility, and a caring attitude. As a leader, you can save time and resources by finding people who possess a persona that naturally allows them to engage using these essential characteristics. Structures such as centers and institutes are university enti-

ties that are often dedicated to addressing community needs. Encouraging faculty to incorporate service and research responsibilities into efforts that include the community and engage students through funded projects, paid and unpaid assistantships, are all ways to grow and nurture community engagement.

Chapter 10
Fundraising

Introduction

Each year there is an increased need for universities to advance through fundraising. This is fueled by constrained support from state and national governments and escalating costs associated with teaching, research, service, athletics, and student support. "Advancement" is often the name of the centralized unit that executes gifts and giving within an institution. Gifts and giving across a university support communities, students, generate an educated citizenry, facilitate discovery, sponsor problem solving, and generate arts and entertainment. Advancement work is primarily focused within academic units, centers/institutes, and athletics. However, student support programming in areas such as health and psychological services, or recreation and club sports are also often in need of fundraising efforts.

Given the diverse areas that need support through gifts and giving, advancement work is an important lever for universities to support their large and complex operations. Gifts can come from many sources including individuals (bequests, general donors, targeted donors, etc.), institutions (grants, foundations, corporations, etc.), and unrestricted funds (used at the discretion of an individual or group). The staffing used to facilitate fundraising activities for a university can vary from a handful of professionals to well over 100 employees. The area of fundraising is dynamic, and depending on the university structure can include alumni relations, a university foundation, prospect research/analytics and fundraising professionals (i.e., development directors), all dedicated to generating resources for the university.

Today, a number of challenging trends influence fundraising across universities. These include downward trending rates of giving, increased competition for obtaining gifts, and granting gifts through Donor Advised Funds (DAF's), which complicates identification of fund sources. At the time of this writing, increases in federal tax rates for gifts have been proposed, which would be problematic, especially for the wealthiest institutions. While these considerations are important in executing effective advancement efforts within a university, this chapter will focus on the traits and approaches of effective fundraisers, e.g., presidents, deans, and athletic directors, and the advancement team that *directly* supports these efforts.

Characteristics of Effective Fundraisers

Individuals with significant responsibilities to raise money and gifts are typically in leadership positions and hold titles such as university president, dean, or athletic director. Other employees may also engage in fundraising and include associate deans, department heads, center/institute directors, vice president of student affairs, or the director of health services. These leaders are almost always paired with a professional or a team of professionals from university advancement who have the full-time responsibility to raise funds. The advancement professionals often have titles such as development director (DD), vice president, or director of advancement. The quality of the fundraisers and advancement professionals is one of the most significant determinants in producing successful giving at a university. I will start by describing the traits, attributes, and approaches of effective fundraisers.

Clearly and Succinctly Communicate Priorities

When considering individuals who have significant fundraising responsibilities such as a president, dean, or athletic director who act as fundraising leaders, they should be able to clearly articulate the priorities of the university or their unit. The ability to explain priorities at a macro-level to potential donors, foundations, corporate entities, university partners, and members of the development team is a critical capability. While additional information may be needed to explain each priority in more detail, maintaining an approach that is clear to diverse audiences and conveys ideas and needs without getting into the weeds is an invaluable skill.

Presenting Priorities

Some fundraising authorities say to never have a presentation that exceeds 11 minutes and to make it shorter if possible (Panas, 2012). It is worth adding that you want to have different versions of your presentations that vary from 15 to 60 seconds to 5 minutes. The 15-to 60-second version is sometimes referred to as an elevator speech, which basically allows for a pitch or overview in the time it takes to ride an elevator. Generally, a potential donor will have interests in areas such as football or cancer research at the university. In short, they want to improve the current state of affairs in their area of interest through gifts to the university. They normally do not want a course in genetics or a dissertation on the internal mechanism needed to move a big idea forward. Donors typically want to help and make a difference, so having a pitch or presentation that meets their needs is essential.

Generate Enthusiasm

In addition to effectively communicating concise and clear priorities, fundraisers need to convey genuine enthusiasm, conviction, and excitement to the donor about funding priorities. As you plan and refine your university and unit advancement portfolio, be sure that something is created that will help you exude these characteristics when you present or discuss your priorities. Remember that despite your genuine enthusiasm for solving your operational problems or shortfalls, most donors do not want to support these needs. One classic example is trying to raise money for staffing or office equipment. These may be an essential need, but they are almost impossible to generate support from donors. Donors desire bold ideas paired with your enthusiasm and commitment.

Once you have some bold priorities, it is helpful to think of the handful of things that you are most proud or excited about in your life. As you consider these items, observe the energy generated when you discuss or think about these meaningful aspects of your life. For instance, it might be your child who successfully graduated from school or excelled in sports, the trip of a lifetime, or a promotion at work that acknowledged your talents. Whatever generates this energy and feelings, you need to tap this source and translate it into your discussions with donors. Often the way you frame your priorities (connecting the priorities to outcomes that are meaningful to you) will grant access to this energy. Like a donor, you need to understand how your philanthropic work is changing lives and making the world a better place (assuming this is your motivation). Once you find this source of energy you will naturally be excited, passionate, and you will not need to remember to smile and act engaged because the work does this for you. Philanthropy is exciting and meaningful work that should generate positive energy. If you are trying to raise support for something you have limited interest or belief in, you will have a difficult time putting forth these important traits. Once you find your energy, fundraising is not work but rather something that is fun and you look forward to doing. Your genuine enthusiasm and conviction for your funding priorities will help create an atmosphere that enables donors to also get excited about giving to your unit and institution.

I once worked with a dean of business and we hatched an idea that business programs needed to be more embedded in health curriculums and health programs need to be more embedded in business curriculums. Succinctly stated, we saw a need for more health in business and more business in health. Over a number of months, we developed this educational programing idea and got excited about the valuable contribution it could provide for healthcare. As we shared this with community members, they also saw the value and were excited about this needed change in the way students were educated across disciplines. This idea took hold with support from individual and corporate donors such as health systems, which created synergy across colleges. As I worked with the other dean it was easy for us to show energy and enthusiasm, which led to fruitful engagement with many donors.

Open Attitude With Thoughtful Boundaries

The fundraising leader, with significant support from the development director (DD), also needs to find ways to match the donor's interest with the university or unit priorities.

While a healthy dialogue communicating everyone's interest is a productive exercise, an open attitude complemented by thoughtful boundaries should be formed. For instance, I once worked with a donor who owned a medical supply company and was interested in giving us supplies and equipment to train students. Some of the items he could provide were not priorities, but we jumped at the chance to refresh our outdated equipment. *What I did not do* is try to convert his offer into a cash gift to support student scholarships, which was a priority. If I were interested in exploring other options with this donor it would be after we accepted the gift he offered, showed him how we were using the supplies and equipment, and demonstrated the difference his generous offer made for students' education. This approach gave us time to get to know each other through a couple of visits and show that we were good stewards of his investment.

Accepting an equipment gift for educational training makes sense because it supports the mission of the university in that it supports quality educational programming. However, there are times where someone has offered a cash gift to initiate a program where we had no faculty expertise or infrastructure to support. In this situation, I had to say that we could not accept the gift because we simply did not have the collective resources to put the programming together, despite their very kind offer. To make this type of decision you need to have boundaries, and once a boundary is crossed, as the leader you need to carefully let the donor know that you cannot accept their gift. Being open to gifts that are not current priorities while setting boundaries on gifts that cannot be accepted is a critical function of an effective fundraising leader. While it may initially be difficult to turn down a gift, if explained well, it is also an opportunity to demonstrate integrity and fiscal responsibility.

How To Create an Open Attitude

Fundraisers can foster an open attitude by listening to donors and understanding their motivations and interests. This can be easier with a foundation because most of this information is typically communicated on their website and a quick conversation with the director or program officer can clarify any questions and provide additional information so your requests align with their giving. However, when working with an individual or family this insight is not as evident and time spent asking questions, probing, and not talking is needed to get this valuable information. This seems simple but many leaders lack this ability because they need to be the focus and then finish the interaction and be on to the next agenda item.

I once worked with a donor who told a story about his wife who had died. His wife was a nurse, and he promised her that he would start a scholarship in her name to support nursing students. He went on to detail how he worked and invested to generate a sizable gift in her honor. He did not want to invest in other health programs, labs, research, or anything else. He took great pride in this gift and was laser-focused on student scholarships for nurses. We took his story to heart and over a decade continued to work with him and received the largest gift the college had ever received from an individual donor. The critical thing we did was to simply listen and follow his request.

Give The Donor Center Stage

As part of your effort to listen and understand potential donors, have the humility to give them center stage. This can be difficult for many leaders because they are often asked to be front and center and over time taking this role is almost reflexive... leaders do this without even realizing that they are doing it. In some cases, having the leader be the center of the stage makes sense because the donor really wants to know and understand the leader. However, many (individuals, groups and entities) who are giving a large gift want the center stage. They want to tell their story and explain how and why they are making a gift. When a donor wants or needs to do this the leader needs to step back, give them the stage, and thank them for their story and gift. If this is something you have difficulty seeing, work with your DD to remind you when you should shift roles and step back so the donor can share their story.

I once worked with the leader of a family foundation where we had received a number of yearly gifts and one very large gift to our college. One year, we took a different approach and asked for a larger gift that went in a new direction. We created a story board and generated a thoughtful presentation that took about 10 minutes. After the presentation, he said that we had created a nice book and that he liked the pictures and university theme. However, what he wanted to know was the impact of last year's donation. We shared this and he was pleased with the progress. He went on to say that he was not interested in what was proposed through the story book and wanted to continue with projects they had funded the previous year. I left the meeting with the unit DD and we both agreed we would never try a new direction through a story book with this donor again. At the end of the meeting, we asked what he was interested in for the next year. He communicated the amount and areas for donation and we thanked him for his support and followed his desires. He clearly wanted the center stage and to have control over where his contributions would go.

Conversation and Stories

As a key fundraiser, being able to converse and get to know a potential donor is also a valuable skill. I once traveled with the college DD to meet with a potential donor in Oregon. The donor was a physician who had retired not far from the coast. The DD had us first meet down on the fishing docks because in retirement the donor commercial fished and prior to going into higher education I was also a commercial fisherman in Alaska. The common experience made for an instant connection and generated a lively conversation. We spent several hours talking and walking the docks before we moved to dinner and conversation about his interests and our college's needs and priorities.

Even though you are meeting with a donor to generate support for your unit or university, they have many interests that provide ways of introducing themselves to you. Similarly, donors are interested in you as a professional, but many want to also know other aspects of your life, especially where there is common ground. Connecting through conversation is important because as a leader you and the DD are often the face of the institution for the donor and they want to know the people and institution they will be supporting. Trust and understanding are key in this relationship. Therefore, as you get to know a donor, be sure and share professional/university information but also open up the conversation to other aspects of your life. Occasionally you will run into a donor who is all business and wants to engage in a transaction. You need to be able to read this and, in this instance, move directly to the business of philanthropy. However, for many a broader conversation about your life can be invaluable in developing understanding and trust.

How To Find Stories

Stories are also useful communication tools that can convey points, demonstrate needs, or show how effectively an investment will be stewarded. Stories tend to be a universal mode to illuminate and engage in an impactful manner. Data and statistics can be useful with some donors but stories and making a connection typically trumps data. As a fundraising leader, work closely with your DD, leadership team, and communication staff to hear the stories that make up the life of your unit or institution. As a leader, especially if the unit has many students and employees, you are often out of the loop when it comes to hearing student or faculty engagement and successes.

One way to get this information is to have your leadership staff share success stories related to your strategic planning at the start of each meeting. If you meet bi-weekly and two to three stories are shared at each meeting, you could hear 50 to 60 stories a year through a meeting that you already attend. Additionally, listening to or reading the stories generated by your communication team can also be a major resource for this material. Look for stories that will resonate with a specific donor, have impact, and move and inspire people within and outside the university. Depending on the depth of the communication you are reviewing, your entire story can be conveyed to you through a 20-minute read. Assuming you have a quality communication team, the information will be accurate, full of interesting information, and quickly available if you need your memory refreshed. A story is much more effective than just making a case or request. A story allows the donor to *feel* the potential impact of a gift rather than just cognitively comprehending their investment. Ideally you want to convey both (feeling and understanding), but feeling is usually the most powerful way to engage a donor.

Meet With The Right People

Occasionally a donor wants to get into the weeds or visit with students or faculty who are conducting research and working directly with students. In this instance, it is important that the fundraising leader provide them with this information or connect them with someone who can communicate the details clearly. This is an opportunity to have the DD work with your communications group to generate impactful communications. A brochure, letter, or video can be helpful in some instances. Similarly, if there are specific questions, your DD can follow-up with the needed information. However, due to the complexity of some topics or the donor's wish to visit with people engaged in an activity, selecting the correct person or group to visit with the donor cannot be overstated. The truth is that some leaders, students, faculty, or coaches are not good at delivering this information and can be a hindrance in obtaining support. Just because someone is a brilliant researcher or a successful coach does not necessarily mean they should be the person who meets with a donor. Therefore, use your judgement, advice from your DD and leadership team, and arrange meetings that have the maximum chance for success. Donors need to meet with someone or a group of people who are clear communicators, succinct, enthusiastic, and engaging.

No funder wants to be overwhelmed with information or have things communicated in a disrespectful manner. As a leader you need to make sure the right people meet with donors.

If You Are Going To Ask You Better Be Giving

If you are a middle-to high-level administrator and part or all of your job is raising funds for your institution, you need to contribute to the university. Sooner than later, you will be meeting with a potential donor and they will ask you how you directed your giving to the institution. If your answer is "I don't give," or "I cannot afford to give," your conversation is likely to be very awkward and will typically lose the interest and possibly the respect of the donor. Think of it this way, you are excited and passionate about your unit or university and want a donor to give money to a priority effort. However, the excitement and enthusiasm are not enough to inspire you to give. The question they will logically ask is, "Well then why should I give?"

As a leader you can give a modest amount regularly and give to something that has meaning for you. If you give $50 to $100 a month, the level can accumulate over time, especially if you are with the institution for a number of years. I have had people ask if I give... I have never been asked how much I give. Therefore, give what you can give at a level that has meaning for you. Additionally, consider a level of giving that makes you part of a group that is distinctive within the university. For employees, often the levels set up by the institution do not require a significant yearly contribution to qualify for this distinction. This suggestion is given knowing that for most people money is tight and there is not typically income that is not already allocated. Giving requires some level of prioritization and sacrifice. It is the same for donors, even if they are wealthy. Therefore, you are simply modeling what you are asking them to do.

If you are going to encourage other leaders in your unit or university to give, be careful of how you go about encouraging this behavior. You can certainly mention that the university is in a campaign and you want to share this initiative with the leadership team and all employees in your unit. It is also appropriate to share that you have selected a fund to donate to and who to contact if they would also like to give to the campaign. However, asking someone who is your subordinate to give could cause issues because giving is not a term of employment and it certainly is not something they are required to do. Therefore, model the behavior and tell your team how this helps you with your donor work and the satisfaction that you personally receive from giving. However, asking them to give is a line you shouldn't cross.

Be a Good Steward

One of the biggest mistakes a fundraiser can make is to have little or no communication with a donor after a gift has been made. Ensuring you maintain these vital connections is something that your university advancement program's customer relationship management (CRM) system and your unit DD can help you execute. The system can send your DD updates to show when, how, and where contact was made with a donor, who was involved with the visit, and a summary of the interaction. With this information the DD can ensure that your time is carefully used and that the unit's donors regularly receive updates (newsletters, magazines, emails, etc.), invitations to celebrations/events (sporting events, student presentations, research exhibits, etc.), and include you in the mix as needed. If your advancement team does not have a CRM you will need to build something in-house so you can track and remember your engagement and relevant information related to these efforts. If you and your DD try to track your work through memory, you will not succeed.

A quality DD will also take time to visit with donors on your behalf and play a key role in keeping them in the loop so they hear about the unit's progress and how their support is impacting the important work of the university. Finding people who are willing and able to contribute to the university often takes significant time to find and cultivate to the point where they are giving university gifts. Through effective stewardship, you increase the opportunity for the donor to engage other potential donors and continue their giving to the university.

I once worked with a foundation that had supported our unit for more than three decades. Throughout the relationship the DD and dean always took time to thank the foundation in multiple ways. First, we mentioned their generosity through our internal and external communications and shared these communications with them. We had a yearly breakfast to discuss the impact of their investments and to make our ask for the next year. The breakfast provided an informal way to catch up and outline our plans for the following year. Based on this discussion, the DD and the foundation staff formalized the conversation so monies could be transferred to the university foundation. The gifts supported student costs for attending school, so we invited members of the foundation to university and college scholarship dinners. This gave the foundation members a chance to meet with the students they were supporting and hear student stories that conveyed appreciation for the support. The dean and the foundation CEO also met each year one-on-one to discuss the future of the college, university, and the foundation, and to examine the overlap between the organizations. The college even created a small book that depicted their contributions and the difference it made for many students' lives over three decades. The DD was in monthly contact with foundation members to check in with staff and keep them up to date. They were important partners, and we made sure they knew this through our stewardship.

The foundation over many years contributed millions of dollars to student scholarships. Their giving increased steadily over time. When asked why they gave to our unit they said there was mission alignment and that our unit did a great job of communicating the results of their investment. They went on to say that not everyone does this and none did it as well as we did. The foundation did not want dinners or celebrations in their honor. In fact, they would not even let the unit pay for breakfast because they wanted resources to go to students. Their requests were simple and straightforward in that they wanted us to document and show the impact of their investment. Without question, the stewardship was critical to our unit's success with this foundation.

Fundraising Leaders Need To Meet With Donors

As a senior fundraiser your involvement with donors is needed and in some instances, they will only want to meet with you. If you work within a university, interacting with a dean, coach, president, or athletic director (AD) may seem commonplace, especially if you work within their unit. However, for some, meeting directly with senior-level leaders within a university carries special meaning, and working directly with these leaders is necessary if they are going to consider contributing. In fact, your title may be a way to schedule a meeting with a donor who is hard to meet with. For instance, some ADs and coaches are memorialized because of their athletic contributions as a student, and possibly as a professional athlete. Someone with celebrity-type status can be very helpful in obtaining visits with potential donors. Similarly, deans or presidents are typically revered as esteemed scholars who lead hundreds of brilliant thinkers, creators, and problem solvers. Meeting with this caliber of a professional can be very appealing.

In most cases, former students will have never spoken with a dean or president during their undergraduate or graduate work at a university. This is especially true at larger universities. Therefore, meeting with these individuals is seen as a rare and exceptional opportunity. In these instances, senior leaders need to be at the table because there is no adequate proxy other than the leader meeting face-to-face with the donor. Cards and letters are nice and a phone call is always appreciated. However, there is no substitute for a face-to-face meeting between the donor and the senior leader. Therefore, if you want to be successful in your fundraising, make time to meet personally with these donors.

Broaden Your Impact...
Include Many in Fundraising

While it is important for senior fundraisers to meet with donors, they do not need to always meet with donors to be effective. As hard as it may be for some leaders' egos, a donor may not want to visit with the AD, dean, or president. I have had several instances where the DD was able to meet with a donor and close the deal without my involvement. Similarly, a donor may want to meet with a faculty member they remember from their college days. Moreover, they may want to meet a researcher, department head, or students. I have observed some leaders who kept strict rules about protecting their access to donors. They needed to be seen as the winner or the person wearing the crown in the fundraising effort. A common sign of a leader who operates this way is bragging about the money *they* raised rather than discussing the money their *team* generated. In other instances, I have seen deans who take on all high-profile donors within their college and vice presidents of advancement who want to personally work with the university's largest donors, even if the donors do not necessarily want their involvement. These practices are not helpful.

It is not necessarily bad protocol to be "the" person who meets with donors, however, as one person you can only touch and manage a finite number of donors. Conversely, if you have a quality DD, leadership team, faculty representatives, and exemplary students, your capacity to engage expands dramatically through these people. Therefore, engaging many simply enhances your unit and college's capacity and impact. I once had a DD who worked with a donor who gave our college a gift in excess of a million dollars. I offered to meet with him, but he liked working with the DD and knew what he wanted to do (student scholarships) and in his mind there was really no reason to visit with the dean. In this arrangement, the donor was happy and our ability to support the college was fully satisfied without my involvement. When it is appropriate, let other qualified people conduct the fundraising.

Invest in Training and Expanding
Your Fundraising Team

Often lead fundraisers do not include members of their leadership team in fundraising efforts and activities. This is a mistake and an opportunity for you to magnify fundraising efforts. Expanding the pool of fundraisers requires that you train your associate deans, divisional deans, department heads, and coaches, because there is an art and science involved with fundraising. The training will not require a lot of time but it does require some investment from you and your team. For instance, you will need to change their job descriptions and support external and internal training for team members. You will also likely need to engage your team in strategic planning efforts focused on fundraising. To be clear, this approach requires your time, energy, as well as the engagement of your extended fundraising team. The time and costs associated with this effort is well worth the potential growth in giving. It will also open and better engage key people on your staff to work effectively with your DD, university advancement, and the community. To maximize impact, strategically expand the number of fundraisers within your unit and university.

At the other end of the extreme, I have seen leaders who have fundraising responsibilities who do not invest in growing their fundraising team and are not interested in meeting or working with donors. This position deprives their unit and the university of needed resources. In these instances, often the leader's focus is more internal and related to academic pursuits, or creating a winning culture in athletics, or personally engaging in writing or research. There was a time when a leader could excuse themselves from this responsibility and largely ignore the work or appoint someone else to take on this obligation. Given the pivotal role that fundraising plays in the success of a university, this approach can no longer be tolerated in higher education. People in roles including president, dean, or athletic director need to be willing to learn how to be successful in fundraising and make a meaningful contribution to this responsibility. If they are not willing to engage in meaningful fundraising, they may need to find another position that aligns with their desired university pursuits and interests.

Creating a Fundraising Team

There are many approaches, factors, and considerations that need to be addressed in the making of a high-functioning advancement team. For instance, having good analytics to identify potential donors is imperative. You can have motivated fundraisers within your unit but if they do not have relationships to cultivate, your advancement efforts will fail. Similarly, ensuring that various positions across the advancement unit are composed of well-trained employees who are up to date in advancement trends, issues, and skills, is invaluable for unit fundraising now and into the future. Furthermore, making substantial investment into technologies, systems, and processes for successful fundraising is necessary. However, the focus of this section is on the various units in a university such as colleges or athletics, and how they interface with university advancement and build a robust team within their unit(s). To this end, we'll discuss potential structures and how members of your unit, especially development directors (DD), can contribute to the creation of a high-functioning fundraising team.

University and Unit Structures

Universities use a number of structures that vary based on the resources, philosophy, size, and approach to fundraising. For instance, some very large fundraising efforts involve several large, decentralized units, e.g., colleges or athletics that work more autonomously. They rely on central advancement business operations associated with fundraising such as maintaining a CRM, conducting financial accounting for the university and/or foundation, and setting, generating, and maintaining university policies and procedures associated with accepting gifts. Others utilize a mix of centralized and decentralized programming whereby the advancement staff formally reports into advancement but the DD may have a split appointment or dotted reporting line to a unit leader. Depending on the approach, the DDs may be housed in the unit or within advancement. Goal setting, evaluation, travel, and event expenses tend to be shared across advancement and the unit. In the third configuration all advancement employees are housed, supervised, and directed by leaders in advancement. In this highly centralized structure, fundraisers are assigned to support a unit or units within the university and facilitate their work through the direction of advancement leadership in concert with a unit leader. Generally, most advancement structures in higher education fall somewhere along a continuum within these three structures.

While all three models have a place in fundraising, the structure that provides a mix of centralized and decentralized characteristics has many attributes. In this approach the knowledge, skills, insights, and problem-solving support that resides within university advancement professionals can be more easily transferred to units. This is helpful because many leaders have very little knowledge or experience with fundraising and need support and direction. Furthermore, splitting appointment(s) and giving the unit leader significant involvement and responsibility for fundraising better engages the leader and unit in this effort. This approach creates buy-in from the unit and allows advancement to have a meaningful role in the oversight and support of the unit's fundraising. Whatever structure is used, it should generate commitment of the leaders who are charged with fundraising responsibilities while providing the disciplinary expertise and services needed through a team of high-quality advancement professionals.

Finding a Development Director (DD)

Without question, the most important match made in fundraising is the effective pairing of the DD with the lead university or unit fundraiser. To maximize this relationship, the two need to work as a high-functioning team. There ideally should be high levels of trust and interdependence to develop an effective fundraising team. The job involves considerable social interaction where these partners interact with donors, future donors, community leaders, and prominent people locally and nationally. The DD needs to become aware of the fundraiser's strengths, comforts, as well as the circumstances where they excel or become anxious and uneasy. In this relationship, it is also helpful if the fundraiser has a similar understanding of their DD's capacity so everyone can work through each other's strengths and comforts. Ideally some of the DD's strengths can fill in some of the fundraiser's weaknesses and vice-versa. Preferably, when a DD hire is considered, the ability to work well with the DD in social settings and how the DD can fill in the fundraiser's gaps should be prime considerations. This is a very unique relationship and the ability to click as a team is paramount.

Candid Open Conversations

In their day-to-day operations, the DD and fundraising unit leader should form an efficient and focused approach to prepare for meetings with donors or potential donors. For instance, in preparing for a lunch meeting the two could discuss past visits, progress, issues, purpose of the visit, and desired outcomes. This process is frequently initiated by the DD reviewing the CRM so the team can become up to date during the walk from the office to the car. This is good use of time and helps focus the visit preparation. For more important or complex meetings, the DD may want to send a preparatory one-page document for the fundraiser to review the day prior to the meeting. During the drive, a candid conversation could review the recommended approach and items that will be addressed during the meeting. The candid conversation allows the DD to push back on the fundraiser's thoughts or approaches and vice versa. This generates clarity and the best approach. The relationship needs to be stable enough so that either player can say, "I don't think it is time to discuss that item... the donor is just not ready." Similarly, the ability to counter and explain why an item should be discussed is just as legitimate and important. Preferably, this is all done in the spirit of making timely and accurate decisions and not an event that devolves into proving who has the most insight. On most items there is typically agreement between both individuals, and this helps increase certainty and confidence in the meeting plan. If agreement does not exist, then further conversation and reflection may be needed before the plan is finalized.

Listen to The DD

Often my DD's visited with potential or current donors one or multiple times before my meetings. One of the things that helped me most was listening to what they had to say based on these interactions. Typically, they were much more informed and closer to the situation than I was and they were all very skillful at reading where the donor was in the giving process. The pre-planing done by the DD before I met with a donor or donor group was invaluable and allowed me and my team to know who to meet with and the purpose of the visit. The direction through the DD's pre-planning was one of the most helpful and essential contributions that I received through this key employee. In some cases, the situation was reversed and I shared updates from my visits and the DD acted as a sounding board based on my interactions. To be clear, I would not do something I was not comfortable with, but I had enough confidence in the DD to generally follow their advice, which was indispensable. After carefully considering their feedback, I would use my style and strengths to execute their advice. As is often the case with a high-functioning team, I would also welcome their feedback on how I planned to execute the meeting.

Essence of a Quality Team

During visits, the fundraiser will usually do more talking than the DD. If the DD arranges the meeting, they often start the session and then let the donor and fundraiser interact. However, during the meeting a skilled DD will interject timely information, cue the fundraiser to share a story or progress in the college, provide important updates, and be able to answer any logistical or process questions associated with giving a gift to the university. This is all done in a very relaxed, positive, and dynamic way as a team. The interactions between the fundraiser and DD are very polished and come across naturally. While pre-meeting preparation is essential for a successful interaction, *the chemistry generated between the fundraiser, DD, and donor creates the essence of the experience.* Strong teams also take advantage of having two sets of eyes and know when a member needs help, clarification, a change in direction, or when someone else should take the lead during the discussion. These connections are hard to teach but are at the heart of a quality fundraising team.

While generating team chemistry needs time to grow, it is hard to force the desired dynamic within a team if it does not organically exist. It is like forcing a friendship that has no basis for success. The dynamic is absent when interactions in social settings only involve one of the members engaging in conversation and the other member becomes invisible. If your DD lacks many of the desirable traits that have been described, you will need to find another partner. However, hiring a new DD can be difficult and time consuming if they have not performed in a way that warrants their removal and similar positions are not available within the university. In this instance, to improve the relationship you should try:

1. Spending more intentional time with the DD to get to know one another.

2. Clearly communicate your approach and style and engage in conversations about how they can complement your engagement with donors.

3. Be patient and give the partnership extra time to grow and solidify.

4. Focus more of the DD's work addressing the logistics or stewardship associated with your development efforts.

5. Look for other strengths that can support your development efforts such as research, data collection, donor identification, or session debriefings (see below).

Even if the chemistry between you and the DD does not exist in preparations for meetings or during the actual sessions, the DD may still have important insights about how the session went through a debriefing. After any meeting, a discussion should take place between team members to share their perceptions of what went well, what connected, and what did not resonate with the donor. The debriefing is essential because often the person who does most of the talking has a different opinion or misses important cues that are picked up by their partner who is more focused on what was taking place during the interaction. Debriefing is something I did with the DD after every meeting and we discussed what went well, what did not go well, and what our next step forward would be based on the interaction. The debriefing was invaluable and often as important as the pre-planning phase of a meeting. Furthermore, taking time to debrief can deepen and grow the partnership with the DD.

The DD Is an Advocate for the
Lead Fundraiser

I once attended an advancement conference for nursing professionals that was primarily composed of DDs from across the country. I was shocked during question-and-answer sessions by the way many of the DDs described their deans and the problems they experienced in their partnership. They complained that their deans were not available for them and lost donors in long-winded conversations clouded by academic jargon. It was as if they were talking about a puppy who peed on the floor and they were not sure if they should hit them over the nose with a newspaper or let it go because a puppy just does not know any better.

A few things came to mind based on this experience. First, DDs, especially new DDs, need to become better aware of a president, dean, or athletic director's job. Yes, fundraising is part of their job but they may also have hundreds of employees in the unit they are responsible for, manage a multi-million-dollar budget, and they may have low enrollments or a series of losing seasons to navigate. In fact, many run a small enterprise and act like a CEO of a company. The president of a university is more obvious, but they have many public relations and political concerns to address, along with the success of the entire university. If DDs have a clear understanding of the fundraiser's other roles they may temper their resentment, belittling, and frustration with their fundraising partner.

Second, you should expect your DD to support and speak favorably of you in any public forum. As a fundraiser you need a loyal DD that you can depend on. At the conference I attended several of the DDs shared stories that were not appropriate for this forum. This kind of behavior is not acceptable and trashing your partner is not a good way to build a high-functioning partnership. As a leader, it is your responsibility to let your DD know your expectations around support and loyalty. A DD simply needs to be very careful about what they say to people within and outside the university, especially if it involves you. Also, if the DD is new to higher education, help them better understand the scope and magnitude of your job so they can understand that fundraising is one of many responsibilities that you have. If the DD still does not support you and speaks despairingly about you within or outside the university after educating and communicating with them, you need to find another DD.

Embed the DD in Your Leadership Team and Community

In some instances, advancement and the DD assigned to units are not accepted into the unit or university. In fact, some view these professionals as salespeople who are only interested in money and not a real part of the university. While some universities have pockets that carry this disdain, higher education has for a while moved from this orientation and see these professionals as an important part of the university. As a leader it is important that you clearly show the importance of these professionals by treating them as an important representative and member of your unit.

Include the DD in Your Leadership Team

One of the things I did as a dean was to include DDs as members of my small and influential college leadership team. This practice is not commonly used in higher education, but I found it to be very powerful. Their inclusion on a team of divisional deans, directors, and associate deans sent a clear message that the DD was an important leader in the college and that their work was essential to our success. This positioning also reduced barriers for the DD and made for easier access to department/school meetings, events and gatherings, so that they could visit with faculty and staff and educate them about our advancement work. Not only could they educate the various sectors of the unit on fundraising, they could engage and generate support more quickly and effectively. The DD was not an outsider but a member of the leadership team. If you give the DD your full support, unit resistance is often reduced and fundraising efforts become reinforced across the unit.

It is interesting to note that at a university level, the director or vice president of advancement is customarily part of a presidential leadership team. Conversely, units within the university such as colleges or athletics do not typically have an advancement person as a part of their leadership team, which isolates them from important information, strategic approaches, decisions, and marginalizes their status in the unit. I remember a dean who was assigned a quality DD but never took the time to engage them as a full member of the college. The final blow came when he took away their office while on vacation and moved their belongings into a cubicle. If you cannot even have the courtesy to tell your partner you're moving them, you have no hope to succeed as a team. In short, not having the DD as part of your leadership team minimizes their success in fundraising. In many ways, the logic of this structural addition to a unit is self-evident but is prevented largely because of tradition and the fear of looking different than other units. As a leader, you can easily make this addition to benefit your fundraising.

Membership on Internal and External Boards

Another way to embed the DD into a unit is to have them on internal and external community boards. Many central university advancement leaders balk at the idea of a DD being on internal/external committees or boards. Their faulty logic is that a DDs job is to be out raising money and that they should not spend time in meetings. Given how much time DDs spend in internal advancement meetings, this position is somewhat befuddling. Nevertheless, generating funds is fundamentally about making relationships and showing that you are a creditable member of a community who will be a good steward of gifts. Having DDs as members of internal and external committees and boards is an outstanding way to form these relationships and generate trust within and outside the university.

As dean of a health college, I chaired a community committee of senior health professionals from across the state. The only other people besides the DD that regularly attended these meetings from the college were the senior associate dean and another associate dean. The membership created powerful connections between the DD and senior leadership across the state. Interestingly, the community leaders were not recruited to raise money for the college, but to give advice and insight into the delivery of health. However, once connections were made, many opportunities developed that allowed the unit to obtain equipment and financial support through these relationships. In fact, some of the board members ended up giving personally because of the relationship formed through their membership on the college committee.

The DDs can also participate on community committees or boards outside the university as a university or unit representative. Like the college community committee previously described, this membership allowed the DD to generate a deeper relationship and understanding of the important community partners' missions and interests. Again, many advancement leaders may not support this involvement because they are worried about the DD being distracted from their work in fundraising. However, this service really deepened relationships and supported the DD in their fundraising efforts. In essence, this is fundraising work.

Including the DD on the unit leadership team and community committees gave them status, but even more importantly, access to information and opportunities for relationship development. This level of inclusion allowed the DD to work with a variety of key individuals on my behalf and expand the work I could do in advancement across the unit. As a leader, find tangible and high-profile ways to make sure that your DD's efforts are respected and supported. Problems can arise if they are on too many committees or boards and the DD is consumed by these efforts. However, this can be easily managed by conversing with the DD before they accept membership to a new committee. Essentially, the conversations serve as a way to gauge and manage their level of involvement. As a leader, particularly a leader within a unit of the university, you may get push-back if you try to engage your DD as a member of internal and external committees or boards. If this happens, you may want to push back because this approach can be a powerful tool for generating support for your unit and university and elevates the status of the DD so they are better positioned to do their work.

A DD Who Cares

While a DD does not have to possess expertise in a particular area such as economics, health, education, sports, or research, it is helpful if they have genuine interest and truly care about the area where they focus their fundraising efforts. This position has been argued and some strongly believe that a quality DD can raise money in any area, even if they have limited interest in higher education as a whole. In short, they are in sales and they should be able to sell anything. While there may be some truth to a sales orientation, there is a risk in this positioning because you will likely have a more motivated employee if they care about the content area or cause. It is more effective to hire someone who has, for example, a passion for music and the arts and sees the importance of this discipline in a university as well as in creating a vibrant community. When you hire someone who cares about an area not only is the DD working for you, but they are able to personally build and support something they care deeply about. In this situation, the DD is more likely to resonate with donors and have more drive, grit, and longevity in the position. Be careful if you are at a university where advancement leadership feel that DDs are interchangeable and that a DD who was effective in athletics will be successful in music. Care and commitment matter.

Consequently, the best scenario is for you to find someone who truly cares and can clearly and vividly explain to you why the area or cause matters to them. As was mentioned earlier, a lead fundraiser is better at their job if they are working for things that they care about. It is also true for the DD. Therefore, when hiring a DD look for someone who cares and is inspired by the area(s) you represent and your productivity and engagement will likely improve because of this orientation.

Reward Excellence

Most units in higher education give rewards to employees for outstanding work performance over the course of a year. Sometimes they are distributed by job classification (classified, professional, and faculty) or they are delivered based on work areas such as community outreach, teaching, research, or administrative support. The awards usually involve a celebration, plaque, and come with some type of cash award. Avoid any type of commission-based compensation like bonus money at different levels of yearly gifting contributions. These compensation schemes create many problems. However, make sure your advancement people are included as candidates for these awards within your unit, just as you would consider any other employee. Furthermore, if they have an exceptional year, you may want to extend a bonus to them for their outstanding work. The awards and bonuses do not cost much ($500-$3,000), but they are a tangible and meaningful way to acknowledge good work.

Address Logistics

If you represent a large fundraising unit within a university there will be a number of meetings, meals, events, and related demands that are a part of your fundraising responsibilities. Organizing lunches, alumni celebrations, scholarship dinners, and donor meetings translate to a pile of logistics that need to be addressed if the events are to be successful. One trait of a successful DD is that they ensure that all of the logistics are taken care of. Notice that phrase describes the DD *taking care of logistics* and not *executing* the logistics. The details of events can range from making sure a lunch reservation for a donor and fundraising team is made and everyone shows up at the right place at the right time for lunch. It can also involve hundreds of participants and a guest speaker in a ballroom. Both require planning, follow-up, and an eye for details.

To make sure meetings and events are successfully executed, the DD will need access to your staff to help them with the logistics, payments, access to special accounts to purchase alcohol, meals, and gifts. They will also need to take control of items that only they can execute. As the unit leader you will not have the bandwidth to worry about these important details. Nonetheless, you need to feel confident that everything is taken care of for small and large events. As your operation grows, the DD may need additional staff to help support the volume of current and future donors, like event planners who focus on fundraising-related events. Whatever the needs, the DD needs resources so actions and efforts are put in place to ensure that the details are worked out and the meetings and events go smoothly. Few things will reduce a donor's interest more than a missed appointment or a failed event.

As dean I worked with the college DD to form a group of physicians who would help advise and support the college. The DD worked hard to recruit almost 20 prominent physicians who were all invited to a Friday evening wine and cheese event to discuss progress and needs within the college. Despite the DD addressing the logistics well in advance, things were not ready for the event. The DD had given a staff person in the college a list of wines to purchase. When she saw the list, she decided to get jug wines because the listed wines were too expensive. Unfortunately, she did not let the DD know about the change. Also, the catering group from the university did not show up with the plates, food, and glasses for the wine tasting. Catering services within universities can vary dramatically in quality and dependability and our services were moderate at best.

Fortunately, the DD arrived early because they knew catering was known to drop the ball. The DD got in touch with catering—who had lost the order—and mobilized them to bring some basic food and utensil items immediately. The DD looked at the wines and saw that the jugs ranged in price from $4 to $8 a gallon! This DD was a problem-solver so armed with their personal charge card, ran to the local grocery store and purchased wines for the event and made it in time for people to get a glass of wine and listen to the dean's opening comments. Even though things were a mess it went well. The story demonstrates that even if you try to address the details, things can fall apart. However, if you have a DD that realizes this inevitability they will double-check, arrive early, and do what needs to be done to ensure the event is a success even when things are a mess.

Creating a Fundraising Team

The importance of having a quality DD has been established in this chapter. Nevertheless, depending on your scope of work, others will be involved to ensure success. If resources allow, part or all of an administrative assistant's time needs to be dedicated to advancement activities within your unit. This ensures that clerical support is available and dedicated for advancement. It makes no sense having your DD filling out forms or going from person to person trying to solve a payment problem. This will help you because the administrative assistant can organize and execute many of the internal and external processes associated with your fundraising efforts and you do not need to solve these problems for the DD.

Furthermore, the various sectors of your unit will need to engage in strategic planning efforts directed by you and/or your DD. The planning will need to be coordinated with the university-level advancement unit through the advancement vice president or associate vice president. In fact, it can be very helpful to have one of these people facilitate some of your unit strategic planning. The strategic planning effort provides a vivid way to engage various sectors of your unit in fundraising and to identify unit-wide priorities. The planning can also be used to let leaders know that fundraising is not just the responsibility of the DD. Some in higher education feel that they simply need to give the DD a list of what they need and the DD will take care of the shopping list with a few meetings or phone calls. However, the truth is that successful advancement programming is everyone's job. It is everyone's job to understand the focus of a campaign and contribute in ways that benefit this effort by finding interested donors, spreading the word, and in the case of your extended leadership team, making it part of their skillset and responsibilities. Inclusive strategic planning and ongoing reminders can be a great way to facilitate this process.

Chapter Summary

1. The topic of fundraising is broad and diverse. The focus of this chapter concentrated on the traits and approaches of effective fundraisers and the advancement team members that *directly* support these efforts.

2. As a fundraiser, make sure you can clearly and succinctly explain your priorities and communicate with genuine enthusiasm, conviction, and excitement.

3. Some donors may want to hear your priorities as a leader and others may tell you what they are interested in supporting. If the donor is sharing their interests, be sure and listen carefully to see if there is a possibility for a match with your priorities and needs. Being open to gifts that are not current priorities while setting boundaries on gifts that cannot be accepted is a critical function of an effective fundraiser.

4. To generate engagement incorporate stories as opposed to just making a case or request. A story allows the donor to *feel* the potential impact of a gift rather than just cognitively comprehending their investment. Ideally you want to convey both (feeling and understanding), but feeling is usually the most powerful way to engage a donor.

5. The lead fundraiser for a unit or university may not always be the person who the donor wants to meet with. Be sure and connect the donor with the right people who can best meet their needs.

6. If you are going to ask for money make sure you are also giving in a way that is meaningful for you.

7. Be a good steward of donations you receive and generate a system that is mindful of your many obligations yet keeps the donor informed and engaged with the university or unit they have supported.

8. Make sure you carve out time to meet face-to-face with donors, but also engage others who work with you to raise funds and broaden the reach of your university or unit's fundraising efforts.

9. There are a variety of university structures that range from university-centered to unit-centered development operations. Typically, something between these two extremes is used to best match the needs of an organization.

10. Without question, the most important partnership in fundraising is the effective pairing of a development director (DD) with the lead university or unit fundraiser. This decision has significant correlation to success in fundraising be-

cause the chemistry generated between the fundraiser, DD, and donor creates the essence of the fundraising experience.

11. Your development director can expand their support and reach by being a strong supporter of you and your work, being a member of your leadership team, representing your unit on external committees/boards, and representing you at events and meetings. Also, find a DD who is good at logistics and can make sure meetings and events run smoothly because things are thought-out and well-prepared.

Chapter 11
Principal Messages and Applications

Overview

In this book we've discussed a number of considerations, approaches, skills, systems, and processes to help leaders in higher education become more effective in the twenty-first century. Many examples came from my experiences over more than 35 years of work in higher education. However, each leader is different and the circumstances they face are unique. Therefore, the final chapter will provide additional direction on how to apply the contents within the book to adapt to your style and needs. Also, a principal or key message distills the essence of each chapter.

How Did the Past Influence Your Leadership?

In Chapter 1, I shared childhood and early work experiences that influenced my leadership. One theme I conveyed is that what might have appeared to be an adverse or difficult part of my childhood turned out to be a trait or insight that helped me as a leader. If you have not done this, it is worth taking time now to reflect on your childhood and early work experiences, both good and bad, to identify attributes that you can apply to your work as a leader. Think of the vivid and impactful experiences that likely influenced who you are today and categorize them under themes. The themes could include the ability to organize, listen, communicate, or connect with people, etc. Often these traits are such a fundamental part of who you are, you may not recognize them. Once the traits and characteristics are identified, you can use this insight as a strength to help you in your leadership work. One word of caution, if you have more than four to five themes, you may be getting too detailed and need to bring them down to a manageable number.

Principal Message #1:

Reflect back on your development to identify innate traits and characteristics that can help you as a leader.

Change

There is a profound need for members of higher education to abandon some antiquated traditions, processes and systems if they are to continue and prosper in the future. Additionally, work needs to be done to maintain and in some instances regain support of the government and citizens of the United States. The reasons for these changes are many and I encourage you to focus on your university and/or system to identify where you are strong and where you need to improve. Every system and/or university is different and the examples I gave throughout the book may or may not be applicable to your circumstances. If there is an unhealthy division between the community and university, find out why. If your state government does not support your university or college, find out why and work to change problematic situations. In short, you need to look within and outside the university to identify opportunities for change so your unit or university can flourish or continue to flourish.

We also explored change in Chapter 2 and the strong resistance to it in higher education. If you think you do not need to change, I encourage you to reconsider this stance, as it could lead to failure. I provide many examples in the second chapter of the strong resistance to change commonly seen across higher education. This can make addressing change a significant challenge, but this is not a good reason to avoid it. Explore your university or unit and find areas where faculty and staff seem intractable in their ability to navigate change. Common areas include degree offerings, delivery platforms, changing direction, degree requirements, etc. However, as a leader you need to identify what areas, items, and issues impact your unit and university and work to shed light on them; then identify a process for creating needed change.

Principal Message #2:

Higher education needs to change and to ignore this imperative will result in failure.

Take Care of Yourself

Early in the book I take on the issue of leaders caring for their health and wellbeing. This is addressed early to help reinforce the importance of this concern. The most consistent and important item ignored by leaders is caring for themselves. Throughout Chapter 3 I mention a number of behaviors and tips to help you engage in this important process. The discussions around mindfulness and the four agreements may have been new to you, while other areas such as sleep, exercise, and nutrition were likely familiar. It is imperative to find time each day to address your health and wellbeing, even if it is only 10 minutes. If you are new to leadership you may have been able to care for yourself prior to this assignment, but leadership can put very different demands on you across all dimensions of health. If you are willing to postpone health care for a day it will likely grow into weeks, months, and years until you find yourself trying to catch up on something that can be challenging to reverse. Therefore, take health very seriously, start today, and make it a regular part of your life. This commitment will make you a better and more sustainable leader and support other critical dimensions of your life. This is one of the most important recommendations I make in this book.

Principal Message #3:

To be a balanced leader you need to engage in health self-care each day... no exceptions.

Being a Caring Leader

In Chapter 4 the term leadership was defined as "the ability to influence." To influence requires that you engage in practices that allow you to get to know and understand your supervisees so that they can be given personalized guidance and opportunities to grow and develop. The focus of this chapter conveys that as part of a professional relationship, the caring elements of leadership are incorporated into your supervisory approach. This professional relationship is fundamentally different from a friendship or a familial connection. The professional relationship incorporates an ethic of care that helps develop and nurture employees while maintaining important boundaries that are part of the supervisor and supervisee roles. How you connect in meaningful ways is up to you, but keeping professional distance while understanding that events and issues outside of work impact employees' lives is your challenge. This is especially true since part of your job is to ensure that employees are productive and held accountable.

How you go about creating this relationship is something only you can navigate. I shared approaches, techniques, and examples of problems in hopes that they help create strategies that can be used to create a caring environment for you and your employees. Taking the time to consider consistent approaches, thoughtful boundaries (which are discussed in Chapter 5) combined with flexibility that addresses individual needs will serve you well as a caring leader. These answers can be best identified through reflection, conversations with trusted leaders/teachers, and being a lifelong learner who seeks out new information and grows from successes and mistakes.

Principal Message #4:

Finding ways to create a professional relationship with subordinates that nurtures and develops them while maintaining boundaries associated with supervisor and supervisee roles is the essence of being a caring leader.

Work Environments

Faculty and staff want to work in an environment where they feel appreciated and safe while knowing their contributions are making a difference. Creating a positive or fruitful environment that is outlined in Chapter 5, is a key responsibility for leaders. Often, enterprises create environments, systems, and processes that do not allow people to prosper at work and prevent them from engaging in what they do best. Your job as a leader is to identify these unit or university-specific problems and to the extent that you can, *free your employees from these constraints.* Take time to consider your direct reports and ask yourself if they are spending time doing the things that they can best address. Many of the questions outlined in the section on performance reviews (Chapter 8) may help you answer these important questions. Your responsibility is to ensure your unit and university are successful and your most precious resource for attaining this outcome is through your people. To facilitate this outcome, consider your approaches (protecting employees from bureaucratic processes, creating effective communications, etc.), reach, authority, influence, and creative problem-solving to create fruitful work environments.

Principal Message #5:

Your job as a leader is to remove barriers that prevent employees from making important and unique contributions to the organization.

Being a Strategic Leader

One of the omissions that most constrains leaders in higher education is not creating and *implementing* a strategic plan. You need to have a plan, people need to understand and buy into it, and you need to ensure it is executed. This is largely facilitated by answering three critical questions: Where are we now? Where are we going? How will we get there? It is like a good class syllabus, it provides direction, outcomes, and a detailed description of what is done each class to achieve the desired outcomes. Have you ever taken a class that had no syllabus or a very poorly conceived syllabus? My experiences were not good, and I often sat in front of an instructor who would say, "OK, what will we do today?" Chapter 6 provides a framework and a number of considerations and cautions related to strategic planning. However, if you can come up with a method that effectively answers these three questions and it is successfully implemented, you will have succeeded. Yes, there are other important considerations such as communication, decision-making, accountability, and resource allocation, but answering these three questions and implementing them is the core of being strategic. In fact, strategic planning and implementation is one of the most important roles you should fulfill as a leader. Therefore, avoid the many pitfalls that come with not planning and make this effort a key priority as a leader.

Principal Message #6:

Develop and implement a strategic plan that illuminates for your organization/unit where you are, where you are going, and how you will get there.

Work Teams

The use of high-functioning work teams can pay powerful dividends for your unit or organization through the synergistic effect that comes from individuals collectively focusing their work, insights, and efforts. Using this approach is very alluring. However, the systematic use and training needed to develop work teams does not commonly exist nor is it supported in higher education. With a few exceptions, most individuals and units have never learned about or effectively used high-functioning work teams. In Chapter 7, the challenges of work teams are discussed at length. Before you decide to use a work team structure as a prominent strategy, be honest and make sure your unit or institution is ready for a big lift. Usually universities will not collectively embrace and support the idea and it will require significant effort that may detract from more important strategic efforts. If you do use this strategy, make sure your unit and/or university is ready and committed and you start at a place that matches your level of readiness.

Principal Message #7:

Be cautious about the use of work teams as a strategy for meeting your strategic efforts. If pursued, develop this approach from a place that matches your unit or university's level of readiness.

Critical Management Skills for Balanced Leaders

In order to be an effective, balanced leader, you must understand and apply basic management skills. While the leaders in higher education are highly educated and knowledge-able in their areas of experience, few step into leadership roles grounded in basic management skills. To be sure, some have learned these skills through previous leadership positions or formal training. While many of the skills such as hiring, performance evaluations, supervision, budget oversight, managing partnerships, creating business structures, and creating effective systems and processes may not seem very glamorous, *they are fundamental to running an effective unit and university.* These important but less than glamorous topics are reviewed in Chapter 8.

Some management skills can be addressed by other employees, assuming you have the resources and expertise on your team to execute these functions. Examples of functions commonly taken on by other employees include financial responsibilities, workforce training, and external projects. However, many management activities require your direct involvement and even if you do not manage the budget, you still need to understand your unit or organization's finances. This does not require you to obtain an MBA, but you will need to obtain training and gain understanding of these management skills. Also, if you learned select skills from a leader who had no management training, you should check and see if their teachings were accurate.

When considering the basic management skills reviewed in Chapter 8, be honest with yourself and identify where the gaps exist. By honesty I mean that you may have received many annual reviews from your supervisor—but that does not mean you know how to conduct quality performance appraisals. Similarly, you may have managed a small line-item budget for a service project, but that does not mean you understand the bookkeeping and revenue generation for a large unit within a university. Your blind spots are not an indication of your ability or effectiveness, rather they simply are areas where you need to broaden your understanding of what it takes to be a manager. The training and information can be found through multiple sources that can bring you up to speed without a lot of effort or time. For instance, there are videos and many books on conducting interviews and performance appraisals that are full of good information and ideas. Also, meeting with someone in human resources who specializes in hiring or performance appraisals can be very informative. Other areas such as understanding how a university's financial system works can take considerably more time, but this is something you can take on in manageable bites (depending on your position). Management training is part of your responsibility as a leader. The only ways to fail in this part of your job are to not follow what you learn or failing to engage in management training and development.

Principal Message #8:

As an effective, balanced leader, you need to understand and be able to apply basic management skills and techniques.

Community Engagement

The need to engage with the external community will vary depending on your position. Nevertheless, effective community engagement is an important part of a successful university. As discussed in Chapter 9, community engagement can be an excellent way to improve university and community relations and enhance the university's standing with citizens and state government. Essentially, you need to consider what your unit or university has to offer, examine ways that the community could benefit from these services, and find a way to align resources with these efforts. Community engagement requires people with community engagement skills (ability to listen, sincerity, humility, caring attitude, etc.) and people with these skills need to be placed in this work. While most units provide some form of service, allocating resources to provide community services is necessary if this work is to take place in a meaningful way. As a leader, your primary challenge is to generate or reallocate resources and give staff and faculty the assigned effort to engage in these activities. Reference these examples in Chapter 9 to determine if some of the approaches may work well in your communities. Additionally, leverage the characteristics and uniqueness of your communities to find creative ways to partner and enhance them.

Principal Message #9:

As a leader in higher education you need to mobilize people with necessary resources to provide meaningful service to your communities.

Chapter 10 Summary

The importance of fundraising has grown steadily in higher education due to accelerated delivery costs and reduced support from the government. Chapter 10 focused on various aspects of the core team directly involved with fundraising activities. Within this team we examined a variety of traits, approaches, and communication styles for effective fundraising. As a lead fundraiser (president, dean, athletic director, etc.) within a university, you will dramatically improve your effectiveness by partnering with a development professional who coordinates your development activities. A strong partnership is critical in creating successful fundraising, so develop or seek out this professional so they can assist you in your efforts. To work effectively with potential donors, you need to refine and test your communications so that you are able to communicate needs and priorities clearly and succinctly. Find stories about your unit or college that move or excite potential donors and deliver these stories with conviction and enthusiasm. You will need to carve time out of your packed schedule so you can meet face-to-face with many of the donors. Often your engaged presence is the only hope for generating support. However, you can also expand your reach by giving others such as your leadership team members and development professional latitude to fundraise on your behalf. To this end, you will need to work with other people in your area who can engage and inspire potential donors and entities to support your priorities. This can only happen by assigning this responsibility, training team members, and giving them needed resources and experiences to become effective at fundraising.

Principal Message # 10:

Your job as a lead fundraiser is to personally recruit gifts while growing a team of empowered professionals who can communicate university or unit priorities in a way that engages others to contribute to the university.

Final Comments

Higher education has done much to improve our society. The higher education system in the United States has been the envy of the world for many decades. However, if support for higher education is to continue, many of the practices and traditions need to change—or be abandoned. This change is essential for the benefits of this enterprise to be actualized by members of society. Balanced leaders are central and essential in this process. I hope some of my examples, thoughts, approaches, and recommendations guide your efforts as a balanced leader who helps higher education prosper and contribute in the years to come.

Bibliography

Allen, D., Swartz, T., & McGinn, D. (2011, May). Being more productive. *Harvard Business Review*, 83-87.

Blanchard, K., & Johnson, S. (1982). *The one minute manager*. Berkley Books.

Bolman, L., & Deal, T. E. (1991). *Reframing organizations: Artistry, choice and leadership*. Jossey-Bass/Wiley.

Buckingham, M. (2015). *Standout 2.0: Assess your strengths, find your edge, win at work*. Harvard Business Review Press.

Buckingham M., & Clifton, D. O. (2001). *Now, discover your strengths: The revolutionary program that shows you how to develop your unique talents and strengths*. The Free Press.

Buckingham, M., & Coffman, C. (1999). *First break all the rules: What the world's greatest managers do differently.* Simon and Schuster.

Chouinard, Y. (2006). *Let my people go surfing: The education of a reluctant businessman*. Penguin.

Christensen, C. M., & Eyring, H. J. (2011). *The innovative university: Changing the DNA of higher education.* Jossey-Bass/Wiley.

Collins, J. (2009). *How the mighty fall: And why some companies never give in*. HarperCollins.

Crow, M. M., & Dabars, W. B. (2015). *Designing the new American university*. John Hopkins.

Crowley, M. C. (2022). *Lead from the heart: Transformational leadership for the 21st century*. Hay House.

Curry, J. R., Laws, A. L., & Strauss, J. C. (2013). *Responsibility centered management: A guide to balancing academic entrepreneurship with fiscal responsibility*. NACUBO.

Deming, W. E. (2000). *Out of the crisis*. MIT.

Doyle, M., & Straus, D. (1976). *How to make meetings work*. Jove Books.

Drucker, P. F. (1990). *Managing the non-profit organization: Principles and practices*. Harper Collins.

Drucker, P., Collins, J., Kolter, P., Kouzes, J., Rodin, J., Rangan, V. K., & Hesselbein, F. (2008). *The five most important questions you will ever ask about your organization*. Jossey-Bass/Wiley.

Duncan, S., Dunnagan, T., Christopher S., & Paul, L. (2001, February). EDUFAIM: A successful program helping empower rural families toward self-reliance. *Journal of Extension, 39*(1), 1-10. http://www.joe.org/joe/2001february/a3.html.

Dunnagan, T. (1987). The development and implementation of the health enhancement curriculum (Master's thesis). Montana State University.

Edersheim, E. I. (2007). *The definitive Drucker*. McGraw-Hill.

Fisher, R., & Ury, W. (1981). *Getting to yes: Negotiating agreements without giving in*. Penguin.

Gunsalus, C. K. (2006). *The college administrator's survival guide*. Harvard University Press.

Hanson. (2024, May 28). *Average costs of college and tuition*. EducationData.org. https://educationdata.org/average-cost-of-college)

Hamel, G., & Breen, B. (2007). *The future of management*. Harvard Business School.

Harari, O. (2002). *The leadership secrets of Colin Powell*. McGraw-Hill.

Hayward, M. (2007). *Ego Check: Why executive hubris is wrecking companies and careers and how to avoid the trap*. Kaplan.

Knutson K. L., Van Cauter E., Rathouz P. J., DeLeire T., & Lauderdale D. S. (2010). Trends in the prevalence of short sleepers in the USA. *Sleep*, 33(1), 37-45.

Lachapelle, P. R., Dunnagan, T., & Real Bird, J. (2011, April-June). Applying innovative approaches to address health disparities in native populations: An assessment of the Crow men's health project. *Community Development, 42*(2), 240-254

Lama, D. (2002). *How to practice: The way to a meaningful life*. Pocket Books.

Lama, D. (2000). *Transforming the mind: Teachings on generating compassion*. Thorsons.

Lencioni, P. (2012). *The advantage: Why organizational health trumps everything else*. Jossey-Bass/Wiley.

Lencioni, P. (2002). *The five dysfunctions of a team: A leadership fable*. Jossey-Bass/Wiley.

Linker, J. K. (2004). *The Toyota way: 14 management principles from the world's greatest manufacturer*. McGraw-Hill.

Liker J. K., & Convis, G. L (2012). *The Toyota way to lean leadership*. McGraw-Hill.

MacKenzie, G. (1995). *Orbiting the giant hair ball: A corporate fool's guide to surviving with grace.* Penguin.

Maxwell, J. C. (2007). *The 21 irrefutable laws of leadership: Follow them and they will follow you.* Thomas Nelson.

McKeown, G. (2014). *Essentialism: The disciplined pursuit of less.* Crown.

Panas, J. (2012). *Asking: A 59-minute guide to everything board members, volunteers, and staff must know to secure and gift.* Emerson and Church.

Pandya, M., & Shell, R. (2006). *Lasting Leadership: What you can learn from the top 25 business people of our time.* Wharton School.

Ruiz, D. M. (1999). *The mastery of love.* Amber-Allen.

Ruiz, D. M., & Mills, J. (1997). *The four agreements.* Amber-Allen.

Ruiz, D. M., Ruiz, D. J., & Mills, J. (2010). *The fifth agreement: A practical guide to self-mastery.* Amber-Allen.

Rumelt, R. P. (2011). *Good strategy/bad strategy: The difference and why it matters.* Crown.

Schloss, E. P., Flanagan D.M., Culler C.L., & Wright A.L. (2009). Some hidden costs of faculty turnover in clinical departments in one academic medical center. *Academic Medicine, 84*(1), 32-36.

Scott, S. (2002). *Fierce conversations: Achieving success at work and in life, one conversation at a time.* Berkley.

Senge, P. M. (1990). *The fifth discipline: The art & practice of the learning organization.* Doubleday.

Temte, A. (2021). *Balancing Act: Teach coach mentor inspire*. Amplify.

Tichy, N. M., & Bennis, W. G. (2007). *Judgement: How winning leaders make great calls*. Penguin.

Tolle, E. (2005). *A new earth: Awakening to your life's purpose*. Viking.

Tolle, E. (2003). *Stillness speaks*. Namaste.

Tolle, E. (1999). *The power of now: A guide to spiritual enlightenment*. New World Library.

Ury, W. (2008). *The power of a positive no: Save the deal: Save the relationships and still say no*. Bantam.

Wakeman, C. (2013). *The reality-based rules of the workplace: Know what boosts your value, kills your chances, and will make you happier*. Jossey-Bass/Wiley.

Wakeman, C. (2010). *Reality-based leadership: Ditch the drama, restore the workplace and turn excuses into results*. Jossey-Bass/Wiley.

Acknowledgements

I want to acknowledge and thank Provost John Buckwalter at Boise State University who supported the writing of this book. I am also appreciative of the insight I gained from working with quality leaders at University of Kentucky, Montana State University, and Boise State University. Additionally, Megan Regnerus was very helpful through her developmental editing of the book, which generated insights and edits that helped create a more cohesive document on leadership in higher education. Similarly, I want to thank Dr. Jowell Powers for her review which facilitated clarity, addressed omissions, and generated narratives that brought additional life and insights to the book. Also, thanks to Dr. Ken Petersen for our many conversations about higher education during our time together at Boise State University. Your insights were very revealing. Finally, thanks to Ryan Bradley for taking the text that was written in a word document and formatting it into a book.

About the Author

Dr. Tim Dunnagan has worked as an innovative leader and administrator in higher education for more that 30 years. Dr. Dunnagan began his career in higher education as Wellness Director for the University of Kentucky (UK) main campus, medical school, and community college system. In this role he successfully worked with university leadership, faculty, and staff to enhance the health and wellbeing of employees across the UK system. He took his first faculty position at Montana State University (MSU) where he obtained the rank of professor. Subsequently, he accepted the position of department head at MSU over a large and complex department. During his tenure as department head, faculty and staff generated a unified vision and strategic plan under his leadership which enhanced teaching and research efforts and created the third largest department on campus. During this time the faculty also experienced substantial growth in research and creative activities. After a successful time at MSU, Dr. Dunnagan accepted the position of dean in the College of Health Sciences (COHS) at Boise State University and remained in this position for more than 14 years. Under Dr. Dunnagan's leadership, the second smallest college on campus grew self-support online programming from 280 students to over 1,800 students generating an additional 35,000 new student credit hours across 12 programs while dramatically growing research activities. Significant growth also took place in face-to-face programming, including the addition of two doctoral programs. In 2025, the college became the largest college on campus and generated millions of dollars of new revenues to effectively support needed health programming and research across the United States. Over his decades of work, Dr. Dunnagan was seen as a collaborative leader who partnered and found ways to support faculty, staff, and students and dramatically grew programming, research, and services across his areas of responsibility. Much of the information in his book, *Finding the Balance: Leadership in Higher Education,* is based on his study of leadership, experiences, successes, and failures as a leader in positions such as dean at Boise State. He provides compelling and applicable insights for effective leadership based on his cumulative experiences.

For access to a free digital edition of this book scan the QR code below or visit: dunnagan.cargo.site